The Moral E
the Madrasa

The revival of madrasas in the 1980s coincided with the rise of political Islam and soon became associated with the 'clash of civilizations' between Islam and the West. This volume examines the rapid expansion of madrasas across Asia and the Middle East and analyses their role in society within their local, national and global context.

Based on anthropological investigations in Afghanistan, Bangladesh, China, Iran, and Pakistan, the chapters take a new approach to the issue, examining the recent phenomenon of women in madrasas; Hui Muslims in China; relations between the Iran's Shia seminary after the 1979 Islamic revolution and Shia in Pakistan and Afghanistan; and South Asian madrasas. Emphasis is placed on the increased presence of women in these institutions, and the reciprocal interactions between secular and religious schools in those countries. Taking into account social, political and demographic changes within the region, the authors show how madrasas have been successful in responding to the educational demand of the people and how they have modernized their style to cope with a changing environment.

A timely contribution to a subject with great international appeal, this book will be of great interest to students and scholars of international politics, political Islam, Middle East and Asian studies and anthropology.

SAKURAI Keiko is Professor in the School of International Liberal Studies at Waseda University, Tokyo. The author of two books on Iran and a book on the Shia, her major interest lies in the analysis of social change in contemporary Iran, with special focus on the role of education.

Fariba Adelkhah is Senior Research Fellow at SciencesPo in Paris. An anthropologist, her main research interests focus on the relationships and interplay between social changes and political transformations throughout the second half of the twentieth century in Iran. She is the author of *Being Modern in Iran*, and her current research deals with the Iranian Diaspora.

New Horizons in Islamic Studies (Second Series)
Series Editor: Professor SATO Tsugitaka

This second series of 'New Horizons in Islamic Studies' presents the abundant results of the National Institutes for the Humanities (NIHU) program for Islamic Area Studies (IAS) carried out in Japan from 2006 to date. This program emphasizes multidisciplinary research on the dynamism of Muslim societies, in both Islamic and non-Islamic areas around the world. By taking a historical approach and adopting regional comparison methods in the study of current issues, the program seeks to build a framework of empirical knowledge on Islam and Islamic Civilization.

Islamic Area Studies is a network comprised of five research centers, at Waseda University, the University of Tokyo, Sophia University, Kyoto University, and the Toyo Bunko (Oriental Library). As of 2008, this network has been brought into the fold of a Ministry of Education, Culture, Sports, Science and Technology (MEXT) program, with the Organization for Islamic Area Studies at Waseda University serving as its central office. As research centers recognized by the MEXT, we aim to promote the development of joint research institutions in the human and social sciences, thereby further developing fruitful joint research achievements.

This publication of the results of our IAS joint research has and will have been made possible through the collaborative efforts of the five IAS centers, and with the financial assistance of the NIHU and the MEXT.

The Moral Economy of the Madrasa
Islam and education today
Edited by SAKURAI Keiko and Fariba Adelkhah

Previously published in the New Horizons in Islamic Studies series

Persian Documents
Social history of Iran and Turan in the fifteenth–nineteenth centuries
Edited by KONDO Nobuaki

Islamic Area Studies with Geographical Information Systems
Edited by OKABE Atsuyuki

Muslim Societies
Historical and comparative aspects
Edited by SATO Tsugitaka

Intellectuals in the Modern Islamic World
Transmission, transformation and communication
Edited by Stephanie Dudoignon, KOMATSU Hisao and YASUSHI Kosugi

Popular Movements and Democratization in the Islamic World
Edited by KISAICHI Masatoshi

The Moral Economy of the Madrasa

Islam and education today

**Edited by SAKURAI Keiko
and Fariba Adelkhah**

Routledge
Taylor & Francis Group

LONDON AND NEW YORK

First published 2011
by Routledge
2 Park Square, Milton Park, Abingdon, Oxfordshire OX14 4RN

Simultaneously published in the USA and Canada
by Routledge
711 Third Avenue, New York, NY 10017

First issued in paperback 2014

Routledge is an imprint of the Taylor & Francis Group, an informa company

Typeset in Times New Roman by
HWA Text and Data Management, London

British Library Cataloguing in Publication Data
A catalogue record for this book is available from the British Library

Library of Congress Cataloging in Publication Data
The moral economy of the madrasa : Islam and education today / edited by
Keiko Sakurai and Fariba Adelkhah.
    p. cm. – (New horizons in islamic studies (Second series))
  Includes bibliographical references and index.
  1. Madrasahs. 2. Islamic education. 3. Islamic religious education.
  I. Sakurai, Keiko. II. Adelkhah, Fariba.
  LC904.M67 2011   2010033208
  371.077--dc22

ISBN 13: 978-0-415-58988-8 (hbk)
ISBN 13: 978-1-138-78904-3 (pbk)

Contents

Illustrations

Tables

Figures

Contributors

Fariba Adekhah is Senior Research Fellow at SciencesPo/CERI, Paris, France. Major publications: *L'Iran*, Paris: Le cavalier bleu, collection Idées reçues, 2005; *Being Modern in Iran*, London: Hurst, 1999 & New York: Columbia University Press, 2000; *Etre Moderne en Iran*, Paris: Karthala, 1998 (new revised edition in 2006, Turkish translation in 2001). *La Révolution sous le Voile: femme Islamique d'Iran*, Paris: Karthala, 1991 (translated into Arabic in 1995, into Spanish in 1996). *Voyages du Développement. Emigration, Commerce, Exil* (with Jean-François Bayart, eds.), Paris: Karthala, 2007; *Ramadan et Politique* (with François Georgeon, eds), Paris: CNRS Editions, 2000.

Dale F. Eickelman is Ralph and Richard Lazarus Professor of Anthropology and Human Relations at Dartmouth College, USA. Major publications: *Public Islam and the Common Good*, ed. Armando Salvatore and Dale F. Eickelman (Leiden: Brill Academic Publishers, 2004). *New Media in the Muslim World: the emerging public sphere*, co-edited with Jon W. Anderson, 2nd edition (Bloomington: Indiana University Press, 2003). *The Middle East and Central Asia: an anthropological approach*, 4th edition (Upper Saddle River, NJ: Prentice Hall, 2002). *Muslim Politics*, co-edited with James Piscatori (Princeton: Princeton University Press; second edition 2003). *Muslim Travellers: pilgrimage, migration and the religious imagination*, co-edited with James Piscatori (London: Routledge; Berkeley and Los Angeles: University of California Press, 1990). *Knowledge and Power in Morocco: the education of a twentieth century notable* (Princeton: Princeton University Press, 1985).

Humayun Kabir received his PhD from the Graduate School for International Development and Cooperation, Hiroshima University, Hiroshima, Japan. Major publications: 'Diversity and homogeneity of Islamic education: colonial legacy and state policy towards *Madrasas* in Bangladesh,' *Journal of Social Studies*, Dhaka: Centre for Social Studies, 120: 1–24 (2008). 'Replicating Deobandi model of Islamic schooling: the case of a Quomi madrasa in a district town of Bangladesh,' *Contemporary South Asia* 17(4): 415–428 (December 2009). 'Exploring disciplinary knowledge of Islam in madrasa schooling in Bangladesh: The allegiance of a *Quomi* madrasa to Deoband,' *Journal of Social Studies*, Dhaka: Centre for Social Studies, 123: 18–38 (2009).

MATSUMOTO Masumi is Professor at Keiwa College, Niigata, Japan. Major publications: 'Protestant Christian Missions to Muslims in China,' *Annals of Japan Association for Middle East Studies*, 21(1): 141–171 (2005). 'Islamic Reform in Muslim Periodicals in China,' *Etudes Orientales, 21/22*: 88–104 (2004). *Study of China's Policy toward Ethnic Minorities* (Tokyo: Taga-shuppan, 1999, in Japanese) (Chinese version, *Zhongguo Minzu Zhengce de Yanjiu*, Beijing: Minzu Chubanshe, 2003). 'Rationalizing Patriotism among Muslim Chinese in Dodoigion,' in Kosugi and Komatsu (eds) *Intellectuals in the Modern Islamic World Transmission, Transformation, Communication* (London: Routledge, 2006).

SAKURAI Keiko is Professor at the School of International Liberal Studies, Waseda University, Tokyo, Japan. Major publications: *Kakumei Iran no kyokasho media: Islam to nationalism no sokoku* [Textbooks Media of Revolutionary Iran: conflict between Islam and nationalism] (Tokyo: Iwanami-shoten, 1999 in Japanese). *Gendai Iran: Kami no kuni no henbo* [Contemporary Iran: change in the land of God] (Tokyo: Iwanami-shoten, 2001, in Japanese). *Nihon no Muslim shakai* [Muslim Community in Japan] (Tokyo: Chikuma-shobo, 2003, in Japanese). *Shia-ha* [Shia Islam] (Tokyo: Chuokoron-shinsha, 2006, in Japanese). 'University entrance examination and the making of an Islamic society in Iran: a study of the post-revolutionary Iranian approach to *Konkur*,' *Iranian Studies* 37(3): 385–406 (2004). 'Muslims in contemporary Japan,' *Asian Policy* 5: 69–87 (2008). 'Une construction des immigrants musulmans: la mosquée, un espace des communautés musulmanes au Japon,' *Revue des mondes musulmans et de la Méditerranée* 125: 89–110 (2009).

SHIMBO Atsuko is Professor at Waseda University, Tokyo, Japan. Major publications: 'Educational support in the areas of ethnic minority,' *Gakujutu Kenkyu*, Waseda University, 51: 1–14 (2003). 'Ethnic minority policy under Japanese occupation', *Studies in the History of Education*, (Japan Society for the Historical Studies of Education), 47: 205–213 (2004) (in Japanese). 'Religious policy and education under the Japanese occupation; focusing on Muslim of North District in China,' *Gakujutu Kenkyu*, Waseda University, 52: 1–15 (2004) (in Japanese). 'School education and family school during the period of foundation of public education', *Studies in the History of Education*, (Japan Society for the Historical Studies of Education), 51: 104–109 (2008) (in Japanese). 'Education and empowerment of Hui Muslim women,' *Gakujutu Kenkyu*, Waseda University, 57: 1–6 (2009) (in Chinese). *Kyouiku wa fubyoudou wo kokuhuku dekiruka* Can education overcome inequality (With Shigeto Sonoda),Tokyo:Iwanami Shoten, (2010 in Japanese).

YAMANE So is Professor at the Research Institute for World Languages, Osaka University, Osaka, Japan. Major publications: 'Saiyid Abu Al-A'la Maududi's Islamic revivalism and the establishment of "Darul Islam",' *Bulletin of Asia-Pacific Studies*, Osaka, 11: 167–210 (2001) (in Japanese). *A History of Afghanistan* (Kawade-shobo, 2002, in Japanese). 'Ghalib's Delhi as Gleaned from His Urdu Letters,' *Bulletin of the Society for Western and Southern Asiatic Studies*, Kyoto University, 56: 61–99 (2002) (in Japanese). 'Horizon of Islam in South Asia: Iqbal and Maududi,' in Komatsu and Kosugi (eds) *Contemporary Islamic Thoughts and Political Movements* (Tokyo: Tokyo University Press, 2003) (in Japanese). *Analysis on Contemporary Pakistan* (Tokyo: Iwanami-shoten, 2004) (in Japanese). 'Sounds of Difference: A Study on Urdu Orthography in India in the Beginning of the 19th Century,' *International Journal of South Asian Studies*, Delhi, Manohar, 2:59–85(2009).

Acknowledgements

This book mainly reflects the findings of researches on madrasas in Asia that were undertaken from 2006 to 2009 thanks to the generous support provided by the National Institutes for the Humanities (NIHU) and the involvement of the Organization for Islamic Area Studies, Waseda University. Fieldworks were carried out and two workshops, first in Tokyo and then in Kuala Lumpur (at the occasion of the International Conference 'New Horizons in Islamic Area Studies: Islamic Scholarship Across Cultures and Continents' on 22–24 November 2008) allowed the whole research team to discuss its findings. Those fieldworks and gatherings were possible thanks again to the funding of the NIHU and the warm support of Professor SATO Tsugitaka (Dean of the Organization for Islamic Area Studies, Waseda University) and Professor YUKAWA Takeshi (Senior Researcher of the Organization for Islamic Area Studies). No words can express our thanks to them for their trust from the beginning and the freedom they gave us to frame this volume in our own way.

Last but not least, they also helped to build this project as a joint venture under an exchange program between SciencesPo, Paris and Waseda University. This was made successful also thanks to Francis Vérillaud (Director of International Affairs Division at SciencesPo, in charge of the exchange program with Waseda) and his counterpart at Waseda University for this exchange program, Professor Yoshiharu Tsuboi, Christian Lequesne (Director of the Centre for International Research and Studies at SciencesPo) and SciencesPo's Asian Study Centre, which offered warm hospitality that allowed the two editors to prepare the manuscript.

We also acknowledge the patience with which Dale Eickelman provided comments and feedback. He went so far as sometimes re-editing the papers and providing new references. He also participated in our Kuala Lumpur workshop. He shared his professional experience and regularly answered our many e-mails calling for help on the spot. Let's just say thank you Dale, thank you.

Such a book never would have reached actual publication without the precious help of some very honorable colleagues. We owe them a lot since, although overwhelmed, they never refused to read and comment on a paper and send interesting documents. Among them, we would like to thank Elisabeth Allès (CNRS, EHESS-CECMC), Talal Asad (The City University of New York), Jean-François Bayart (CNRS, SciencesPo), Leila Cherif-Chebbi (OFPRA-CECMC),

Gilles Dorronsoro (Sorbonne I, Carnegie), Tatsuya Kusakabe (Hiroshima University), Roland Marchal (CNRS, SciencesPo), Olivier Roy (CNRS, EHESS, European University Institute in Florence), and Masahiko Togawa (Hiroshima University).

Our special thanks go to all institutions and people in charge, who facilitated our researches by understanding our project, by warmly welcoming our questions, by opening their library to us, by giving us their precious time, and by sharing their very experiences.

Let's not forget to thank Islamic schools and universities throughout our field works, national archives centres, *Waqf* institutions, ministries of education, etc. in all those countries in which research was carried out.

Last but not least, we would like to warmly thank Miriam Perier and Ryuichi Sugiyama for helping us to put our manuscript to the standards required by Routledge.

Note on transliterations

This book draws on source materials in Arabic, Persian, Afghan, Urdu, Chinese, Bengali, transliteration conversions preferred by Muslims as well as non-Muslims, writings in English or in French, and colloquial as well as literary uses in these languages. As consistently as possible, we use the system adopted by the *International Journal of Middle East Studies*, except for proper names, substantives such as titles (ayatollah), institutions (hoseynieh) and places (Karadj). These words are part of our daily usage on the Internet and for the sake of coherence we decided not to modify them. Also we omit diacritics. Although religious terms often derive from Arabic—for example, the Arabic *sunna* (tradition) becomes *sunnat* in Persian—we decided not to impose the Arabic where it does not accurately reflect local or regional usage. When appropriate, the common origins of such terms are indicated in the glossary. Likewise, the plural of most foreign terms, especially those derived from Arabic, is indicated by the addition of an 's' to the singular.

1 Introduction

The moral economy of the madrasa

Fariba Adelkhah and Keiko Sakurai

Learning the sciences and disseminating knowledge are important duties for Muslims, and this is why places of teaching have been given a special status in Islam. Irrespective of the name given (such as madrasa, *hawza, maktab, kuttab*, and *jamia*), the places where knowledge is imparted are highly regarded by Muslim communities around the world. In fact, numerous *hadith*s, or sayings of the Prophet, underline the need for knowledge: 'Seek knowledge, from the cradle to the grave, even if it is to be found in a place as distant as China,' although, as Keiko Sakurai rightly reminds us in this book (chapter 3), women were excluded until modern times.[1]

Since knowledge is considered a religious duty, mosques (*masjid*s, literally, places of worship) were the first institution of learning in Islam (Makdisi, 1981: 10). Whether viewed as an institution or simply as a 'venue of convenience' (Berkey, 2007: 42), whether viewed as a formal or as an informal institution (Berkey, 1992a),[2] they play an important role in the organization of classes and lectures: two perfect examples are those of the Zeitouna mosque in Tunisia (established on 731) and the Sheikh Ansari mosque (also called Masjid-e torka)[3] in Najaf (Iraq), where Khomeini used to pray and impart his teachings during his long exile (1963–1977). Furthermore, other sites of education have come into existence over the centuries such as *khanqah* (Sufi hospice), *maktab* (place for writing) and, of course, madrasa[4] (literally place of teaching, or place for teaching law). Subsequently, larger and more ambitious institutions like universities were also built, such as al-Azhar in Egypt (established in 972), Nizamiyya in Baghdad (established in 1067).[5] This multiplicity of institutions scattered all over the Muslim world has broadened the possibility of religious education and the development of different trends in the understanding and teaching of Islam, as Muslim scholars are traditionally encouraged to move from place to place in order to look for knowledge (Gellens, 1990). The renowned centers of Islamic knowledge have evolved over centuries in places like Kufa, Baghdad, Damascus, Cairo, Tunisia, Cordoba, Najaf, Isfahan, Qom, Delhi, Deoband, Lucknow and, as desired by Afghan Shia quite possibly in the future, Kabul.

Although Islamic knowledge does not build a united *umma* by itself, it has always been used as an instrument of power. In fact, this is why knowledge has also been a subject of debate, rivalry and conflict among various religious authorities and believers throughout the centuries. To a great extent, this friction explains the variety of schools of *fiqh* (Islamic law): from the early stages of Islam they included the Hanafi, named after Abu Hanifa al-Numan (d.767); the Maliki, named after Malik ibn Anas (d.795); the Shafii, named after Muhammad ibn Idris al-Shafii (d.820); and the Hanbali, named after Ahmad ibn Hanbal (d.855). The Shia and Ismaili communities follow the Jafari school, named after Imam Jafar Sadiq (d.765). Later the Wahhabi school, named after Muhammad Abd al-Wahhab (d.1791) and the Bahai school, named after Bahaollah (d.1892), follow the reformist paths of their founders. One should also underline that the strengthening of one of the most prominent educational institutions, the Nizamiyya school in Baghdad, is the consequence of opposition to the divisions of that time, such as the Mutazalites in the eleventh century (Sikand, 2005: 27; Malik, 2008: 4). It worth adding that the term madrasa seems to fall within the scope of this Nizamiyya tradition (Fischer, 1980: 38–39). Besides, conflicts have not only existed between different schools of *fiqh* but also within each school, as people who were educated in the madrasa could take up positions that are important in any Muslim community: *muftis*, judges, bureaucrats working in religious institutions (such as *waqf*, or pious endowments), and others who are supposed to regulate everyday life (weddings, funerals, religious gatherings, pilgrimages, mosque). Moreover, conflicts could also be rooted in the economic power of the learning institutions as they often possess substantial financial resources (Berkey, 1992a: 112–116).

Religious learning institutions and the madrasa, despite being one of the oldest Islamic institutions—some date from the eleventh century—have often been looked on with suspicion by modern states, whether Western or Muslim. More recently, a not-so-interested or even ignorant international (i.e. Western) community also became openly distrustful of them when Islamic extremism was linked to the teaching of the madrasa. While this perception crystallized with the Iranian revolution in 1979 and the terrorist attacks that took place in the subsequent decade in Europe and the Middle East, it was strengthened by the takeover of Kabul in 1996, as the Deobandi madrasa provided the rank and file of the new Afghan regime—the well-known Taliban. The September 11th tragedy further radicalized this belief. The common understanding nowadays is that Islam is both a religion and a political entity, and that in order to control one of its dimensions, one has to control the other.

Numerous authors, many among those we are referring to in this volume, have argued against this view, showing it to be too simplistic and lacking any logical grounding. While sharing their concerns, we intend to change our analytical approach from the available literature on this subject today. Our intention is not to offer a discursive analysis of the syllabus of representative madrasas and how they have changed over time or in various social and political contexts. Our goal is not to illustrate their adaptation, flexibility or even modernity in order to contradict the criticism that views these schools as outdated institutions.[6] We do not deny that a disposition to violence has also been one of the possible outcomes of madrasa education, in the past as well as today, not because of poverty (Saleem, 2008), but because if knowledge means power, it is possible that power could spring from knowledge, including knowledge imparted within or because of these religious institutions. Our primary goal is to assess the activities of institutions dedicated to religious knowledge in the same way we assess other knowledge institutions that are influenced by their environment and try to change it, even though the agenda of madrasas is indeed broader. In other words, we would like to deal with what Dale Eickelman, following and commenting on Pierre Bourdieu, although very critical of his misrecognition of the historical context in which his work is produced, calls 'the political economy of meaning,' or 'the reproduction and transmission of systems of meaning and how these shape and in turn are shaped by configurations of power and economic relations among groups and classes in different societies' (Eickelman, 1979: 386; 2009). In this perspective we look at the inevitable interactions between more traditional (and religious) institutions and the more modern ones in order to grasp the dynamics at play. By illustrating their connections with the past and the scholastic tradition and their enrolment in modernity (Asad 1993), we intend to describe the historical context, during the last three decades, in which Islam contributes to integrating categories that were marginal for different reasons: pluralism, new identities, equality of rights and development. Following Dale Eickelman's seminal comments on the sociology of education, he writes, 'Durkheim in his *Evolution of Educational Thought* was explicitly concerned with the historical problem of change in dominant ideologies of higher education and how these ideologies were related to the conflicting interests of class and social groups and were manipulated by them' (1979: 392). These conflicts create opportunities that might lead to violent action but also to the improved communication and dialogue essential for creating a shared public space (Eickelman and Salvatore, 2004). We do not want to use dichotomies to analyze madrasas such as good versus bad, liberal versus totalitarian, or tradition versus modernity. One should not deny the continued relevance of these schools, whose impressive development over the last thirty years tells us much about the blind spots of our modern yet Manichæan understanding of religion and tradition (Hefner and Zaman, 2007).

In this perspective, analyzing madrasas necessitates a semantic clarification. These institutions lie at the crossroads between religious and secular realities, between the national and the transnational, or between faith, Islam and its desire to have dialogue with the rest of the world, including the West, as well as lay and secular milieus. Bear in mind that 'laïcité,' as the French say, is a 'political choice defining the place of religion in an authoritarian and legal sense,' and that the phenomenon of secularization is first of all a process: 'it is when religion ceases to be the focus of men's lives, even when they still define themselves as believers [that] men's actions and the meaning they give to the world no longer come under the sign of the transcendental or the religious' (Roy, 2005: 19–20).

Madrasas are general training and educational (from elementary to tertiary) institutions, geared towards producing and transmitting knowledge. Are they also institutions devoted to religious education, general instruction, or they are religious institutions devoted simply to religious instruction? Are they run by clerics, or can lay people also take a part in their management?

It will quickly become apparent that the answer is not in fact that simple. After all, a state-run university can offer theology courses, and religious schools can offer secular subjects. The terminology current in Muslim countries reflects this indeterminate state. In Arabic, the word madrasa signifies a teaching institution of various levels. As it happens, teaching and research institutions were religious in ancient Muslim societies, as were the first universities, such as Bologna and the Sorbonne, in Christian Europe. But the identification of the madrasa with the religious educational field is in a sense accidental, even though it is a constant in most South Asian countries. In Iran, for instance, the word madrasa refers generally to state schools, and religious schools are known as *maktab* or, for the training of clerics, *madrasa-i ilmiyya* or *hawza-i ilmiyya*. In this book, we will be dealing solely with contemporary madrasas in the religious sense of the word, as institutions in which students receive religious teaching, which can offer complementary modern teaching as well. The main point to grasp at this stage is that madrasas are geared first and foremost towards producing and transmitting knowledge, starting with reading and writing the language of the sacred book, the Quran. As such, they have a relationship with power. We could refer to them with the concept of 'power-knowledge' coined by Foucault, or we could speak of hegemony, citing Gramsci. Either way, madrasas have a role in defining and reproducing epistème, 'sens commun,' consensus and domination. This is what George W. Bush understood in his own way when he tried to force Pakistan to reform its madrasas in the wake of September 11th, within the framework of the strategy of 'democratizing' the 'Greater Middle East.' This will leave some people affirming that madrasas are one of the keys to the 'clash of civilizations,' likening them to recruiting offices for potential terrorists (Riaz, 2008: 20–51). It is true that madrasas are one of the issues—or even one of the causes—behind the often-violent clashes between Muslims and the West. But these conflicts initially tore apart Muslim societies themselves, by putting clerics and lay intellectuals at loggerheads with each other, but also by promoting discord among clerics or among lay intellectuals. The antagonisms that agitated madrasas were mainly internal Islamic ones. Some divided religious and secular people with respect to the content and direction of social change. Others carried the seeds of theological, legal, confraternal and sectarian divisions sometimes leading to schisms, at the extreme exclusion and persecution, as with the Bahai in Iran and the Ahmadiyya in South Asia.

Working on knowledge and its production will not lead us to favour the role of ideas, belief or culture. As Paul Veyne (2007: 228–230) demonstrated with respect to ancient Christianity, people's ideas tend to match their practices, not the opposite. Granted, ideas have their own autonomous lives, which often last longer than those of the relevant practices and have their own validity. Knowledge contributes to creating or forming a tangible social situation. It is a speech act or 'speech event' (John Bowen, 1993: 9). From that perspective, madrasas should by their very nature be seen as part of a specific historic and social situation, that they themselves help define. On the one hand, they are not static, as they span the centuries. On the other hand, their course/development is not identical from one country to another.[7] In this book, we speak of the full diversity of contemporary madrasas in five different countries, namely Afghanistan, Bangladesh, China, Iran and Pakistan. This will show that the lowest common denominator is to be found in their relationship with public, state or modern—i.e., non-religious—teaching.

Contemporary madrasas are educational institutions that are not disconnected from the transformation of society itself. So-called 'Muslim' societies have undergone profound change in recent decades: their demographics have changed, they have become more urbanized, state centralization and bureaucratization has progressed, the organization of economic life has changed, international migrations have taken place, and the list goes on.

For instance between 1980 and 2005, the population increased from 13 million to 24 million in Afghanistan, from about 90 million to 150 million in Bangladesh, from 980 million to 1.3 billion in China, from about 39 million to 70 million in Iran and from about 85 million to 159 million in Pakistan.[8] According to the latest data, adult literacy (15 years and over) has increased from 29.2 to 53.5 per cent (1981–2007) in Bangladesh, from 5.5 to 93.3 per cent (1982–2007) in China, from 52.3 to 82.3 per cent (1986–2006) in Iran and from 25.7 to 54.2 per cent (1981–2006) in Pakistan.[9]

The impact of these transformations on madrasas is evident, and madrasas can no more escape them than can state school systems. Moreover madrasas have been evolving by constantly supplying increasing demand for education, which in many cases was neglected by the state. The increase in the number of madrasas since the 1980s is clear evidence of how madrasas have evolved in line with the changing environment. Thus, madrasas are mass educational institutions all facing the economic disorder, and specifically the property speculation sparked by rapid urbanization. They must deal with states that have differing degrees of centralization and bureaucratization, but also with local government and NGOs that are emerging as a potent force in planning and development (Eickelman, 2007: 146). They have had to deal with major political events such as the consolidation of state power by the secularist Communist Party in China, the independence of Bangladesh, the 1979 Iranian Revolution, the Soviet occupation of Afghanistan and the ensuing civil war, or the 'fight against terror.' They have reacted to these upheavals or shocks by adapting themselves and innovating, in their organization, their teaching methods or their curricula. We describe diverse situations in this book, and one must bear in mind that contemporary madrasas have tended to adopt the bureaucratic model of modern state education, with the notion of courses and prerequisites, the spatial organization around classrooms, lecture theatres, libraries and IT rooms, the financing of study by means of scholarships granted by the bureaucracy on the basis of academic achievement, standardized and merchandised teaching manuals, the splitting of the school or academic year into semesters and vacations, and, in some cases, social protection akin to that of a Western welfare state.

Like the students of France's most prestigious higher education institutions, such as the *Ecole normale supérieure* or *Polytechnique* (*Ecole nationale d'administration*), the *talib*s (students of religion) are akin to civil servants, receiving wages, and also enjoying paid leave and other advantages that are no doubt not for nothing in the appeal of their courses. Thus, the teaching of Arabic, which provides access to the Quran, no longer involves the teaching of civilization, but rather the study of a grammar book, purely instrumental and disconnected from history. This makes Arabic a communication tool, a technique, on the same level as calligraphy, which is still widely taught, but as an art, if not a handicraft. The Quran's supporting material—printed version, CD-Rom, filmed version—is trivialized: the mass reproduction of holy books means that people take less care when handling them, and students can stop or fast-forward a recording or switch from one support to another as they please (Adelkhah, 1999a: 107–108). Religious knowledge becomes a corpus of practical and utilitarian solutions for the problems of modern-day life. Lastly, madrasa administration is increasingly influenced by management science, with accounting and financial rules, bureaucratic procedures, ledgers, human resources management, user-consultation processes. This makes them a competitive and challenging field occupied by players moved by different and varied contemporary motivations.

This means that madrasas are a reflection of the societies in which they have grown, while at the same time they contribute to building these societies. The most important point is that they help make education more widely available, to the point where it is now widely deemed to be essential. They offer access to knowledge that is all the more precious that the state school system cannot provide it, either because the financial resources are lacking or because of its outrageously elitist character, and because state schools, in insufficient numbers, are more often than not concentrated in the larger cities – and often in their center. In any event, madrasas often come across as better adapted to social conditions, and are considered effective because of their flexibility, a bit like *hawala* and the interest-free loan chests, which are better suited to the needs of the population, in some milieus, than banks. This reasoning goes for the education of the girls and young women sent to madrasas, if only because they represent a non-negligible slice of the school market. This is because madrasas, which help make education more widely available, also help make education a marketable commodity. For education is indeed a market, increasingly occupied by businessmen, often expatriates, or politicians. These people are sometimes looking to make a profit, against the backdrop of the deregulation and privatization of public services (Herrera, 2006: 39–42). Often, they are also looking to move up the social ladder, bearing in mind that the founders and benefactors of madrasas can generally hope to reap social recognition, or even electoral benefits. Thus private madrasas provide a link with globalization. At the very least, they relay the global lingua franca, English, as well as information and communication technologies, including audio, video, IT and the Internet.

As we will see, the development of madrasas is not simply a religious phenomenon in the strict sense of the term. In Pakistan for instance, the government's goal of cheaply improving national educational statistics and to respect the desiderata of multilateral institutions has prompted it to foster the creation and development of madrasas, which have taken their place in the official teaching system (Saleem, 2009: 105–106). And in numerous least-developed countries, including Afghanistan and Pakistan, as well as a lot of sub-Saharan African countries, Islamic teaching is the only sort available to poor people, and even some members of the middle classes (Rahman, 2004: 91–92). Periods of economic crisis and structural adjustments have reinforced their appeal. However, it would be a big mistake to reduce madrasas to schools for underprivileged people. Just as adherence to Islam is far from being restricted to desperate people and can extend into higher socioeconomic categories, including intellectuals, engineers, doctors and the owners of large stores, madrasas also take in children from the middle and even upper-middle classes, in addition to the fact that they help their promoters move up the social ladder, as we pointed out earlier. As social institutions, they illustrate and support the ascension of the middle class that has gone hand in hand with urbanization.

From this perspective the various chapters in this book will tend to imply that madrasas are not, or not only, the expression of an identity and a lack of openness specific to Muslims. They were open to the world, and vice versa, and some believe that their organization based on *waqf* provided the model of the university endowment in Oxford (Makdisi, 1981; Gaudiosi, 1988). *Hawza* in Iran has perpetuated the original scholastic tradition, by accepting the Greek philosophical heritage and the pedagogy of paideia, as demonstrated by Michael Fischer's (1980) and Roy Mottahedeh's (1985) impressive studies.[10] In India, at the end of the nineteenth century, madrasas opened up, albeit in a critical and reactionary manner, to Western thoughts (Metcalf, 1982), while in Najaf, in the 1970s, Muhammad Baqir al-Sadr, the great theorist of Islamic economics, was not indifferent to the socialist way of thinking, something for which he was often criticized (Mallat, 1993: 142; Walbridge, 2001: 136–137). Madrasas are faced with the social, cultural, religious, and educational pluralism that characterizes contemporary Muslim societies. This interaction is not devoid of difficulties and occasionally degenerates into conflict, if only because of the need for the reciprocal distinction that both systems suppose. Religious or secular radicalism is often the price to pay for this interaction. We do not see this in ecumenical terms. By definition, this interaction involves the antagonism and passion transmitted by difference, the competition for resources or access to power, and increasingly, proximity as religious teaching becomes more bureaucratic and rational. And paradoxically, madrasas, as a framework for teaching, end up by contributing in their own way to a certain secularization: by legitimizing the need for universal education, even for girls or for various ethnic or sectarian minorities; by competing against, complementing and offering synergies with state schools; by adjusting to a constant play between educational supply and demand; and by 'nationalizing' themselves and validating the established state framework.

The latter point is of particular interest. On the one hand, madrasas increasingly exist within a national space that bends them into compliance with public policy or ideology. These policies and ideologies in turn help affirm a national form of Islam. The identification of the Islamic Republic of Iran with Shiism and the transformation of Qom into a major holy city are an extreme example of this. Nevertheless, in Afghanistan, Shia madrasas also aspire to making the country a new magnet for Islamic teaching, comparable to Qom or Najaf. And in China, madrasas have appropriated the benefits of Communism, particularly in terms of the emancipation of women, and are in turn 'nationalizing' themselves.

On the other hand, madrasas continue to perpetuate the transnational dimension of the *umma* and to look abroad for models (Noor *et al.*, 2008: 17–18). The al-Azhar in Cairo is legendary, in a positive sense in most Sunni countries, particularly in Southeast Asia, or in a negative sense, by dint of the contestation it inspires, as in Iran (Zaman, 2007: 251–252).

The ambivalent relationship between Shia madrasas in Afghanistan and Iran is also very telling with respect to the interaction between the nation state and the transnational dimension. The creative tension between Islamic teaching and state schools is compounded by tension stemming from the simultaneous desire to move beyond national borders and to reinforce them. Contrary to what state authorities and some intellectuals contend, the transnational dimension does not necessarily preclude the nation and its state and it can contribute to state formation (Bayart, 2007). Obviously, the synergy between one and the other gives rise to numerous conflicts that in turn help turn madrasas into spaces of secularization.

Madrasa are a meeting place between the holders of state power and other members of civil society, particularly benefactors working to establish and run schools. The two can cooperate, but they can also be in conflict. This is not to say that managers and students of madrasas are particularly active in the political and electoral arena or in social organizations, if the Iranian example is anything to go by. But the status and financing of Islamic education informs a critical debate between the respective roles and responsibilities of state and madrasa, and the virtues of the market and the private sector. The question of schools, including madrasas, cannot be dissociated from the public debate on political economy, and beyond that, globalization. At the same time, madrasas, which are built on confidence—confidence of families vis-à-vis an institution deemed pious and not-for-profit, confidence of the state vis-à-vis an apolitical institution that is helping rebuild the nation's moral fiber in the face of the communist peril and secular materialism—are today faced with the vital need for accountability, not only in the face of the government, from which they must gain recognition and whose regulations must be respected, but also vis-à-vis students, who need to be able to use their education in the job market and who become users—or rather consumers—by virtue of the fact that they pay school fees. In other words the issue of madrasa is related to the concept of the moral economy in the sense it refers to the issue of legitimacy and social justice, their representation, the 'deep emotions' they raise, and their materialization (Thompson, 1963: chapter 3; 1993: 336ff). In fact, by using the concept of the moral economy of the madrasa, we would like to emphasize not only the 'moral' dimension of the economic practices, but also the economic dimension of cultural and religious practices. Here, Islamic education appears to be the ground of interaction between moral and political economy.

Given the prevailing polemical view of madrasas, it may appear surrealistic and naive to emphasize the interaction and complementary nature, albeit rooted in conflict at times, between madrasa and state schooling. Both these systems now rely on each other, in some countries at least, and this interdependence is an opportunity as much as a constraint. It will appear even more surprising that we see in madrasa the possibility of 'emerging from the minority,' whether it be for women, ethnic or sectarian minorities, people from rural milieus or underprivileged families; and, from the perspective of the *umma* and each of the countries that make it up, a way of maintaining rank on the international stage by emphasizing its respectability and identity in the name of the legitimate and universal quest for knowledge.

However, post-revolutionary France has already shown us how outrageously religious teaching, the chief goal of which was to turn the republicans' own cognitive arms against themselves, ended up by secularizing the very Catholic western provinces, and particularly Brittany (Lagrée, 1992). Comparisons have their limits. But this detour through history and religious sociology allows us to reintroduce the notion of duration. However diverse the social phenomena represented by madrasa, teaching, including Islamic teaching, is now a critical issue in political, social and theological debate in Muslim societies. Now that madrasas are part of mass education in countries where access to knowledge has become a vital need for families, offering a key to the world, they find themselves outside the strict religious and clerical boundaries, at the very heart of public life.

Notes

1 It is by no means underestimating the importance of some rare exceptions such as the one during the Mamluk rule (1250–1517) in Egypt where religious education was never exclusively for the elite but was open to all—including women and the 'common people.' See Berkey (1992b).

2 Jonathan Berkey describes the transmission of religious knowledge as a highly personal process, one dependent on the relationships between individual scholars and students. The great variety of institutional structures, he argues, supported educational efforts without ever becoming essential to them.

3 We do not know when this mosque was built, but this place is closely associated to Sheikh Mortada Ansari, Ayatollah Khomeini's most influential mentor, who was born in Iran and buried in Najaf (about 1799–1864). He was also the first marja to develop the theory of Zeynabieh, see Momen (1985: 311).

4 According to Jamal Malik, darasa, the root of the word madrasa, refers to an institution supporting Muslim scholastic philosophy and law (2008: 4–5, 49). This is a common idea among specialists of India.

5 For an erudite development on educational institutions in Islam, see George Makdisi (1981).

6 This period change is strikingly attested by the stance taken by one of the most brilliant scholars, Nikki Keddie, who, although very cautious, actually thought in the 1970s that religious institutions were rooted in the past of Islam and had little future as such, especially in the field of education in the Middle East (1978: 7). On a different

note and analysing Islamic education, Dale F. Eickelman recalls the extent to which historians and sociologists have tended to take at face value the ideological claim in Islam of the fixed nature of religious knowledge (1978: 490).

7 For instance and referring to Ibn Khaldoun, Dale F. Eickelman underscores that the role of memory was stressed more in Morocco than elsewhere in the Islamic Middle East (1978: 490).

8 United Nations Population Division, World Population Prospects: The 2008 Revision Population Database. <http://esa.un.org/unpp> (accessed 10 January 2010).

9 UNESCO. <http://stats.uis.unesco.org> (accessed 10 January 2010).

10 Jonathan Berkey (2003: chapter 21) argues that much that we take as characteristic of Islam is in fact the product of the medieval period.

2 The rise of new madrasas and the decline of tribal leadership within the Federal Administrated Tribal Area (FATA), Pakistan

So Yamane

In 1996, in a Pakistani village known as 'T' within the Federal Administrated Tribal Area (FATA), around fifty Arabs, who wanted to control the area, suddenly entered the village and fought against the tribals who did not want the Arabs to control them. The Arabs were able to enter the area because some tribal youngsters let them in; these Arabs were fighting the internal war in Afghanistan with the Taliban and were looking for a place to hide. As the Arabs entered, they shot at the gate of the tribal chief's residence killing some tribe members. The angry tribal chief ordered the entire tribe to fight the Arabs. As a result of the severe gunfight, the tribal members succeeded in killing some of the Arabs and got rid of them. According to the tribal chief, since then, neither the Arabs nor the Taliban have attempted to enter this area.

Twelve years later, in the spring of 2008, bombs fell on the *jirga* meeting in FATA, causing numerous casualties. It is said that those who opposed the traditional tribal system carried out this attack.

According to the tribal chief, the situation in the tribal area has now become unstable. The tribal leadership that had been traditionally held by the elders has been transformed into a newly-emerging religious leadership, and the new leaders are being trained at the newly-established madrasas in the area.

It is common knowledge that the ethnic majority of the Taliban is Pashtun: 'The tribals of the area are known to be ethnically and ideologically linked to the Taliban and Pashtuns, and South Waziristan—with nearly three hundred kilometres of border with Afghanistan—has become the hub of the Al-Qaeda and Taliban elements' (Nuri, 2005: 130).[1] Most of these soldiers, who had voluntarily joined, were once Afghani refugees belonging to the madrasas in Pakistan. They were treated as guests by the local traditional society where the traditional tribal code of life—*Pashtunwali*—has been in effect. However, some of the mullahs and madrasa students opposed the traditional leadership. The above-mentioned cases are examples of such opposition.

The authority of the tribal leaders in FATA has been challenged by the mullas and the students of the newly-established madrasas in two ways. First, the students are not necessarily Pashtun, and they neglect the Pashtun tribal code and seniority system. Second, the students challenge the tribal peoples' understanding of the coexistence of Islam and the tribal code by introducing politicized Islam.

In this chapter, we intend to describe in details this dual challenge to the tribal elders' authority, by analyzing the context in which the madrasas have developed. Of particular relevance is the fact that the primary explanation encompasses political and financial aspects throughout the Soviet Union presence in Afghanistan that was reinforced by migratory dimension and not essentially linked to the resurgence of a trend of political Islam polarized by holy war. This analysis provides therefore a historical background that help us understand that madrasas are not only tools for mobilizing people but also give an opportunity to renew the political or religious hierarchies.[2]

Pashtun society and FATA

In 1947, Pakistan—a country that comprises different ethnic groups possessing their own language and cultural heritage, such as Panjabis, Pashtuns, Sindhis, Balochis, and Kashmiris—became an independent country. Currently, 96.28 per cent of the total population is Muslim (*Population Census of Pakistan, 1998*),[3] 75 per cent of the Pakistani Muslims belong to the Sunni sect,[4] 20 per cent are Shiite and the rest are mostly Hindus and Christians.

The North-West Frontier Province (NWFP), which borders Afghanistan, was created by British India under the FCR, Frontier Crimes Regulations, in 1901. Pashtun is the major ethnic group in this border area. The 2,500 kilometer-long border, called the 'Durand Line,' between Pakistan and Afghanistan was set by the British and Afghanistan in 1893. This border was inherited by Pakistan; but when Pakistan became independent, after the 'Pakistan Movement', in 1947, the Pashtuns led a movement of their own toward autonomy, and this was called the 'Pashtunistan Movement,' which was supported by the government of Afghanistan. This movement rendered Pakistan's situation extremely fragile. After several political discussions, some of the Pashtuns agreed with the ideology of the Pakistan Movement and decided to join Pakistan, while at the same time remaining autonomous in their tribal area that then became the 'Federal Administrated Tribal Area' (FATA; see Figure 2.1). It consists of seven Agencies and six Frontier Regions whose total population amounts to 3,138,000 with a low level of literacy of 29.5 per cent for males and 3 per cent for females (Zaman, 2005: 73).

According to Article 1 of the Constitution of Pakistan, FATA is treated as a separate entity, and following Article 247, it is administrated by the Federal Government.[5] Therefore, although FATA is part of the NWFP, it is outside its executive authority, and the Governor of the NWFP, in his capacity as an Agent to the President, is in charge of regulating its affairs (Hussain, 2005: 5). Thus, we can say that there exist institutional differences between FATA and the NWFP. For instance, 'a man who committed murder in broad daylight and in front of witnesses in the Tribal Areas would not be tried according to the laws of the land prevalent in the rest of the British Indian Empire. He would be tried according to

Figure 2.1 Map of FATA

the laws of Pashtunwali—the customary and traditional Code of the Pashtuns—as interpreted by the *jirga*' (Ahmed, 1986: 135). During the British rule in India, the British left the tribal structure largely untouched (Ahmed, 1986: 135). Tribal structures were allowed to function uninterrupted and undisturbed; their tribal 'purity' was thus ensured (Ahmed, 1986: 131).[6] This is why the tribal areas have been called 'the last free place on earth' (Ahmed, 1986: 135). Every foreigner who intends to enter this area has to first obtain permission from the government of Pakistan. Even Pakistani governmental officials, including army personnel, cannot move freely inside the area. In contrast, the Pashtuns living in the NWFP can move about freely, as it is regarded as part of '*Pashtunistan*.' For example, the Salarzai tribe lives across the border in Afghanistan. Until a few decades ago, kinsmen on both sides of the border followed the tradition of cross-migration every few years and used to live in the homes and lands of their cousins across the border. This was of course a tactic that was used to give the Pashtuns the opportunity to take advantage of the economic conditions that prevailed in the valley on the other side of the border (Hussain, 2005: 4).

Although the people in FATA and those living in South Afghanistan seem to share the same history, there are a few differences between them, especially in their degree of acceptance of modernization. People in South Afghanistan, especially those in the towns, enjoyed modern education until the 1970s, since King Amanullah had started to modernize the country in the early 1920s. In contrast, people in FATA were unable to obtain regular education in their area for a long time. This was due to the fact that since the area had been uninterrupted and undisturbed, in other words, since it was rather backward in terms of the social infrastructure, no modern educational system was introduced for a long time. Another difference between these two areas lies in the fact that the presence of Sufi Saints in South Afghanistan was traditionally accepted. This acceptance was demonstrated by the political system, which did not prevent the Sufi leaders from becoming political leaders.

The Pashtun society consists of clans and sub-clans comprising families and *maliks*, and the tribal chiefs head each sub-clan. The Pashtun are known for their tribal code of life, called *Pashtunwali*. This is not a written document, but a code of ethics understood by all Pashtun. *Pashtunwali* consists of the basic concepts of social life, including honor (*nang*), reciprocity (*badal*), compromise (*nanawatay*), hospitality (*milmastiya*), *jirga* (council of elders), and so on. In addition, the Pashtuns have a loosely collected set of old customs called *riwaj*. In the FATA area, both Pashtunwali and *riwaj* are the basic codes of life.

The federal civil bureaucrats or political agents represent the government in the area. They act as magistrates and are in charge of appointing the members of the *jirga*. For instance, in South Waziristan of FATA, the political agent is called the 'King of Waziristan' (*de Waziristan badshah*) (Ahmed, 1986: 75). Nevertheless, in spite of his vast authority, he has to pay respect to the tribal code of life. The political agent controls the tribes and keeps a close eye on any particular ebb and flow of the tribal customs. He acts as an executive, a judge, and a revenue collector.[7] He does not often interfere with the domestic affairs of the tribes as these are regulated by a rigid, unwritten code of conduct or 'code of honor' (Khan, 2005: 89). Many important matters are decided according to the *riwaj* in contradistinction with the Islamic law or even the official law implemented by the government (Teepu, 2008: 101). In case of any problem in the society, the *jirga* examines the issue and presents the verdict before the magistrate. Then the magistrate examines the proceedings of the *jirga* to determine whether justice has been done as per the *riwaj* (Hussain, 2005: 5). The *jirga*, especially the tribal *Wulasi Jirga*, is strictly dominated by the local *riwaj*, and the Islamic law is rarely applied during its proceedings.[8] If the verdict seems to be correct, the magistrate announces it as a decision of the court; if not, he remands the case back to the *jirga* to ensure the correct and just application of the prevalent *riwaj* and holds a new *jirga* again. This traditional system of *jirga* has been paid utmost respect by the government. The government gives the *jirga* members the title of *maliks* or *lungis* and awards them regular allowances called *mawajib* (Hussain, 2005: 7). The *maliks*, or tribal chiefs, are paid a hereditary allowance of *mawajib*, whereas the *lungis* are given an allowance for services rendered at a particular time, and the allowance ends with the death of the individual concerned (Hussain, 2005: 7). Therefore, the status and authority of the elders of the Pashtun society was protected not only by their tradition but also by the government.[9]

According to Asta Olesen, although it may be argued that *Pashtunwali* formed the ideological basis of the Afghan state from 1747 to the mid-nineteenth century, this does not imply that *Pashtunwali* constituted the main ideological frame of reference of the ethnically heterogeneous and divided society (Olesen, 1995: 36). Anthropologists have often pointed out the coexistence of both Islam and the traditional codes of conduct in Pashtun life. Ahmed Akbar goes further and underlines the fact that Islam and Pashtunness coalesce and overlap (Ahmed, 1986: 90). Although there is often a divergence or clash between the *riwaj* and Islamic law, in some matters, for example, in the case of giving a share of inheritance to the daughter, the edicts of the Islamic law are avoided under the *riwaj* (Teepu, 2008: 101). In fact, not only was Islam part of the legal and moral basis of society, mediated through and coexisting with the tribal code and local customs, but also, for many centuries, all learning and education in the country took place within an exclusively religious framework.

In the traditional hierarchy, both the elder *jirga* members and the religious leaders had their own authority. Islamic religious groups that provide leadership in society may be broadly divided into three categories. The first two are defined by their function in society and the third by its genealogical links with holy ancestors. The first, the *ulama*, is defined by religious and legal learning and includes a *mufti*, *qazi*, *maulana*, and *maulvi*. The second category, defined by esoteric, sometimes unorthodox practices, includes groups like the Sufis. The third category includes the *sharif* or *sayyid* (descended from the Prophet), and the *mian* (descended from holy men) (Ahmed, 1986: 85). However, one more religious authority—the mullah who appeared at the local level—is, according to Ahmed Akbar, difficult to list in these three categories because these individuals neither possess the *sanad* (certificate of religious education) nor are they a part of the descendents of holy men, and they can hardly be classified as sufis or esoteric men. This is why, when, in 1997, Mullah Muhammad Umar—the pioneer and leader of the Taliban movement—was nominated as 'Amir al-Muminin' or the Caliph of Umma, he was hesitant to accept the title since he was unable to complete his religious education and had no sanad when he joined the jihad of the anti-Soviet war. In other words, although an unclassified category, the mullas enjoy authority in the local areas and exert their influence especially upon the young people, both religiously and politically. In our discussion, we will further elaborate on this special context through which the Taliban, led by Mullah Umar, was able transcend the local border areas and seize power in Afghanistan.

Madrasas in FATA and its surrounding regions

The formation of madrasas underwent three phases in South Asia. The first phase is the era in which traditional Quranic studies were imparted at privately supervised madrasas.[10] Such madrasas have been seen in many places including the FATA, notably because young girls are allowed to learn only the basic religious principles and practices (Zaman, 2005: 8). The second phase started in the mid-nineteenth century. The modern educational system was introduced in traditional madrasas as part of the Islamic revival movement brought about by the *ulama* of the Deobandi seminary. Under the British government, Indian Muslims who were influenced by European science and knowledge sought a new manner of Islamic education. Some established modernized colleges; Sar Saiyid Ahmad Khan, who established Aligarh College in 1875, emphasized the merits of modern science. Others established madrasas where traditional Islamic education was imparted through the modernized system. The Dar al-Ulum madrasa in Deoband is the most famous one; it was established by Muhammad Qasim Nanotavi and Rashid Ahmad Gangohi in the village of Deoband, north of Delhi, in 1867 (Metcalf, 1982).

In the mid-nineteenth century, the British government requisitioned the *awqaf*, on which many madrasas have been financially dependent. Madrasas were then unable to obtain financial assistance from the *awqaf* without the permission of the British government. This meant that the religious institutions came under the control of non-Muslims. The Deobandi did not comply; they gathered financial assistance from not only the rich Muslims merchants but also common people. This gave the madrasas the ability to maintain their economic and religious independence. At the same time, the Dar al-Ulum madrasa started systematic education not only in Islamic studies but also in modern Western thought and philosophy (Khalid, 2002: 100). They created a council in the administration of madrasas, most of which were run by individuals. After several decades, the Deobandi seminary became popular in South Asia where the *ulama* and students were deeply involved in the anti-British political movement in the early twentieth century. Some Deobandi scholars started Islamic revival movements such as Jamiat al-Ulama-i Hind, which was established mainly by the Deobandi *ulama* in 1919, Tablighi Jamaat—a missionary movement started by Maulana Muhammad Ilyas in 1926—or Maulvi Ashraf Ali Thanavi's religious education for Muslim women through the book of *Bihishti Zewar*. In 1924, a Jamiat al-Ulama-i Hind committee was established outside Peshawar (Haroon, 2008: 51), and in order to focus on the national political objectives in the NWFP, it announced the establishment of the Jamiat al-Ulama-i Sarhad.

The main discussion in such madrasas was focused on the issue of jihad and its necessity at that time. Members of the *Faraizi* Movement in Bengal and those of the Deobandi seminary insisted that India was a *dar al-harb* (land of the war) and that the Indian Muslims should continue to wage jihad against non-believers, as Sayyid Ahmad Barelvi had done against both the Sikhs and the British in the mid-nineteenth century. In 1922, Abul Kalam Azad, a Deobandi scholar and politician of the Indian National Congress, declared a fatwa against the Indian Muslims, stating that India was no more *dar al-Islam* (land of Islam) but *dar al-harb* under the British control and that the Muslims should migrate to Afghanistan, which was *dar al-Islam* and had maintained its independence even after three wars against the British. In view of this order, more than 20,000 Indian Muslims attempted to migrate from India to Afghanistan; however, the Afghani government refused to allow their entry into the country. This incident implies that the Indian Muslims considered Afghanistan a *dar al-Islam* during the British rule. Muhammad Iqbal, the national poet of Pakistan, too praised the independence of Afghanistan in his poetry as the 'Thought of Afghani Mihrab Gul.' Moreover, others, like the members of the Bareli seminary, Sar Saiyid Ahmad Khan's Aligarh Movement, and other Deobandis, claimed that as far as Muslims could complete their religious duties in a given land, as was the case in India, that land should be considered *dar al-Islam*. Later on, these independent madrasas made a great contribution to the independence movement by training many Muslim leaders at the beginning of the twentieth century.[11] Jamiat al-Ulama-i Hind played a major role in the independence movement and supported the Indian National Congress, whose assertion was opposed to the independence of Pakistan. In the mid-1940s, most of the Deobandi *ulama* in the NWFP were pro-Congress, but by 1947, the majority of NWFP *ulama* supported the Muslim League idea of Pakistan because of the long-standing relations between the Jamiat al-Ulama-i Sarhad and Muslim League (Haroon, 2008: 58). Finally, Jamiat al-Ulama-i Hind was divided into two groups— one stayed in India and the other established Jamiat al-Ulama-i Pakistan after the independence of Pakistan. Even after the independence of Pakistan, some *ulama* studied in Deoband in India, but they were small in number. Despite making use of the Deobandi name, madrasas in NWFP developed according to the local politics after 1947. In the same manner, in FATA, madrasas began to be established, but most of them were under the control of the local authority—the *maliks*.

The third phase was the establishment of madrasas for political purposes as bases for mujahidin in the 1980s, which involved the training of religious students who would join the jihad movement of the anti-Soviet war in Afghanistan. Most of the newly-established madrasas in both NWFP and FATA were called 'Dar al-Ulum,' which was also the name given to the traditional local madrasas since they also imparted Deobandi-style education. However, the nature of these madrasas differed from the traditional ones as they were established for political purposes and had close links with the Ministry of Interior, the NWFP government, Intelligence, or religious parties that had close links with the government. During the anti-Soviet war, the local *maliks* were quite satisfied with the support that they got from the western countries through the religious parties and intelligence of Pakistan. However, soon after the anti-Soviet war, with the cessation of support from other countries and the lack of attention paid to the area, social disorder, influenced by the internal war in Afghanistan, became a serious problem in FATA. The *maliks* were helpless in this situation and were rapidly losing their local authority. Soon, the *ulama* of the newly-established madrasas, instead of the *maliks*, began to emerge in the society.

Towards the increased institutionalization of madrasas

According to an economic survey published in 2001, 1,065,277 students in Pakistan attended 6,761 madrasas, while 6,089,139 students attended 36,096 private schools, and 16,213,438 students attended 199,676 public schools.[12] For public education, the government of Pakistan invested 34,872 million rupees—2.2 per cent of the GNP—in 1993–4 and 72,237 million rupees—2.3 per cent of the GNP—in 2000–1. It is worth mentioning that the registered madrasas received public subsidies from the government. In this manner, they were granted 137,000 million rupees in 1988–9 and 1,654,000 million rupees in 2001–2.

Following independence, fresh attempts were made to reorganize the madrasas, which were the legacy of the ancient religious education system, into five main organizations or boards:

1   The *Wafaq al-Madaris al-Arabiya* was established in Multan in 1959 and belongs to the Hanafi Deobandi seminary.
2   The *Tanzim al-Madaris (ahl-i Sunna)* was established in Lahore in 1960 and belongs to the Hanafi Barelvi seminary. All the madrasas that belong to this organization maintain a close relationship with each other and hold examinations at the same time.
3   The *Wafaq al-Madaris al-Salafiya* was established in Faisalabad in 1955 and belongs to the Sunni Ahl-e Hadith (Salafiya) seminary.
4   The *Wafaq al-Madaris al-Shia*, established in Lahore in 1959, belongs to Shii Islam.
5   The *Rabita al-Madaris al-Islamiya* was established in 1983 at Mansura, and its headquarters of Jamaat-i Islami are situated in Lahore. This organization does not belong to any particular branch of the religion.

The restructuring or institutionalizing of the madrasas through the establishment of these five madrasa boards seemed to be a real achievement after the establishment of the foundation of the Deobandi School in the mid-nineteenth century. It might also be considered a challenge to the modern educational system in Pakistan toward which the madrasas reacted.[13]

For instance the *Rabita al-Madaris al-Islamiya* consists of 531 madrasas in total. Although its headquarters are located at Mansura in Lahore, its biggest madrasas are located in the NWFP and in Sind. Around 36,364 male and 13,190 female students attend these madrasas, while it has 1,754 male and 954 female teachers.[14] While around 27 per cent of the students are women, they compose 35 per cent of the teachers.[15]

It is also worth mentioning that the *Rabita al-Madaris al-Islamiya* has three committees: *Majlis-i Umumi* (General Body), *Majlis-i Mushawat* (Advisory Committee), and *Majlis-i Intizamiya* (Administrative Committee). The General Body consists of every representative of each madrasa and elects the members of the Advisory Committee, which covers the general activities of the organizations and elects the members of the Administrative Committee every three years. This committee can change the regulations of the organizations if two-thirds of all the members agree. The general meeting of the committee is held once a year. The Administrative Committee operates according to the regulations and discipline dictated by the Advisory Committee.

This organization set the educational curriculum in 1986. In this curriculum, subjects (Quranic study, Hadith Study, Arabic metaphysics and grammar, biography of the Prophet, logics, Islamic jurisprudence, history, etc.) and the titles and authors of textbooks are introduced. These subjects are added up into the number of marks that will be given during the examination. At the same time, some schools such as the Iqra Rozatul Itfal Trust (IRIT) combine government curricula or the elite private curriculum with elements of the formal Islamic-education curriculum (Fair 2008: 8). Algebra, Urdu, and English classes were also added to the curriculum. Urdu class is set according to the public school program, and all the Urdu textbooks are the same as those used in public schools.

On an official note, the government of Pakistan issued the educational policy in 1979, which explicitly recommended, for the first time, the establishment of religious institutions where modern subjects could be taught together with specializations in religious disciplines; the President of Pakistan, Zia al-Haq, appointed a Madrasa Reform Commission (Rahman and Bukhari, 2005: 65). Although the physical structure of the madrasas and their organization have been modernized, the basic curriculum of subjects remains more or less the same despite the discussions with regard to the question of whether or not to add new subjects to the current curriculum. For example, this question arises in the necessity of education in science and English, as well as in the history of Islam and the philosophy of Shah Waliullah (Hashmi, 1987: 201). The need to teach history, geography, politics, Urdu and Persian poetry of Muhammad Iqbal or Akbar Alahabadi (Kakakhel, 1987: 207) and the utilization of computers for Quranic studies were all important issues discussed among madrasas' authorities ('Ali, 1987: 240).

Financial support for madrasas

Madrasas have various resources, of which the benefits from religious taxes such as *zakat* and *ushr* are a part. According to a report by the Ministry of Education in 1988, 935 madrasas (67.4 per cent) received a total of 25,591,200 rupees that year. Although under specific conditions, the government of Pakistan has also been providing financial support to madrasas. For example, in the years between 1985 and 1988, the government created a three-year project of education in English, social studies, and Pakistani studies for madrasas and contributed a sum of 1.9 million rupees to the project. In the same manner, six years later, it created a three-year project (1994 to 1997) for education in English, social studies, and Pakistani studies only for the ninth and tenth grades, which cost 19.95 million rupees. In order to promote the progress of education at madrasas at an intermediate level, the government provided each of the fifty major madrasas with computers and printers from 2000 to 2003, which cost 30.45 million rupees. In fact, it seems that this policy was generalized to other madrasas up to 2004 (Khalid, 2002: 184).

The establishment of the five madrasa boards, as mentioned earlier, was also an opportunity to settle financial difficulties as a result of the establishment of a strong accounts section. According to the Institute of Policy Studies in Islamabad,[16] the reason for the increase in the number of madrasas even after the anti-Soviet war and 11 September is that the newly established madrasas could easily obtain financial support through the section account.

The issue of the provision of subsidies from foreign countries had divided the mujahidin groups during the war. For instance those groups based mainly in the NWFP or FATA received huge support from Western and Middle Eastern countries through Pakistan. For instance, Abud al-Rasul Saiyaf, the head of Ittihad-i Islami bara-i Azadi-i Afghanistan, received financial support only from Middle Eastern countries, on the other hand, Yunus Khalis, the head of Hizb-i Islami, never rejected 'non-Islamic' Western aid through Pakistan, even though he insisted that financial and material support should only come from Islamic countries (Rais, 1994: 185–186). Gulbuddin Hekmatiyar, the head of another sect of Hizb-i Islami, who had separated from the Khalis' party, was openly supported by the government of Pakistan. As we said before, having a great concern about the 'Pashtunistan' issue, Pakistan wanted Hekmatiyar to be an influential pro-Pakistan Pashtun leader in Afghanistan. Jamiat-i Islami's Burhanuddin Rabbani was also not opposed to Western financial and military support via Pakistan but was not willing to get political influence from other countries. He argued that Afghanistan's political independence should be the major concern (Rais, 1994: 182–183).

One should not underestimate the support of the Tribal Areas, which assumed a new and extremely important role during the war where the entire regional administration and organization was subservient to its objectives (Khan, 2005: 38–39). The mujahidin, who were living in FATA and the NWFP, welcomed all financial support. This maintained the financial balance between the traditional leaders and newcomers. The newcomers in the mujahidin began to play a more effective role in the Tribal Areas with the help of outside financial and military support. After the withdrawal of the Soviet troops, some of the members of the mujahidin went back to their own homes, but some remained at the madrasas. Besides, some ex-mujahidin members in the Tribal Areas even became bandits during the internal war in Afghanistan with the help of their weapons. The internal war and brigandage brought about disorder in the Tribal Areas, and the tribal chiefs were unable to restore effective order in their areas. When the Taliban, instead of the local chiefs, established safe conditions in the border areas between Balochistan and Southern Afghanistan in November 1994, merchants at the bazaar in Quetta were asked if they supported the Taliban. The answer was, without any surprise, positive, since the promise of reopening a safe trade route to Central Asia was at stake. All the more, since the members of the Taliban in that area were considered innocent students with pure minds, they were financially and emotionally supported through notable traders' donations to the madrasas.

Political background of the establishment of new madrasas

In 1973, a pro-Soviet government was established by a coup in Afghanistan. Western countries worried about the situation in Afghanistan and began to train anti-government elements in the country. The students, who had established Islamic study groups and prepared the anti-Soviet movement at Kabul University, escaped arrest by the Afghanistan government and moved to Pakistan. Most of them settled in Peshawar City, the capital of NWFP and the seat of the Pakistani government, led by Dhu al-Fiqar 'Ali Bhutto, who helped them. Nasrullah Khan Babur, who was the governor of NWFP at that time, helped and trained these Afghan refugees. The Western countries offered humanitarian assistance to those Afghani refugees through the Pakistani government, and part of the assistance was used to build madrasas not only in the border areas with Afghanistan but also everywhere else in the country.

For markedly different reasons, Western as well as Muslim countries subsidized the development of madrasas. The anti-Soviet war in Afghanistan was called a 'proxy war of the Cold War.' The issue of 'proxy' had been given a very precise meaning and no foreign country was officially allowed to send weapons and soldiers to Afghanistan. One should keep in mind that the real reason that many Afghans lived in refugee camps and participated in the jihad movement totally differed between Western and jihadist views of the proxy war. The latter was part of the elite crowd and very often either belonged to Kabul University, such as Gulbuddin Hekmatiyar and Ahmad Shah Mas'ud, or were under the influence of Arab professors as some of them had been studying in Egypt, such as Abu al-Saiyaf and Burhanuddin Rabbani. While the leaders were concerned about the establishment of an Islamic state, which was entirely supported by Islamic countries such as Saudi Arabia, the Afghani refugees in camps fought against the Soviet Union because the social revolution initiated under the influence of the Soviet Union had broken the entire traditional social hierarchy based on the feudal system. The jihad movement was even stronger since the new system was advantageous to neither the landowners nor the farmers. Moreover, the sufi leaders and landowners participated in the movement, and both led the resistance. Since jihad was the top priority, everything else was subservient to its objectives; the administration and local resources were geared towards serving jihad (Khan, 2008: 41).

The presence of Afghani refugees became one of Pakistan's major foreign policy planks (Ahmed, 1986: 166). In addition, the government led by Zia al-Haq promoted Islamization, including the introduction of *zakat*. The Inter-Service Intelligence (ISI) and Jamaat-i Islami (JI)—the largest and most organized religious party in Pakistan, founded by the Islamic thinker and journalist Abu al-Ala Maududi in 1941—functioned as a gateway for international support from both Western and Arab countries.[17] Once the US began pouring in billions of dollars in order to finance the Afghani jihad movement, Pakistan became a hotbed of religious extremism and their main recruits were the youth, who very often come from deprived socioeconomic backgrounds with no prospect of finding jobs in a stagnant economy (Jalal, 2008: 274–275).

Newly developed madrasas

At the time of independence, only 245 madrasas were recognized in West Pakistan.[18] In 1960, this number increased to 464 and many of the madrasas were located in the countryside and rural areas (Jalal, 2008: 277).[19] A great increase in the number of madrasas occurred in the 1980s when the number reached 2,056—including 1,012 in Punjab, 426 in NWFP, 318 in Sindh, 1,135 in Balochistan, 29 in Azad Kashmir, 27 in Islamabad, and 47 in Gilgit-Baltistan formerly known as the Northern Areas. Although there is no data concerning the number of madrasas in FATA until 2000, it has been reported that two-thirds of the madrasas in Balochistan are located in FATA.[20] A very interesting report, using data from the 1998 Census, states that the top ten districts, in terms of the madrasa market share, are all situated in the Pashto-speaking belt along the Pakistan–Afghanistan border in Baluchistan and the NWFP.[21]

The number of madrasas doubled from 1988 to 2000 at each level, but the increase rate differed according to the madrasa board to which each madrasa belonged. For instance, the number of madrasas in *Wafaq al-Madaris al-Arabiya* (Hanafi Deobandi) increased from 840 in 1988 to 1,947 in 2000—an increase of 232 per cent. On the other hand, the madrasas of *Tanzim al-Madaris Ahl-i Sunna* (Hanafi Bareli) increased from 363 to 717 (198 per cent), while the madrasas of *Wafaq al-Madaris Salafiya* (*Ahl-i Hadith*) increased from 161 to 310 (193 per cent); *Wafaq al-Madaris Shia* increased from 47 to 297 (632 per cent), and the rest increased from 96 to 2,653. The average increase in madrasas in Pakistan during that period was from 2,861 to 6,761 (236 per cent).[22] In this report, the increase in the number of Shia madrasas is remarkable.[23] It may be explained by the fact that in the democratic era, organizations could establish new madrasas more easily than during the marshal law regime (Khalid, 2002: 176).

This remarkable growth in madrasas was closely related to the external and internal politics of Pakistan. During the Cold War period, especially during the anti-Soviet war in Afghanistan, Pakistani president Zia al-Haq supported the establishment of madrasas in the context of Islamization.[24]

The transformation of tribal leadership in FATA

Many Afghani refugees studied at the madrasas established in Pakistan in the 1970s and 1980s, of which 45 per cent belonged to the Deobandi or Hanafi Schools and were accordingly registered by the Ministry of Interior.[25]

At first, the madrasas and mosques in FATA were built by the local chiefs such as *maliks* (landowners), were located near their residences and were thus easily accessible to the children.[26] This indicated that the tribal leaders had considerable influence on religious affairs as well as traditional leadership as owners of religious institutions. However, the newly established madrasas for refugees and mujahidin in FATA were built and administrated by others who had no relationship whatsoever with the local authorities, for instance, governmental authorities or foreign NGOs. Therefore, these new madrasas were built far away from the local chiefs' residences. The local chiefs' administration became ineffective under the sudden and huge increase in the population, as a result of the influx of millions of refugees from Afghanistan and fighters from other countries (Khan, 2008: 42).

During the anti-Soviet war, more than three million refugees from Afghanistan entered Pakistan. Those refugees were not only Pashtuns living in neighboring FATA, but also Tajiks, Uzbeks, Hazaras, and Arabs. As a result, the students and teachers of the newly established madrasas mingled with students and professors coming from outside the area from places such as Punjab and were deeply influenced by politicized Islam, which emphasized jihad.[27]

Therefore the Pashtun community in both NWFP and Balochistan, which traditionally welcomed many Pashtuns from Afghanistan, also received many foreigners. If the former refugees—most of whom belonged to their ethnic groups—were Pashtun, they were treated like relatives; yet, the aliens were very different from them. Many of these new students from outside were not necessarily familiar with the Pashtun tribal code. These young students, or mullas, came either from other parts of Pakistan such as Punjab or Kashmir, including university students, or from Afghanistan, Middle Eastern countries such as Saudi Arabia, or Southeast Asian countries such as Malaysia and Indonesia. They, being influenced by the Soviet invasion of Afghanistan, felt the need for jihad and entered the FATA to join the holy war. After entering the area, they stayed at the newly established madrasas in the refugee camps or in the tribal, rural Pashtun area and studied the newly introduced concept of jihad. Many of them were then recruited as the most favorite by the Student Front, which belonged to traditionalist parties, notably that of Muhammadi.[28] These parties claimed that Islam and justice were not a radical political ideology and that these ideologies together helped unify all these different groups (Rubin, 1995: 140).[29]

However, as these students gradually accomplished their goals and studies and became mullas, they started addressing political issues and justifying the war against the Soviet in the light of Islam. These students went on to become the mujahidin—fighters of a holy war—and alternatively, we may say that the fighters in the battlefield were students of the madrasas. In the name of humanitarian assistance, the *ulama* and mullas gained access to the huge financial and military help and also received political support from the government of NWFP, the government of Pakistan (Afghan Desk), religious parties such as Jamaat-i Islami or Jamiat al-Ulama-i Islami, and the international community. These mujahidin stayed at madrasas or mosques in FATA near the border of Afghanistan. They began to take leadership not only of the madrasas but also of the community itself.[30]

As mentioned previously, these madrasas and their students were first welcomed by the local community, who respected and supported them, because they were fellow Muslims (Ahmed, 1986: 66). However, gradually, the antagonism between the local *ulama*, supported by the tribal authorities and the mujahidin, came out into the open and the two parties began condemning each other. The former claimed that the mujahidin ignored the value of Islam and disrespected the traditional society and tribal code, and the latter reciprocated and criticized the private and traditional madrasas for depriving the students of the acquisition of political consciousness and modern education.

In other words, as the young mujahidins strengthened their political power, they became critical of the conservative elders of the society. The newcomers and new generations, influenced by their theological education at the madrasas, discovered that the traditional tribal code and Islam were not fully congruent. For the tribal chief, it seemed that there were two kinds of madrasas and students; some were simple and good madrasas where poor children studied the Quran, and the others were madrasas established during and after the war for private benefits and were therefore considered illegal and far from being Islamic. As one might understand, despite the fact that there is no major contradiction between Pashtunness and Muslimness, this conviction has not prevented clashes between the traditional and religious authorities. The history of this area is full of such conflicts, which divided the population whenever there was such a clash.[31]

However, the consequences of the last conflict seemed to have brought about a dramatic change in the organization of the leaderships and the tribal authorities in this area, which led to the rise of the Taliban. Since the refugees became a major part of the total population of FATA,[32] the mullas became the legitimate authorities who could solicit aid for the refugees; thus, they effectively emerged as new leaders in this area, and the local administration was helpless, especially because the newly emerged leaders (mullas) were heavily armed (Khan, 2008: 45).

The following interview with a tribesman can help understand this situation better. 'After the so-called religious people arrived in the tribal territories, the routine of the once-peaceful common people of FATA was destabilized. On routes leading to the remote, inaccessible areas of the tribal territory, the Taliban, who are not appreciated by the local people, have established many unauthorized barriers. The people face tremendous difficulties while traveling within the tribal areas, passing through valleys and encountering barriers along roads. They are stopped, spoliated, terrorized, and insulted. Their belongings are checked and the Taliban hold innocent people for long periods under *habeas corpus*, against their will. The Taliban have never been a threat per se, but the militants are disrupting the organization of everyday life, which is no longer possible for the local tribal people. If *Pashtunwali* is facing difficulties that's because the Taliban do not care about the *jirga* decisions, and they would rather destabilize the old traditional system in order to gain a vested interest in society. The Taliban do not bother to shed the blood of the innocent in order to create terror and intimidate the local community. At present, the *jirga* is disrupted and manipulated by Taliban militants established in the areas.'[33]

It seems obvious that what was at stake at that time was the elders' authority and responsibility towards maintaining order in the society. Routine matters were tackled by those who were unaware of the traditional code of conduct of the tribal people. In fact, some local scholars were assassinated because they dared to openly preach against suicide bombing attacks, stating that these were non-Islamic. Some of the newly emerged mullas were not only against the modern school system but were also against the education of girls, and they intended to paralyze the social system.

The Taliban as a challenge to the tribal order

After the withdrawal of the Soviet army, there was hope for peace and rehabilitation in Afghanistan, but instead, the situation became worse. Despite the establishment of the mujahidin's government in 1992, the rivalry among different political and ethnic groups caused fierce fighting and brought about an era of civil war. The political vacuum led to an escalation in robbery and murder. During the summer of 1994, some of the students at madrasas near and around Quetta and Kandahar planned to establish a group for the recovery and restoration of law and order in the southern part of Afghanistan. It is said that this initiative was supported, if not planned, by the Pakistani ISI. On 1 November 1994, Pakistan's Interior Minister Nasrullah Khan Babur declared that the Pakistani government would reopen the road from Quetta, the provincial capital of Balochistan, to Turkmenistan through the southern area of Afghanistan.[34] The government of Pakistan sent thirty-one trucks full of goods to Turkmenistan, calling them 'a gift for the people of Central Asia.' Soon after their departure, however, these trucks were assaulted at the border town of Spin Bordak in the Kandahar Province of Afghanistan.

Around twenty Afghani students who were put up at madrasas in Pakistan—mainly based in Balochistan and NWFP—roused themselves to prompt action and rescued the aid trucks on 4 November. They executed the bandits in conformity with the Sharia Law. Then the Taliban gathered the weapons from the people and succeeded in demilitarizing the area. They instructed the bandits to obey them by saying that if they surrendered, they would only have to forfeit their arms; however, if they did not do so, the Taliban would impose a 'punishment' on them. During the first stage of their reign, the Taliban did not utilize their weapons very often, which is why the locals welcomed them as 'pure-hearted students.' Furthermore, the merchants supported the Taliban in order to get rid of the bandits who were often responsible for causing trouble in their business. They made donations to the madrasas in the name of Islam because the Taliban eliminated the bandits and assured them of secure trade with Central Asia.

In 1995, many students of the Dar al-Ulum madrasa, located at the corner of a refugee camp in a suburb of Peshawar city, arrived in Afghanistan to join the Taliban movement.[35] Many buses full of students crossed the bother to join the jihad movement. The movement was officially treated as a self-repatriation of refugees. A printed fatwa, signed by more than thirty local mullahs, claimed, endorsed by Quranic verses, that the fight going on inside Afghanistan was against Islam and that the robbers should be executed. The fatwa was the sign of a new movement led by the newly-emerged mullahs who were distinguishable from the traditional leadership. When the Taliban captured the capital city of Kabul in September 1996, they established their own government in Afghanistan and set up the *shura*, a consultation assembly, which was entirely composed of mullahs. They set up local *shura*s in major villages for administration. The Taliban's *shura* system exercised a great influence over the neighboring FATA area, and the tribal leaders in this area claimed that the newly-emerged mullahs and students did not pay any respect to the *jirga's* decisions, that is, the new mullahs' decisions were not based on the traditional *riwaj*, which had long dominated the *jirga's* decisions. They also criticized the mullahs for challenging the traditional authority and social equilibrium.

Although, in 1997, the Taliban controlled almost 90 per cent of Afghanistan, the situation changed dramatically after September 11, 2001. Towards the end of that year, and in the name of anti-terrorism, the Taliban regime was ousted by the US military and a new Afghani government was established. Pakistan's debt was waived and the state even obtained financial assistance for cooperating in the anti-terrorism war; the US provided Pakistan with $700 million for this purpose. When the Pakistani government conducted investigations on the madrasas and launched an anti-terrorism operation against the Taliban in the FATA area,[36] the Taliban retaliated to the attacks both in Pakistan and Afghanistan. Strangely, the students of the newly established madrasas, especially in Pakistan, who had joined the Taliban's jihad movement, were now described as the 'local Taliban.' Despite the heavy pressure on and the attacks against the Taliban, private support for new madrasas and the Taliban is still pouring in. Pakistani army has been continuing a sweeping operation against the Taliban especially in the South Waziristan area where the base of Tahrik-i Taliban Pakistan (TTP) is located. In January 2010, a political agent of South Waziristan called a *jirga* of about 300 Mehsud tribal elders to hand over 378 wanted militants, including the leader of TTP, to the government. But tribal elders did not promise to do so as according to the elders the issue was so complicated that it may involve a large conflict.

Conclusion

In brief, the rise of the Taliban movement in FATA might be related, firstly, to the arrival of emigrants and refugees from other regions of Pakistan and from Afghanistan since the 1980s, and, secondly, to the importance of Western and Arab aid in support of the Jihad movement against the former-USSR. This context has revealed and amplified a double rupture between the Taliban movement and the traditional, tribal Pashtuns in the one hand, and moreover, emphasizes their autonomization on one hand, and between the Taliban movement and the traditional religious hierarchy, on the other. The Taliban Movement, far from being the affirmation of the Pashtun tribal fact in FATA, seems to find its origin in the destabilization of the tribal leadership, notably the Pashtun leadership, and in the reconfiguration of what being a Pashtun means. Therefore, it seems that what is at stake, through the development of madness, is hardly Muslimness or Pashtunness, but the flow of merchants and the balance of power in this new context left behind after the war.

Notes

1 NATO accused the people of FATA of providing shelter and support to the Taliban and Al-Qaeda (Gul, 2008: 68). Shinwari (2008: 12) writes 'Poverty, illiteracy, lack of resources and opportunities and exclusion from the mainstream political process are the factors that provide an ideal scenario for extremism and militancy to take roots in a society.' Although there are some tribesmen who joined the Taliban (Gul, 2008: 76), we should note the situation of severe fighting between the Taliban and the local tribal leaders in FATA in 2008 and 2009.

2 Studies on madrasas in Pakistan have focused on their politicization. Rahman discussed how the politicized ulama's rejection of traditional education of madrasas brought about the existence of militants (Rahman 2008) and Candland refers to the US policy of pouring dollars into madrasas at the time of anti-Soviet war (Candland, 2008: 104). But these articles have not discussed the transformation of tribal leadership we are focusing on in this chapter.

3 The total population of Pakistan (which includes East Pakistan) was 93.83 million in 1961. The census of 1998 is the last one we have had access to. Moreover, one should mention that a census was conducted in 1980, before the war against the Soviet occupation in Afghanistan, and since 1998 there has been no compiled census. Of course this might help us to better understand the context in which madrasa was developing in Pakistan, as the field which as early as 1980 became a supporting battlefield to the war in Afghanistan.

4 Sunni Muslims in Pakistan mostly follow the Hanafi School of law, but they belong to different seminaries. Some belong to Deobandi seminary and others to Bareli seminary. There are many Muslims in Pakistan who celebrate the anniversary of Sufi Saints at their tombs. Those Sufi Saints belonged to four major sufi orders: Chishtiya, Nakshbandiya, Suhrawardiya, and Qadriya.

5 Following the establishment of FATA, and according to Article 246(b), another subdivision was set in its neighboring area, PATA, Provincial Administrated Tribal Areas.

6 Before the independence of Pakistan, on July 30, 1947, Muhammad 'Ali Jinnah made it clear that 'as regards the tribal areas … the government of Pakistan has no desire whatsoever to interfere in any way with the traditional independence of the tribal areas. On the contrary we feel that as a Muslim state we can always count on active support and sympathy of the tribes' (Bangash, 2005: 48).

7 This strong role of the Political Agent was set in Sections 40 and 44 of the Frontier Crimes Regulations (FCR), introduced by the British in 1901 and inherited by the Pakistani government. There are some arguments about amendments to FCR, for instance, about the separation of the Political Agent's judicial and political powers (Shinwari, 2008: 4).

8 There are three levels of jirgas, that is to say, the local Maraka Jirga, the tribal Ulasi Jirga, and Grand National Assembly Loya Jirga.

9 At the independence of Pakistan, there were almost two hundred maliks in FATA (Shinwari, 2008: 3).

10 It is said that madrasa education in South Asia started just after the establishment of Muslim rule, in the era of Qutb al-Din Aibak, who governed Delhi and died in 1210. Sultan Shams al-Din Iltmish (d.1236) established his own madrasas and Muhammad Muiz al-Din Ghori established a madrasa in Ajmer, which is famous for the tomb of Sufi Saint Muin al-Din Chishti. In this way, the number of madrasas increased as Muslim governments developed. Since Sultan Abu al-Qasim Mahmud Ghaznavi (d.1030) belonged to the Shafi school of thought, the madrasas also belonged to this school; later, the Hanafi School of Law became popular in South Asia and this School of Law became dominant in this area. The names of madrasas in South Asia are Jamia, dar al-Ulum, and Madrasa Arabiya (Ahmad 1986: 21). The curriculum of

these madrasas has been edited by Allama Nizam al-Din Shahid Sahalvi (d.1747 / 1161H.); it was written in Arabic and consists of an eight- or nine-year course. Since the majority of Sunni Islam in Pakistan belongs to the Hanafi school of thought, it is traditionally led by ulama. These ulama are linked mostly to the Bareli branch of the Hanafi school, which accepted the Sufi network. The ulama regarded this Sufism as truly representative of Islam and the people have followed the sayings of pirs, the spiritual leaders of Sufism. Ulama teach Quranic studies at madrasas in a traditional system of individual tutoring. Most Muslims in Pakistan like to visit dargah or mazar, the tomb of a Sufi Saint, and enjoy the music of qawwali, the sayings of the Saint. People have learned religious teachings either through the qawwali or at madrasas. Olesen considers the madrasa students in rural Afghanistan, pointing out that those students come from poor, landless families with no other prospects in life than to become mullas. This can be seen in Pakistan as well. Thus, this kind of traditional Quranic education has been most active at madrasas in Pakistan.

11   One of the most famous madrasas of the late Mughal period is Farangi Mahal in Lucknow. Farangi Mahal is highly developed in the study of law, philosophy, and theology and has produced a large number of qazis, judges and muftis. In addition, this institute fixed the religious curriculum systematically, called 'dars-i Nizami.' In the same period, Madrasa Khairabad, led by Fazl-e Haq Khairabadi and his son Abd al-Haq Khairabadi, was established in northern India, where many scholars appeared. Thus, the nineteenth century was a very important era for Islamic study in South Asia. In 1893, Nadwat al-Ulama was established in Kanpur, where classic literature was translated and published in order for the people to understand the heritage of Islamic culture of the past. This institution transferred to Lucknow in 1898, where madrasa Dar al-Ulum was built and both Islamic and English education began. In this way, modern education was brought to madrasas through the British governance of India. Later, at the beginning of the twentieth century, the Deobandi madrasas began to issue fatwa for the purpose of emphasizing Islamic teachings, preaching against the governance by the British, or kafir. They stressed the non-cooperation movement against the British. Thus, the Deobandi madrasas sometimes caused the political movements as well. Some famous activists of the Pakistani independence movement belonged to the madrasas of this seminary.

12   There are 36,096 private schools in Pakistan, which include 28,811 privately owned schools, 2,580 NGO schools, 1,134 trust-based schools, 746 foundation-based schools, and 2,825 others (Economic Survey of Pakistan 2000–2001).

13   It is unknown what the literacy rate was in Pakistan at the time of its independence, but in 1981, the total literacy rate was 26.2 per cent, within which male literacy was 35.0 per cent and female literacy was 16.0 per cent. In the report from 1998, the literacy rate in FATA was only 17.4 per cent; the rate for males was 29.6 per cent, while the one for females was only 3 per cent (Population Census Report 1998). Such a low rate of literacy is highly disappointing, but even this small degree of literacy can be regarded as progress. When the British left the area and Pakistan became independent in 1947, there was not a single school, dispensary, electric bulb, or government post in the Mohmad Agency (Ahmed, 1986: 121). Among these Agencies and Frontier Regions, the region with the highest literacy is Peshawar, but the total literacy rate is 29.31 per cent, within which the male literacy rate is 52.76 per cent, while the female one is 5.26 per cent. In all of Pakistan the total literacy rate was 45 per cent in 1998: 56.5 per cent for males and 32.6 per cent for females. 72.6 per cent of males and 55.6 per cent of females in urban areas were literate, while 47.4 per cent of males and 20.8 per cent of females in rural areas were. The number of schools in FATA in the year between 2001 and 2002 amounted to 3,184 primary schools (1,931 for boys and 1,253 for girls), 367 middle schools (272 for boys and 95 for girls), and 197 high schools (179 for boys and 18 for girls) (Zaman, 2005: 74). The figure of enrolment at primary schools in FATA for 2001–2002 was 284,264 in total, within which 208,842 were male and

75,422 were female pupils (Bureau of Statistics NWFP). The enrolment in middle and high schools was 41,495 (male 36,903 and female 4,592). School enrolment increased by only 1.3 per cent from 1999–2000 to 2001–2002 (Zaman, 2005: 76). Enrolment is still low, as the rate of students who drop out before completing primary school is still high. This rate in Pakistan between 1998 and 1999 was 16 per cent in total, 11 per cent in urban areas and 18 per cent in rural areas. The most common reason for which 44 per cent of students drop out of primary school is that the students do not want to continue school life—this is true for 41 per cent of students in urban areas and 45 per cent of those in rural areas. The second most common reason is that parents do not allow their children to go to school; this applies to 25 per cent in total, 21 per cent in urban areas and 27 per cent in rural areas (Pakistan Integrated Household Survey 1998–1999). From these figures, it is obvious that the literacy rate is lower in rural areas than in urban areas in Pakistan, and that FATA is a backward area when it comes to education. Zaman (2005: 76–78) quoted Zeba Mehsood's pointed problems on education in FATA, such as staffing positions, unavailability of infrastructure for water, lack of latrines, boundary walls, and residential facilities, which amount to a problem in the quality of education.

14 A report given by Jamaat-i Islami, Pakistan. This report shows that the organization has 113 madrasas in Punjab, where 8,627 male and 4,399 female students are taught by 387 male and 205 female teachers. The 183 madrasas in NWFP have 9,047 male and 3,504 female students, 431 male and 330 female teachers; the 124 madrasas in Sindh have 11,556 male and 2,703 female students, 584 male and 297 female teachers; the 21 madrasas in Balochistan have 1,355 male and 77 female students, 70 male and 15 female teachers; the 14 madrasas in FATA have 1,360 male and 77 female students, 113 male and 12 female teachers; the 4 madrasas in FANA have 175 male and 113 female students, 6 male and 4 female teachers; the 64 madrasas in Azad and Jammu Kashmir have 3,744 male and 1,702 female students, 143 male and 77 female teachers; and the 8 madrasas in Islamabad have 500 male and 413 female students, 20 male and 14 female teachers.

15 Jamaat-i Islami has its own education office, namely Nizamat-i Islami, to favorably influence young people toward Jamaat-i Islami ideology. It oversees some 2,000 private schools throughout Pakistan and Jamaat-i Islami members may privately establish schools beyond the purview of the Nizamat-i Islami (Fair, 2009: 21).

16 IPS was established by Jamaat-i Islami in the mid-1970s.

17 'Following the Soviet invasion of Afghanistan in 1979, the Jamaat-i Islami found the opportunity to make a decisive breakthrough in Pakistani politics. By throwing its weight behind the Afghan resistance movement, the organization catapulted itself onto center stage in the American-backed jihad orchestrated with the help of the Pakistani army and its intelligence services' (Jalal, 2008: 274).

18 121 in Punjab, 59 in NWFP, 21 in Sindh, 28 in Balochistan, 4 in Azad Kashmir, and 12 in the Northern Areas. Jalal gives another source, as there were only 137 madrasas in 1947. She adds, 'the number rose from 210 in 1950 to 563 in 1971, and during the early 1980s, 893 larger and smaller Pakistani madrasas were in existence, with a total of 3,186 teachers and 32,384 regular students' (Jalal, 2008: 277).

19 195 madrasas in Punjab, 87 in NWFP, 87 in Sindh, 70 in Balochistan, 8 in Azad Kashmir, 1 in Islamabad, and 16 in the Northern Areas.

20 The report shows that the number of boys increased by 211 per cent and girls by 161 per cent. According to the records there are 300 madrasas. Among these, 72 were 'daura-i hadith,' 71 'moquf aliya,' 120 tahtati, 20 'hifz' or 'tajviz,' and 17 'nazira.' The report shows that the number of madrasa students almost doubled between 1988 and 2000: 'nazira' students rose from 296,090 (1988) to 611,165 (2000); 'hifz' madrasa students went from 91,224 to 204,230; 'tajviz' or 'qurat' from 45,719 to 83,015; 'tahtati' from 59,775 to 112,308; 'moquf aliya' from 12,363 to 29,714; and 'daura-i

hadith,' from 12,845 to 24,845. On average, the number of madrasa students increased by a factor of 204 per cent over a period of twelve years (Khalid, 2002: 170).

21   The report is based on the investigation by Andrabi team. These districts are Lasbela, Kharan, Kalta, Kohlu, Loralai, Kila Abdullah, Khob, Pishin, Hangu, Zarak, Lower Dir, Shangla, Buner and Chitral. With the exception of Lasbela, in Balochistan abutting Karachi, all of these high-intensity madrasa districts are along the Afghanistan–Pakistan border. But Andrabi team could not evaluate the important areas of FATA because census data were not available for FATA (Fair, 2009: 36).

22   Khalid explains that in the census of the year 2000, the number of madrasas belonging to any organization was 4,108 and the number of others was 2,701 (Khalid, 2002: 176).

23   We do not know whether the increase in the number of Shia madrasas in Pakistan was influenced by the Islamic Revolution of 1979 in Iran.

24   Jalal also shows that once Pakistan was awash in greenbacks, maulvis rushed to fill the demand for recruits by offering their students for jihad. Since they are a means of establishing political dominance, self-proclaimed religious parties of all sectarian denominations, as well as the Jamaat-i Islami, set up madrasas in places where they saw opportunity to extend their influence (Jalal, 2008: 277).

25   Most of the financial support was given to the madrasas of the Deobandi school, which upset the sectarian balance. State patronage of Deobandi imams in government-run mosques and the rise of the sect's militias spurred both the Barelvis and the Ahl-i Hadith into action, and the contempt for secular and rational forms of knowledge transformed madrasas into factories for turning out a lethal kind of religious bigotry (Jalal, 2008: 276–277).

26   Not only in FATA, but also in other rural areas of Pakistan, the distance between the children's residence and the madrasa has been a problem. In a 1966 report on education in FATA, the distances between the two middle schools or high schools are given as follows: 4 miles in Frontier Region Kohat, 5 miles in Malakand, 40 miles in Dir District, 5 miles in Kurram Agency, 8 miles in South Waziristan, 20 miles in Dera Isma'il Khan, 6 miles in Waziristan (Barelvi, 1980: 218–219).

27   The concept of jihad was theoretically discussed in Urdu language by Maududi. Maududi justified the right of jihad in his book Al-Jihad fial Islam (Jihad in Islam) in 1930 in order to protect Muslims from the criticism of non-Muslims who said that Islam was related only to violence.

28   Nabi Muhammadi, a famous Sufi in Southern Afghanistan, led the political party called the Islamic Front of Afghanistan.

29   Rubin adds an example of one journalist as follows: 'If a reporter asks a Talib what kind of rule he wants in the future, he will answer "Islamic," because that is the only word he knows for the rule of law Afghanistan so sadly lacks. One might also note that Southern Pashtun tribes represented by the Taliban had little if any representation in the leadership of the parties that were involved in the negotiations. Few Qandaharis had attended the modern state educational system, and they were consequently absent from the principal political elites of the mujahidin, the Communists, and even the old regime' (Rubin, 1995: 140).

30   According to the report of NGO, CAMP (Community Appraisal & Motivation Program) of 2008, in a response to the multiple choice question 'Law and Order in tribal areas can better maintained through ...', 44.7 per cent of respondents favored the Islamic law, while 36.2 per cent believed that jirga can effectively maintain the law and order situation in FATA (Shinwari, 2008: 59).

31   For instance, in South Waziristan. In the late 1960s, a mulla who migrated from the neighboring Bannu District built a beautiful mosque and a complex of schools and dormitories and began to grow powerful in local politics. A rivalry sprang up between the tribal leaders; both mulla and tribal leaders began to accuse one another, regarding each other as kafir. They even used the word jihad to refer to the tribal fight. At last,

the mulla was arrested. Thus, the fact that religious and tribal codes complement each other does not prevent competition and conflict among tribal leaders and religious authorities (Ahmed, 1986: 77–82).

32 For example, according to Ahmed (1986: 174), about 50,000 refugees were said to be living in South Waziristan Agency. Of these, about 20,000 are officially registered and are thereby entitled to standard measures of official aid. Out of a total population of 300,000 tribesmen, some 50,000 are 'outsiders.' A proportion of 1:6 of such outsiders in any total population is a high one to feed and support. The problem is more acute in North Waziristan Agency, where the number of officially registered refugees is almost 120,000 (making the refugee-to-local ratio 1: 2).

33 Interview with a tribesman.

34 Babur was the governor of NWFP in the 1970s. He played an important role in supporting Afghan mujahidin based in NWFP. When the Taliban emerged, he said in an interview that 'the Taliban are my children.'

35 In the 1990s several Jamiat al-Ulama-i Islami / Deobandi madrasas became notorious for education Taliban leaders and supporting the Taliban in Afghanistan politically, financially, and even militarily (Fair, 2009: 57).

36 Education Sector Reform, which includes the reform project of madrasas, was launched by Musharraf's government in January 2002. One of its major objectives was development of a more secular system to stave off the ever-mounting international pressure to counter Islamist extremism (Fair, 2009: 40).

3 Women's empowerment and Iranian-style seminaries in Iran and Pakistan

Keiko Sakurai

Although an oft-quoted adage from the *hadith* states that 'seeking knowledge is a duty of Muslim males and females,' the access of Muslim women to education has historically been limited to the *maktab* (Quranic school) or private tutoring at home, and women have been excluded from attending Islamic seminaries[1] or theological colleges teaching Islamic science, though there were a few exceptional cases.[2] Therefore, female education has lagged far behind male education in Muslim societies such as Iran and Pakistan.

Ironically, the right of Muslim women to learn was officially acknowledged after the introduction of modern schooling, under the growing influence of the West. In Iran, Reza Shah, the founder of the Pahlavi dynasty, introduced state-controlled schooling in order to educate experts and bureaucrats who were loyal to the monarch. Under his reign, women were admitted to elementary and secondary schools, and for the first time in 1935, they were even allowed into institutes of higher learning (Menashri, 1992: 107–110). In Pakistan—a part of colonial India until India's partition in 1947—a small number of private colleges offered education to Muslim girls, mostly from well-to-do families,[3] but Pakistan's state-controlled education system has not contributed significantly to the improvement of women's access to higher education.

In the process of the expansion of state-controlled schooling, the seminary system was marginalized and even stigmatized as out-of-date; however, the seminaries in both Iran and Pakistan, while remaining male-dominated institutions, continued their teaching activities. In Iran, where the majority of the population is Shia, the seminaries successfully evaded state intervention while claiming to be, after Najaf, the seat of higher learning and religious authority for the Shia. On the other hand, in Pakistan, where only about 15 per cent of the population is Shia (Momen, 1985: 282), the Shia seminaries could develop only to a limited extent, and they were obliged to send their students to either Iran or Iraq for higher learning. This situation made Pakistani seminaries dependent on Iranian or Iraqi ones.

Half a century after female students were first admitted to institutes of higher learning under the reign of Reza Shah,[4] Khomeini decided to officially authorize the establishment of women's seminaries. Khomeini, the founder of the Islamic Republic of Iran, was counted as one of the *marja-i taqlid* (source of emulation), or the highest clerical authority, when he overthrew the government and established a regime based on the principle of *vilayat-i faqih* (guardianship of the jurisprudent authority) in 1979. Armed with double legitimacies, he simultaneously represented the state and the clerical authority. He emphasized the role of women in society by stressing their three complementary roles of mother (*madar*), militant (*mubariz*), and Muslim (*musalman*) (Adelkhah, 1991: 42–43). It was under Khomeini that the first full-scale women's seminary, Jamiat al-Zahra, was established in 1984. In the 1990s, the concept of women's seminaries became increasingly popular and spread rapidly across Iran as well as to other countries, such as Pakistan. The development of this concept marked the beginning of a new chapter in the Shia history of Islamic studies on various levels.

In this chapter, I would like to analyze this new phenomenon of women's seminaries in order to gain a clear understanding of the extent to which the religious and traditional educational practices at the seminaries could, in fact, open the door to two major complementary innovations. First, through the establishment and development of women's seminaries, the Islamic Republic of Iran seemed to have developed a new seminary model that occasioned the transformation of the seminary—previously considered a stronghold of religious tradition—into a revolutionary agency whose primary role was to train propagandists (*muballigh*) of *vilayat-i faqih* both inside and outside the country, such as in Pakistan. As opposed to the men's seminary model, which had a long pre-revolutionary history and had enjoyed autonomy from the state for centuries, the Jamiat al-Zahra and other major women's seminaries in Qom were established under the initiative of the clerical leaders of the state, who were eager to mobilize the support of women in their political cause. This subordination of women's seminaries to the state and the 'étatisation of Islamic education' (Hefner and Zaman, 2007: 13) facilitated the application of bureaucratic management and the adoption of modern school arrangements, such as common examinations, standard curricula, modules, semesters, an academic credit system in the seminaries, and a systematic acceptance of international students with special courses designed for non-Iranian students (*tullab-i ghayr-i Irani*).[5] These measures minimized the differences between the seminaries and the state-controlled university, reduced the burden of seminary studies, and popularized seminaries among young women as a new option for higher education.

The international students who graduated from the Qom seminaries are currently scattered all over the world, and many of them are actively engaged in activities focusing on education and propagation. Since the 1979 revolution, Pakistani students at the Qom seminaries have outnumbered those from other countries. The role of the Shia women's seminaries in Pakistan, mostly run by Pakistani female graduates from Iranian seminaries, will be subsequently examined in this chapter as an example of how the Iranian seminary model is implemented in places outside Iran, where the Shias are in a minority, in addition to how it functions in a different context.

Second, regardless of the initial reasons for the establishment of the women's seminaries, women's acquisition of the right to study at seminaries opened up new possibilities for them to change the balance of power, not only between men and women at the familial and societal level, and among clerical institutions, but also between women and the state in the context of the Islamic Republic of Iran, through becoming a strong social group.

The growing presence of seminary-educated women in the official religious sphere dominated by revolutionary discourses elevated the position of women in the largely male-dominated clerical hierocracy. Moreover, the active participation of seminary-educated women in the public religious sphere has made 'the women's issue' an important topic for clerical discussion and has initiated debates over Western versus Islamic ideas of women's empowerment.

Growth of the seminary

Before the 1979 Islamic Revolution, women had no official means of accessing seminary education, which was often limited to some *maktab*[6] for women, such as the Maktab-i Narjis in Mashhad;[7] the Maktab-i Tawhid,[8] and the women's section of the Dar al-Tabligh[9] in Qom; the Maktab-i Fatimah established in Isfahan[10] and the Maktab-i Zahra in Shiraz[11]—all of which were run privately, with little coordination. Although Ayatollah Qudsi and Hojjatoleslam Shari initiated some efforts towards the institutionalization of women's seminaries before the revolution, the full-scale institutionalization began only under Khomeini's sanction (*hukm*). Jamiat al-Zahra commenced in the academic year 1985\86, and all the existing *maktab*s in Qom were merged into it.[12]

Jamiat al-Zahra offers full-time study courses, ranging from secondary high school diplomas to doctorate degrees, for residential as well as non-residential students. Students can also avail of part-time study programs and correspondence courses. The Jamiat al-Zahra's Department of International Affairs manages courses for international students. Students are admitted on the basis of their performance in the entrance examinations, and all the courses, which are taught over two semesters, are modular. According to the 2006–7 brochure of Jamiat al-Zahra, the seminary has over 12,000 students studying in its various departments and over 16,000 students have graduated from Jamiat al-Zahra since its establishment (Jamiat al-Zahra, 2006–7: 5).

The establishment of Jamiat al-Zahra and its resounding popularity prompted the clerics to open other women's seminaries, thus boosting the number of women's seminaries in the 1990s. However, until the establishment of the Management Centre for Women's Seminaries *(markaz-i mudiriyat-i hawzaha-i ilmiyya-i khaharan)* in 1997, there were no statistics on women's seminaries available to the public. According to the data publicized in 1997, there were 11,255 students and 1,102 (685 female, 417 male) professors at 138 women's seminaries countrywide. In addition, Jamiat al-Zahra itself had approximately 8,000 students and 137 professors.[13] The number of students enrolled at the seminaries under the control of the Management Centre for Women's Seminaries rose to 20,000 in 2002. It seems that Khorasan, the largest province before its division into three provinces, with 15 million pilgrims visiting it annually, enjoys a special status since it is not included in these statistics. In 2002, approximately 8,000 students were studying at 35 seminaries in Khorasan (Shirkhani, 2005: 100). The capacity of all these seminaries still appears to be insufficient, because in every academic year, the seminaries are unable to accept more than 10 per cent of the total applicants.[14]

Figure 3.1 shows the number of women's seminaries under the supervision of the Management Centre for Women's Seminaries by year of establishment. It also reveals that the real boom in women's seminaries began in the 1990s. We must bear in mind that along with the increase in the number of seminaries, female enrolment in government-run higher education institutes increased at a correspondingly rapid pace, to the extent that it exceeded male enrolment in 2003.[15]

Unlike the men's seminary, with its long historical precedents, the women's seminary is a new phenomenon with few historical examples. The founders of women's seminaries are usually clerics who are eager to set up their own seminaries in their hometowns in order to reach out to the female population in the area. These seminaries often start out as small classes for imparting religious education and gradually expand in size and organizational scale. According to the directions for administrating women's seminaries issued in 2006, a seminary of the smallest scale comprises 15–30 students, one principal, one teacher, and one administrator.[16] This relative ease in opening women's seminaries provides opportunities for clerics living outside Qom to expand their range of social activities and consolidate their position in local settings.[17]

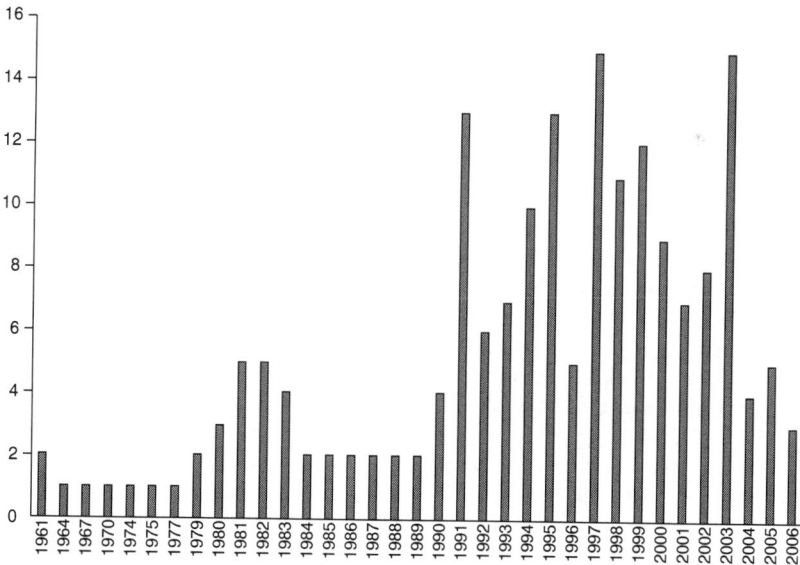

Figure 3.1 The number and year of establishment of Shia women's seminaries in Iran

Source: adapted from http://www.whc.ir/forms/schoollist.php?start=6~267 accessed September 2007.

Women who wish to proceed to post-secondary education face many hurdles. The shortage of seats in universities faced by those with a strong desire to acquire a tertiary degree and the lack of public space to engage in meaningful activities are pressing matters for young women. Under such circumstances, seminaries are regarded not only as another option for those who fail to obtain a seat in a university—since the application of the university-style system to women's seminaries has made seminary education equivalent to secular higher education—but also as a suitable place for those who want to pursue religious knowledge, those who prefer to study in a 'segregated space,'[18] and those who prefer a more intimate study environment than a university.[19] In addition, the high demand for seminary graduates in the fields of education and religious propagation has provided a favorable environment for seminary expansion.

Towards an Iranian model of the seminary

Although seminaries were marginalized in the process of the expansion of state-controlled schooling that started in the 1920s, they survived as independent institutions falling outside state control and maintaining their own management and teaching style in Iran. In contrast to 'Western Europe's examination-giving and degree-granting universities' (Hefner and Zaman, 2007: 9), the seminary education system in Iran has been characterized by the lack of a defined curriculum or standardized examination and evaluation system. Neither were there any age restrictions on admission into these seminaries nor was the duration of study defined. Before the spread of universal primary education after the Second World War, boys who completed their basic studies at local quranic schools could enter the seminary in Qom at around 12–14 years of age. The first level of study in these seminaries is called 'preliminaries' (*muqaddamat*), comprising the study of grammar, rhetoric, and logic. The middle level of study is called 'texts' (*sutuh*), in which students learn theology, law, and jurisprudence, based on the textbooks.

Only a limited number of students are able to proceed to the third and most advanced level of education, called 'beyond texts' (*dars-i kharij*), wherein they receive training to become a *mujtahid*, an expert who can issue an authoritative opinion on Islamic law (Mottahedeh, 1998: 451–452). When a mentor is satisfied that his student has acquired the ability to issue a competent legal opinion, he issues an *ijaza*, a certificate authorizing the student as a *mujtahid* in his own name. Therefore, it is not the institution but an individual *mujtahid* who issues the certificate (Mottahedeh, 1998: 454).

The highest-ranking clerics were powerful enough to avoid state control and enjoy full independence owing to their independent financial resources, derived from religiously lawful funds such as the zakat, *khums*, *waqf*, and donations paid to their office to maintain seminaries and distribute scholarships. However, after Khomeini and his clerical followers seized power, they proclaimed that since an Islamic state had been established, the state would subsidize seminaries in order to meet the increase in the demand for religious experts who could engage in policy-making, deal with socio-economic problems in government organizations, and simultaneously propagate the official ideology of Islam (Shirkhani, 1384: 56–64). They also attempted to control seminary affairs by establishing the Management Council of the Qom Seminaries (*shura-i mudiriyat-i hawza-i ilmiyya-i Qum*) in 1980.[20] Although the council formulated various proposals for restructuring the management style of seminaries and their curriculum, it failed to occasion substantive changes in the face of resistance from the seminary heads who were circumspect about accepting grants from the state treasury in an effort to retain their autonomy (Shirkhani, 1384: 58).

In 1991, after the death of Khomeini, his successor, Khamenei, established the High Council of Seminaries[21] (*shura-i ali-i hawza*) and its executive organ, the Management Centre for Seminaries, which was another step towards the institutionalization and rationalization of seminary activities. Khamenei's intention was to extend the state's control over seminary affairs, which were still in the hands of senior clerics whose religious rank and prestige were much higher than his own. Backed by overwhelming resources, Khamenei's policy was successful in unifying the management and applying the university-style education system to many seminaries; however, a few prestigious seminaries such as Ayatollah Golpaygani's seminary and the Fayziyya va dar al-Shifa seminary continue to remain independent.[22] Moreover, some *mujtahid*s seem to have adopted a middle path and have accepted the centralized management and standardized selection, curriculum, and evaluation up to the intermediate level; however, they have reserved the right to manage the advanced courses and issue the *ijaza* in an individual's name. This has resulted in a dual system of management, notably, in the men's seminaries.

Unlike men's seminaries, women's seminaries—a relatively late phenomenon—have generally welcomed centralized management. In February 1997, the High Council of Seminaries established the Management Centre for Women's Seminaries and gave it the mandate of developing the curriculum, conducting entrance examinations, and consolidating the unified program. Students are admitted in the seminaries on the basis of a combination of their scores in the common entrance examination, which consists of a written examination and an interview, and their high school grades (Markaz-i Mudiriyat-i Hawzaha-i Ilmiyya-i Khaharan, 1383–4\2004–5). The common entrance examination is conducted by the Management Centre for Women's Seminaries, and applicants are required to take the examination on a particular date at the nearest examination centre, at least one of which is established in each province.[23] Currently, the courses offered at the women's seminaries have been standardized, as shown in Figure 3.2.

The courses include a three-year preparatory course (*daura-i pish hawzavi*) for junior high school graduates and a one-year course for high school graduates. The four-year general course (*daura-i umumi*), divided into Levels 1 and 2, is equivalent to an undergraduate course. Level 3 covers the six areas: study of the Quran and *hadith*, philosophy, *tabligh*, history, ethics, and Islamic education; this course is equivalent to a master course. After taking this master's-level course, students can opt for another three-year special course (Level 4) and an even more advanced extra special course comprising *ijtihad* 1 (Level 5) and *ijtihad* 2 (Level 6).[24]

	Seminary		Government school

			Junior high school (3 years)

| Preparatory course (3 years) | | (1 year) | High school (3 years) |

| | | | Pre-university (1 year) |

| General course | level 1 (2 years) | | Undergraduate course (4 years) |
| | level 2 (2 years) | | |

| Special course | level 3 (3 years) | | Master's course (2 years) |
| | level 4 (3 years) | | Doctoral course (3 years) |

| Extra special course | level 5 (at least 3 years) | |
| | level 6 (at least 4 years) | |

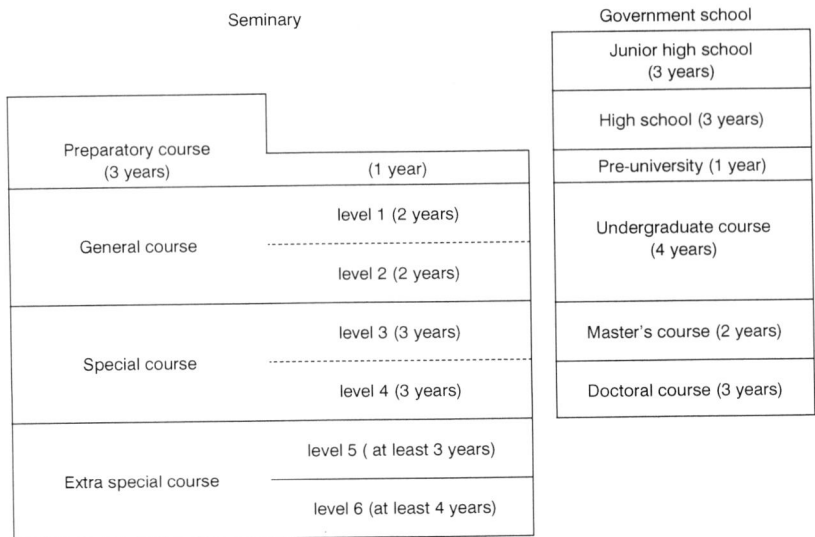

Figure 3.2 The women's seminary system in Iran

Source: adapted   from   http://www.kowsarnoor.net//knn/html/moarefi/sakhtar.html accessed 25 April 2007.

The academic year is divided into two semesters, each semester extending over 18 weeks. To pass examinations in each subject, a student has to obtain more than 12 points out of 20, and the acquisition of credits is a requirement for graduation.

An applicant to a seminary is required to have the following qualifications: be loyal to the *vilayat-i faqih* and the regime, a citizen of the Islamic Republic of Iran, not be ethically corrupt, and be physically and mentally healthy. Apart from these, there is an age restriction. Applicants for the three-year preparatory course should not be over 17 years and should have completed eight years of general education. Similarly, applicants for the one-year preparatory course need to have a higher secondary certificate and not be over 21 years. In the case of applicants who have finished junior college, the maximum age for application is 22; for those who wish to pursue a bachelor's degree, it is 24; for the master's degree, it is 26; and for the doctoral degree, it is 28. However, if the applicant is a wife or daughter of a martyr or someone wounded in war, or a sister of a martyr, the age restriction is extended by two years; for married women, it is extended by three years.

According to the application booklet of 2004, 16 seminaries offered a seven-year course to 266 local and 66 non-local applicants who had finished junior high school, while 163 seminaries offered a five-year course to 3,840 local and 394 non-local applicants with high school graduation certificates; the completion of these courses would be equivalent to attaining a bachelor's degree. Judging from these numbers, the dormitories can accommodate only about 11 per cent of the total number of students, which presents a striking contrast to the men's seminaries, where the students are mostly boarders. The number of applicants to women's seminaries is twice the number of applicants to men's seminaries, and in some provinces, the number of applicants may be as high as 15 times the number of seats. At present, approximately 15 per cent of those who finish Level 2 (equivalent to a bachelor's degree) proceed to Level 3, or the master's degree course.[25]

Unlike men who, after a long period of study, assume a clerical role for a living, women are pressured to complete their studies in order to get married and have children. Therefore, a university-style system in which students can obtain a formal degree after the completion of each stage fits their needs. The formal degree also improves the employment prospects for women. Hence, it is not surprising that many of them work as religious teachers at various institutions, including schools, where such degrees are considered to be the basic requirement. Therefore, for graduates of women's seminaries, a degree that certifies the completion of studies to a certain level is more valuable than the traditional *ijaza* that guarantees the transfer of knowledge from teacher to student.

Tabligh: Political mobilization

In the course of the revolutionary movement, the clerics and seminary students were also mobilized along with other social groups such as workers, students, and intellectuals. Although these experiences divided the clerics, they were convinced of the importance of gaining control over social affairs, including education. The Cultural Revolution that began in 1980 was considered as an opportunity to not only expel the anti-revolutionary elements from universities but also restructure the educational institutions in accordance with the official ideology, by controlling students and the contents of textbooks.

Ironically, it was easier for the new Republic to impose the official ideology on schools and universities than on the seminaries, since, at least in theory, the high-ranking clerics who taught at the seminaries were entitled to follow their own interpretations and could not be forced to follow Khomeini's diktats.

This explains, in part, the necessity of the regime to create new institutions in order to support and disseminate Khomeini's new Islamic ideology—the philosophy of *vilayat-i faqih*. For example, Khomeini's disciples, who were actively engaged in preaching during the revolution, established the Islamic Propagation Office of the Qom Seminaries (*daftar-i tablighat-i hawza-i ilmiyya-i Qum*) in 1979.[26] In 1984, in order to recruit qualified female preachers, this office opened a women's section, offering a one-year short training program and a four-year long one.[27] In 1998, this branch, which was called the Women's Education Centre (*markaz-i amuzish-i khaharan*), started a course entitled 'Introduction to Islam and Its Propagation' (*daura-i maarif-i Islami va tabligh*).[28] At present, the objectives of the Women's Education Centre are to enhance women's knowledge on Islam, and train preachers and dispatch them to various parts of the country. To this end, the centre's activities include developing propagation programs and encouraging research on Islam. The basic requirements for applying to this centre are: the applicant should have completed high school graduation; should be a resident of Qom; should have passed the written and oral examination; and should have a husband, father, or brother who is a cleric. The motive of training women from clerical families is to dispatch them to places to propagate, along with their husband, father, or brother. The number of religious gatherings organized by the centre steadily increased from 314 in 1979 to 9,127 in 1992. On various occasions, the centre organizes and dispatches female preachers for religious gatherings at schools and other places.[29]

In 1991, in order to improve the training of experts in propagation, the Management Centre for the Qom Seminaries established an education centre specializing in propagation (*markaz-i amuzishha-i takhassusi-i tabligh*), thereby joining the domain of propagation activities (Shirkhani, 1384: 77). When the Management Centre for Women's Seminaries was established in 1997, education, research, and propagation were identified as the major educational fields in women's seminaries. Although the Shia seminaries have a historical presence of over a thousand years, many of the traditionally studied texts and curricula of these seminaries do not suit contemporary needs. Therefore, the women's seminaries were specially equipped with 90 textbooks customized to suit modern requirements. Every year, approximately 3,000 students graduate from the seminaries, ready to carry out propagation activities; therefore, the development of an efficient curriculum for propagation is a very important issue. In addition to basic seminary studies, such as literature, the Quran, Islamic jurisprudence (*fiqh*), principles of jurisprudence (*usul al-fiqh*), ethics, theology (*kalam*), and logic (*mantiq*), seminaries teach subjects such as 'introduction to the other religions,' 'the political system of Islam,' 'women in Islam,' 'introduction to Western culture,' 'Arabic literature,' and 'English communication skills.'[30]

Besides the propagation activities organized by the seminary and other organizations, the neighborhood religious gatherings held by traditional women at private homes or in the *hoseynieh*[31] provide a platform for seminary-graduated women. Traditionally, privately trained 'freelance female preachers' have led these gatherings (Adelkhah, 1991: 143–147; 1999a: chapter 3; Torab, 2002: 147). However, since the early 1990s, young seminary graduates with formal training have been gradually taking charge of such gatherings (Adelkhah, 1999a: 109; Kamalkhani, 1998: 63). These seminary graduates reconcile women's non-formal religious activities with the official Islamic ideology dominated by male clerical authorities, thereby mobilizing women's participation in the official cause (Torab, 2002: 153). In addition to this, a popular preacher can gain respect in society as well as economic independence (Adelkhah, 1999a: 109–110; Kamalkhani, 1998: 65); this provides women with a good incentive to pursue seminary education.

Besides Iranian women, international seminary students have become an important focus for propagation activities. Before the revolution, the Qom seminaries (*hawza-i ilmiyya-i Qum*) accepted students from across the border irrespective of nationality. However, after the Islamic revolution, the Qom seminaries became the stronghold for the 'export of the revolution' and represented the foreign policy of the Islamic Republic of Iran.

In this context, students from outside Iran were categorized as 'non-Iranian students.' Further, in order to facilitate the training program for potential non-Iranian preachers, the Council for Supervising Non-Iranian Seminary Students (*shura-i sarparasti-i tullab-i ghayr-i Irani*) was established in 1979.[32] This organization was reorganized as the International Centre for Islamic Studies (*markaz-i jahani-i ulum-i Islami*)[33] in 1986, and it played a prominent role in developing the seminaries and their curricula, including Persian language training[34] for non-Iranian students, as well as recruiting students from various countries. Though the Qom seminaries are far from monolithic, the International Centre for Islamic Studies has been successful in representing the Qom seminaries in the international arena. The systematic acceptance of non-Iranian students has made these seminaries more accessible and has attracted many of these students. At these seminaries, non-Iranian students are first required to undergo intensive Persian language training, since most of the texts, including the writings of Khomeini and other Islamic revolutionary ideologues, are in Persian. This has inevitably enhanced the position of Persian as 'the language of the revolution'[35] in the Qom seminaries and at other places, and has promoted the 'Persianization' of Shia sciences.[36]

Currently, the International Centre for Islamic Studies supervises more than thirty schools and affiliated educational, cultural, and research-oriented centers. Among them, Bint al-Huda in Qom is the first women's seminary exclusively for non-Iranian female students. Bint al-Huda was established by a group of clerics under the leadership of Ayatollah Asefi in 1982, and it previously offered courses in Arabic mainly for students from Iraq and the Gulf region. However, it was placed under the supervision of the International Centre for Islamic Studies in 2000 (Markaz-i Jahani-i Ulum-i Islami, 2007: 251), following which it introduced courses in Persian to facilitate the acceptance of students from five continents. In 2006, 235 students of Bint al-Huda, most of them from Iraq, Pakistan, and Afghanistan, graduated from this seminary,[37] and in 2008, 550 students from 25 countries were engaged in studying various courses.[38]

Bint al-Huda offers a two-year post-high school course, undergraduate courses, and a master's course. A doctoral course began in 2008. In order to obtain credibility abroad, the graduation certificate of Bint al-Huda is issued by the Ministry of Science, Research and Technology.[39] Even before graduation, the students of Bint al-Huda engage in propagation activities within as well as outside Iran.[40]

For example, one of the Pakistani students at Bint al-Huda visited the city of Sukkur in the Sindh province of Pakistan for 12 days during the month of Ramadan for propagation activities. According to her, Shia constitute 25 per cent of the population in Sukkur; however, their knowledge of Shiism is minimal and most of them follow Sunni practices. She says that the men of Sukkur think that women have no right to education. In view of this situation, she organized many classroom-style meetings for the young women of Sukkur and discoursed on topics such as the religious connotations of fasting during the month of Ramadan, Islamic moral codes, and ideal Islamic women such as Khadija and Fatima Zahra.[41]

Another Pakistani student of Bint al-Huda talks about her experience of propagating in her native city of Skardu in Baltistan. Her father is a cleric who studied at Najaf for 14 years; he is a representative of Ayatollah Sistani and Ayatollah Khamenei at Skardu and has founded seminaries for men and women in Skardu.[42] According to the student, people in Skardu have immense respect for those who have studied in Iran. She gives an example: she was appointed to introduce the 'feast of duty' (*Jashn-i taklif*), a ceremony for girls who have reached puberty;[43] this ceremony was initiated and popularized in contemporary Iran. Girls who had recently reached the age of nine years were invited to the ceremony and were offered a headscarf and Khamenei's canonical guide.[44]

To gain admission in Jamiat al-Zahra, foreign students are required to have completed high school and be aged between 17 and 25 years for residential students and 16 and 35 years for non-residential students; admissions are on the basis of the candidate's documents and a personal interview. The applicants are required to complete a six-month Persian language program and a four-and-a-half- or five-month foundation studies program before enrolling for the two-year diploma or four-year bachelor's course. A two-year master's course is provided to those who are interested in advanced studies. Unmarried students can seek accommodation in the residential halls on campus; however, there are many non-Iranian students living in Qom with their husbands, who themselves study at one of the men's seminaries in Qom.

According to the undersecretary of the international division of Jamiat al-Zahra, 900 non-Iranian students from 40 countries are currently enrolled in the institution.[45] Graduates from Jamiat al-Zahra have served as teachers or principals in Islamic schools in their respective countries such as Pakistan, India, Bahrain, Lebanon, and Bangladesh.[46]

They belong to various backgrounds; for instance, a woman from Thailand, born in 1980, narrated her story as follows. Her family converted to Shiism when she was seven years old. She entered Jamiat al-Zahra in 1998 and studied there for a while. For the last five years, she has been teaching at al-Mahdi seminary (*hawza-i ilmiyya al-mahdi*) in Bangkok, which currently boasts 17 female students aged between 17 and 22 years; only local teachers are employed at this seminary, and some of them have graduated from Jamiat al-Zahra. When she was a student at Jamiat al-Zahra, she visited schools in towns such as Babol and Sari during the *dah-i fajr-i inqilab*,[47] where she, along with other foreign students, talked about the revolution and Islam—which was welcomed by the Iranians. These experiences helped her organize various propagation programs for the al-Mahdi seminary, in which both Shia and Sunni students participated.[48]

Maktab-i Narjis in Mashhad also accepts non-Iranian students. It was established in 1966 by Fatemeh Khamoushi; however, the Pahlavi regime grew suspicious about its activities and even forcibly closed it down for three years. After the revolution, Maktab-i Narjis was free to redouble its activities. Ever since, it has accepted 315 students from 21 countries and regions including Indonesia, Albania, Azerbaijan, Afghanistan, the US, Myanmar, Pakistan, Thailand, Turkmenistan, China, Iraq, Kyrgyzstan, Kashmir, Congo, Malaysia, India, and various Arab and

African countries; of these, 230 students have already graduated. The students of Maktab-i Narjis have been dispatched to various places such as schools, offices, universities, and mosques for carrying out propagation activities. For example, in the 2003 academic year, a total of 2,635 gatherings were organized; these gatherings involved 97 preachers in propagation activities during the month of Ramadan. As many as 1,054 gatherings were organized by 56 students in the months of Muharram and Safar. A total of 680 students were sent to 18 places for youth recreation programs.[49] After graduation, most of the non-Iranian students return to their country of origin and engage in preaching and teaching in their community.[50]

Implementation of the Iranian model in Pakistan

Pakistan and Iran both have Shia populations; however, in contrast with Iran, where Shia form the majority, they constitute only 15 per cent of the population in Pakistan. The rest mostly comprise Sunnis, but they are divided into sub-sects, namely, Deobandi, Barlevi, Ahl al-Hadith, and Jamaat-i Islami. Each sect and sub-sect has its own madrasa board to recognize and supervise the madrasas belonging to its own sect.[51] Relations between the Islamic seminaries and the state-controlled schooling are different in both countries. In Iran, seminaries are regarded as institutes of tertiary education to which students may be admitted after the completion of compulsory education. However, in Pakistan, seminaries are called madrasas (*dini madrasa*, pl. *dini madaris*), and they range from institutes that offer primary- to tertiary-level education; moreover, most of the students attending these madrasas have never received any formal schooling.

At the time of India's partition in 1947, there were 245 madrasas in Pakistan, of which 7 were Shia. By 1988, the total number of madrasas had risen to 2,861, of which 47 were Shia.[52] By 2002, the number of madrasas in Pakistan had increased to 9,880, with 419 of them belonging to Shia.[53] By 2004, there were 458 Shia madrasas, and 84 of these were for females (Kazmi, 2004; Durrrani, 2002). Pakistan is composed of diverse regions and various ethnicities (see Figure 3.3); the largest Shia population can be found in the Punjab province. In all, 58 per cent of the Shia madrasas for men and 65 per cent of those for women are located in the Punjab province, followed by the Sindh province and the Gilgit-Baltistan of Pakistan.[54]

The political situation surrounding the madrasas changed dramatically with the rise of Zia al-Haq, a general who seized power in 1977. Zia Islamized the legal system and implemented interest-free banking and the compulsory deduction of zakat from bank-account holders[55] in order to legitimatize his military rule. However, the Shia regarded Zia's Islamization, which was based on the Sunni Hanafi school of law, as a threat to their beliefs. They protested against Zia's Islamization and eventually compelled Zia to exempt the Shia from the compulsory collection of zakat.[56] Zia also attempted to improve the economic conditions of madrasas so as to integrate them into formal schooling through financial assistance; to this end, he decided to distribute the collected zakat money to registered madrasas.[57]

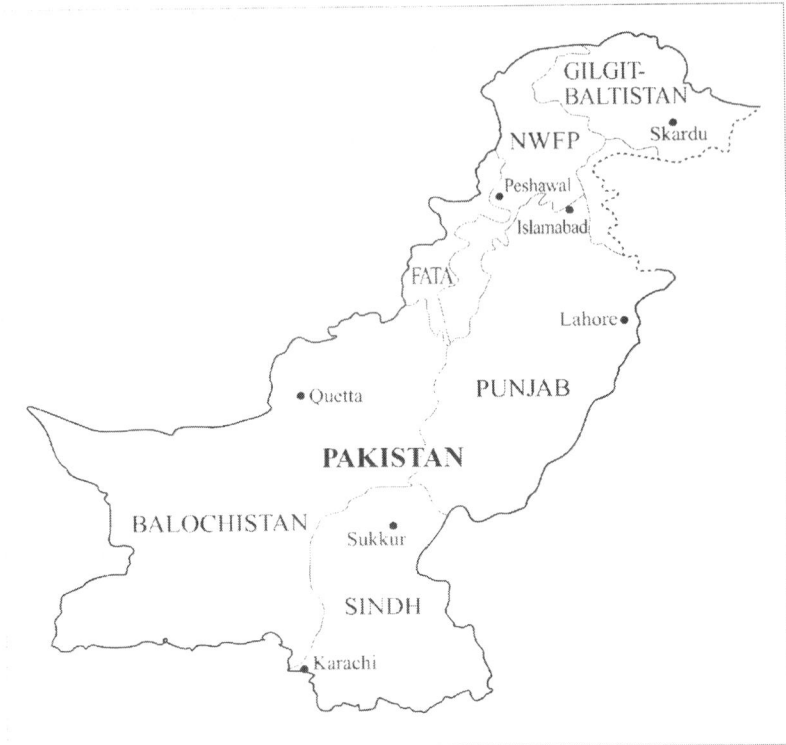

Figure 3.3 Map of Pakistan's provinces

According to Islamic law, it is not permissible to use zakat money for funding madrasas; however, this sponsorship was justified because the majority of the students studying at madrasas came from families in need.[58] In addition, Zia tried to modernize madrasa education by granting formal recognition to the final examination certificates conferred by the madrasas.[59] In 1981, the highest of these certificates, issued by the board of madrasas, was recognized as being equivalent to a BA or MA degree in Islamic studies (*Islamiyat*) or Arabic, on the condition that the student should pass in the examination of these two subjects.[60]

Zia's Islamization politicized a religious matter and aggravated sectarian divide and conflict. This situation was intensified by the establishment of a Shia theocratic regime in Iran and the 1979 invasion of Soviet troops in Afghanistan. Due to these events, the Pakistani Shia were emboldened by the success of the anti-US Islamic revolution in Iran and politicized their identities (Nasr, 2000a: 175). On the other hand, the Zia government entered into an alliance with the US in support of the Sunni Afghans and mujahidin fighters who were fighting against Soviet troops in Afghanistan. These ongoing efforts to save their Afghan compatriots provided Pakistani Sunnis with a golden opportunity to augment their power in the religious and political arena.

Under these conditions, the madrasas, especially those of the Deobandi sub-sect, proliferated rapidly.[61] The Shia, whose positions were threatened by the Sunni-oriented Islamization, sought support and guidance from Iran. Many of the Pakistani and Afghani Shia youth, mostly Hazara[62] refugees living in Pakistan, were eager to study at Iranian seminaries; this led to an increase in the number of Pakistani and Afghani students in Qom.[63]

Shia youths in Pakistan usually begin their education at the local madrasa. The Shia madrasas in Pakistan are private organizations run by local clerics. Although the Shia Madrasa Board (Wafaq al-Madaris al-Shia, Pakistan) in Lahore provides the curriculum, examination, and certification of the degree, other decisions, namely those regarding administration, recruitment, collection of alms, financial management, selection of textbooks, level of study, and criteria for the acceptance of students, are left to the discretion of each madrasa.

Shia students who wish to proceed to a higher level of study, which is beyond the capacity of Pakistani clerics, apply for the examination organized by the Shia Madrasa Board. Iranian delegates from the Qom seminaries visit Lahore to conduct interviews with students that have acquired the highest scores in the final examination and choose students on the basis of these interviews to admit into the seminaries at Qom. Many of the successful male students come to Qom along with their wives and daughters and let them study at Jamiat al-Zahra. Female students without a companion are offered rooms in the dormitory attached to the seminary.

The number of female Pakistani students at Jamiat al-Zahra and other Iranian seminaries increased rapidly in the early 1990s, and after returning home, many of them engaged in teaching at the women's madrasas. In many cases, the founders and principals of women's madrasas in Pakistan are male clerics; however, a substantial number of madrasa managers and teachers are graduates from women's madrasas.[64]

As shown in Figure 3.4, the number of madrasas increased in the 1990s, particularly in the mid-1990s; however, according to the directory of Shia madrasas in Pakistan, five women's madrasas were established in the 1980s. Among them, the Madrasa al-Zahra,[65] founded in 1988 by Husayn Najafi in Lahore, grew to be one of the best-organized madrasas in Pakistan. In the beginning, it was a small religious center offering basic teaching three days a week for boys and girls aged 10–12 years. Gradually, it developed into a madrasa with a hostel that could accommodate 12 students. In 1997, this center was named Madrasa al-Zahra, and it subsequently obtained a place within the premises of Jamiat al-Muntazar,[66] the best-organized Shia men's madrasa in Pakistan, in which the Shia Madrasa Board has its office. In 2006, Madrasa al-Zahra obtained a large plot for building classrooms and a hostel in the suburbs of Lahore.[67] Graduates from this madrasa contribute to promoting Islamic education for Shia girls in various parts of Pakistan and have until today opened at least seven madrasas (Kazmi, 2004: 585–587). At present, this madrasa offers a five-year course focusing on

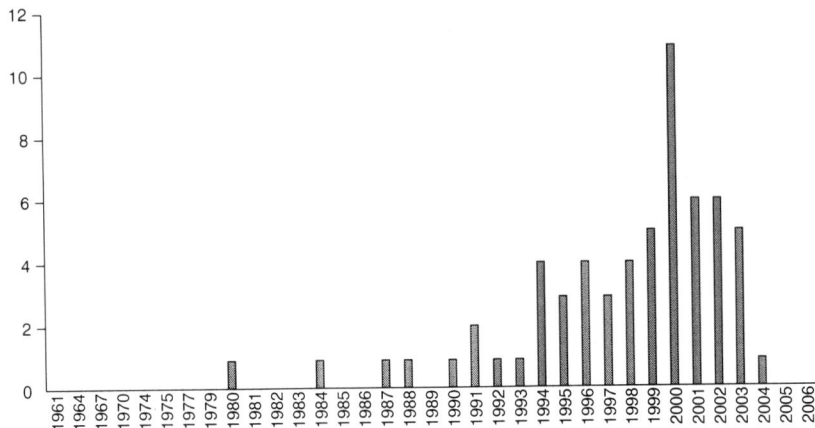

Figure 3.4 The number and year of establishment of Shia women's madrasas in Pakistan

Source: adapted from (Kazmi, 2004)

religious subjects, and an applicant is required to have completed the tenth grade or preferably the twelfth grade from a government-controlled school.

In addition to the Madrasa al-Zahra, the following three madrasas can be introduced as good examples of well-organized women's madrasas in Pakistan. Jamia Zainabiyya is a women's madrasa with a hostel that was established in Lahore in 1998 by Idara Minhaj al-Husayn.[68] It is a Shia organization founded by a Pakistani cleric, Muhammad Husayn Akbar, who studied at a Qom Seminary. His wife, who also studied at a Qom seminary, is the one who actually manages the daily classes at the madrasa. Applicants are required to have the minimum qualification of the completion of ten years of study, and students are accepted after a few months of provisional admission. Students have to appear for examinations twice a year, and one of these examinations is conducted by the Shia Madrasa Board. The madrasa is run using *khums*, zakat, and local donations.

Jamia Narjisiyya was established in Lahore in 1996. The founder of this madrasa was a Pakistani cleric who had studied at Qom for 12 years, and during that time, his wife studied at Jamiat al-Zahra. When he returned to Pakistan, he sold his property to purchase land in Lahore, where he built his home and a madrasa with a hostel. He has designated this madrasa as a *waqf* and runs it on *khums* and local donations.[69] Students receive free education at this madrasa, though they must provide for their own textbooks. The completion of the tenth grade is the basic qualification for applying to this madrasa, and students can study both religious and secular subjects in order to obtain a two-year higher secondary certificate, namely FA.[70] After the completion of four years of study, students have to take an examination conducted by the Shia Madrasa Board to acquire a degree from the madrasa. Every year, 10–12 students graduate from this madrasa.

Sakina bint al-Husayn is a women's madrasa established in Lahore in 2000 by Ghulam Husayn Najafi, who completed his higher education at Najaf after six years of studying at Jamiat al-Muntazar. He returned to Pakistan in 1970, started teaching, and eventually became the vice president of Jamiat al-Muntazar. In addition to teaching, he wrote many books to counter the negative propaganda against the Shia. His daughter serves as a principal of Sakina bint al-Husayn. In April 2005, while travelling in a car along with his daughter,[71] Ghulam Husayn Najafi was shot dead in a sectarian attack that also injured his daughter.[72] However, his daughter, the principal of Sakina bint al- Husayn, coped resolutely with the tragedy, and her courage was widely admired and praised; this made the madrasa extremely popular among the Shia. This madrasa accepts students of all ages, regardless of their educational background, provided they show a strong will to study. The madrasa offers different courses for students in the primary, eighth grade, tenth grade, and BA levels.[73] Since the Shia are in a minority in Pakistan, this madrasa specially focuses on educating Shia women to defend Shiism and provides clear and logical answers on the differences between Shiism and other sects.[74] In order to achieve this goal, students are specially trained to perform the ceremony to mourn the martyrdom of the third Imam, Husayn, in which the tragedy of Karbala is described and re-enacted. The madrasa also provides short-term courses for not only school and college students but also housewives and working women, thus offering a learning opportunity to everybody. The madrasa is financed by local donations such as *sadaqa*, *khums*, *zakat al-fitr*, proceeds from the sale of skins of slaughtered animals, and monetary offerings to the twelfth Imam.[75]

Table 3.1 provides data regarding the four above-mentioned madrasas, collected by means of a questionnaire survey.[76] Except for a few local students, the majority of the students of the four madrasas reside in the respective madrasa hostels.

Table 3.1 shows that the average level of students' education before entering the madrasa is higher than the national average,[77] while Table 3.2 reveals that madrasa students have strong educational aspirations. Table 3.3 shows the breakdown of students hoping to serve as religious experts such as religious teachers, preachers, and *zakira*s,[78] or wishing to start their own madrasa. The reason why fewer students aspire to be *zakira*s as compared with those who wish to be preachers is partly because the role of a *zakira* has been traditionally assumed by women with no formal religious education and who have learnt the skill from other senior *zakira*s, thus leading to the development of views often bordering on heterodoxy (Abou Zahab: 128–129). Therefore, the conflict between the traditional and religiously trained *zakira*s has reduced the popularity of being a *zakira* as a career option among students. Several students stated that their goal was to be a scholar, which requires advanced education in Iran. Table 3.4 shows that a considerable number of students have at least one madrasa-educated person in their family or among their relatives.

In Pakistan, especially in the rural areas, women's opportunities for social participation are extraordinarily limited; however, men can hardly find a pretext

Table 3.1 Four women's madrasas in Lahore

	Madrasa al-Zahra	Jamia Zainabiyya	Jamia Narjisiyya	Sakina bint al-Husayn
Number of questionnaires collected	42	28	37	58
Year of establishment	1988	1998	1996	2001
Average age of a first-year student (in years)	17.9	17.2	18.8	16.4
Age of the youngest student (in years)	15	13	16	10
Average years of education completed by students before entering the madrasa (in years)	10.1	–	–	9.0
Percentage of students hailing from villages	35%	32%	35.1%	44.8%
Percentage of students hailing from towns	22.5%	8%	16.2%	8.6%
Percentage of students hailing from cities	42.5%	60%	48.6%	46.5%

Table 3.2 What would you be doing had you not been admitted into the madrasa?

	Madrasa al-Zahra	Jamia Zainabiyya	Jamia Narjisiyya	Sakina bint al-Husayn
I would be studying.	78.6%	71.4%	89.1%	56.9%
I would be working.	9.5%	14.3%	5.4%	18.9%
I would be staying at home, preparing for marriage	9.5%	7.1%	2.7%	24.1%

Table 3.3 What do you want to do after graduation? (Multiple choices permitted)

	Madrasa al-Zahra	Jamia Zainabiyya	Jamia Narjisiyya	Sakina bint al-Husayn
I want to open my own madrasa in the future.	35.7%	17.8%	35.1%	51.7%
I want to be a zakira.	28.5%	32.0%	16.2%	27.5%
I want to be a religious teacher.	50.0%	35.7%	40.5%	12.0%
I want to be a preacher.	50.0%	46.4%	37.8%	53.4%

Table 3.4 Is there a madrasa graduate in your family and among your relatives?

	Madrasa al-Zahra	Jamia Zainabiyya	Jamia Narjisiyya	Sakina bint al-Husayn
My father is a madrasa graduate.	19.0%	3.5%	0%	10.3%
My mother is a madrasa graduate.	4.7%	3.5%	0%	6.8%
There is at least one madrasa graduate in my family or among my relatives.	57.1%	42.8%	43.2%	75.8%

for restricting women from attending religious gatherings which provide them with a rare opportunity for socialization. Therefore, religious experts are in great demand in such areas, and women have very few culturally relevant options, such as being a preacher, a teacher, or a *zakira*. In addition, being a religious expert earns a person respect as well as economic benefits, since such women are remunerated for their religious services at women's gatherings.

It is worth mentioning that these four madrasas are quite unlike the typical Pakistani madrasas. According to the statistics for 2000, 76 per cent of the female students enrolled at the madrasas of all sects attend primary-level courses (grades 1–5) and only 6.3 per cent of the female students pursue higher-level studies (grades 11–16) (Institute of Policy Studies, 2002: 31).

The founders' educational experience at Qom or Najaf not only influences the educational arrangements of the madrasas but also reflects on the credentials and status of the madrasas they run. For this reason, some madrasas are adorned with pictures of high-ranking *marja*s such as Khomeini, Khamenei, Khui, or Sistani inside the building to signify their direct or indirect mentorship. However, under the growing influence of anti-Shia Wahhabism in Pakistan, these credentials can become a double-edged sword and inflame sectarianism. In view of this situation, in recent times, even the madrasa founders educated at Qom seminaries have begun to adopt a cautious attitude towards the *vilayat-i faqih*, so as to protect themselves from the accusation of being a subordinate of Iran or conspiring towards an Iran-inspired revolution.

Feminization of the seminary

The Islamic revolution transformed the 'women's issue' (*masala-i zanan*) from being a 'taboo subject' to one that is widely discussed in the scholarly works of high-ranking clerics (Mir-Hosseini, 2002: 74). Since the Islamic Revolution, numerous articles and books on gender-based issues have been written from various viewpoints. These publications can be roughly categorized into two groups: works written from an outsider's or secular perspective and those written from an insider's or participant's perspective, which regard Islam as the source of their legitimacy (Ahmadi, 2006: 34). However, this division is too vague to reflect the wide-ranging contemporary debates on gender-based issues in Iran, and it is beyond the scope of this chapter to deal with such details.

The dominant view on gender-based issues within the Qom seminaries is represented by the writings of influential clerics such as Morteza Motahhari,[79] Javadi-Amoli,[80] and Ebrahim Amini.[81] They justify the differences with regard to the rights and obligations of the sexes on the basis of innate gender differences. According to Motahhari, 'Islam does not believe in uniformity between men and women. But at the same time, it does not give preferential treatment to men in the matter of rights' (Mutahheri 1992: 65). Motahhari's assumptions have been widely used as the basis for arguments put forth by the clerical establishment. Khamenei shares this assumption: 'From the viewpoint of the value of human beings, Islam sees men and women as equal. However, from the viewpoint of assigned duties, this is not so. Islam believes in a special duty for women, which is not lighter than that for men' (Banki Purfard 2002: 24–25). On the basis of this assumption, he emphasizes that women should prioritize their roles of being a good wife and mother, even though scientific, economic, and political avenues are open to them (Banki Purfard, 2002: 30–31).

These clerical viewpoints on gender-based issues have been disseminated through various organizations associated with the Qom seminaries. The Islamic Propagation Office of the Qom Seminaries (*daftar-i tablighat-i Islami-i Qum*) advocates its view on gender-based issues through the *Payam-i Zan* (women's message), a journal seeking to explore an Islamic solution to women's issues (Mir-Hosseini, 1999: 84). In addition, the Office of Research and Study of Women's Issues (*daftar-i mutaliat va tahqiqat-i zanan*), which was established as an institution affiliated to the Management Centre of Women's Seminaries, publishes books and magazines.[82] The office has played an important role in advising the government on gender policies. The objective of the office is to present new methods of explicating the characteristics and rights of women from the following perspectives.

1   Equality of women and men in terms of humanity;
2   Equality of the ethical and social values of men and women;
3   Differences in God's expectations from men and women;
4   Existence of innate differences between men and women;
5   The complementary nature of men and women at the familial and societal levels;
6   Existence of gender values;
7   Essential nature of the masculine and feminine gender roles and people's obligation to protect the gender roles in that form;
8   Importance of maintaining a balance between rights and duties in a manner that assures the dignity and guarantees the equality of women and men.[83]

Even the clerics who admit the need for change in order to meet the requirements of contemporary society[84] dismiss the idea of gender equality as a Western concept and refute the feminists' claim for equal rights. The head of the Office of the Research and Study of Women's Issues, Zibainejad, insists that the 'acceptance of the innate difference between men and women makes the Muslim view different from that of the feminists' (Daftar-i Mutaliat va Tahqiqat-i Zanan, 2006: 11).

Although it is the male clerics who justify the differences regarding the sexes in Islamic law on the basis of innate gender differences, these viewpoints are widely accepted among the female seminary students at Jamiat al-Zahra, which is regarded as the stronghold of male-centric Islamic jurisprudence (Mir-Hosseini, 1999: 243).

As mentioned earlier, one of the primary motives for the establishment of women's seminaries was to educate women to become experts in propagation. Hence, female seminary graduates were trained to propagate the concept of women's rights within the Islamic context, as defined by the verses of the

Quran and Islamic law, to a female audience. The aphorisms of Khomeini and Khamenei, which uphold the value of the family as a basic social unit and the role of women in the family, are often cited by these graduates; they also dwell on the scholarly works of theologians such as Motahhari, Amoli, and Ebrahim Amini. Accordingly, women's seminary graduates, who themselves constitute a part of the clerical establishment, are trained to defend the male theologians' interpretation of women's rights as being authentic from the religious point of view. The active participation of female religious experts in socio-religious activities is regarded as a success in the implementation of Islamic women's empowerment. For example, in the twenty years of its history, Jamiat al-Zahra has produced many female religious experts who are qualified to teach higher-level courses originally taught by male clerics. As a result, except for the board of trustees, whose members are all male *ayatollah*s, all the eleven members of the academic board of Jamiat al-Zahra are women who have mostly completed Level 3 of seminary education. Likewise, one-third of the members of the management board are women, and the nine research groups at the institution are all headed by women who have attained Level 3 or even higher degrees of education.[85] Consequently, the major activities of Jamiat al-Zahra are now carried on by women who are highly respected and recognized as religious experts.

However, their high educational achievement and important role in seminaries so far does not seem to be a threat to male dominance in the clerical hierarchy. The majority of female students leave the seminary after completing Level 2, and very few students proceed to Level 3,[86] which is still insufficient to be a *mujtahid*. Therefore, in spite of the rapid growth in women's seminaries, female *mujtahid*s such as Nosrat Amin[87] and Zohreh Sefati continue to be exceptional figures. Sefati complains about the current scarcity of female scholars who have the ability to issue their own legal opinion. She criticizes the fact that 'many female scholars see no future in attaining the degree of *ijtihad* as long as they cannot be a source of emulation;'[88] however, 'the responsibilities of a *mujtahid* are not only limited to being a source of emulation' and '*mujtahid* women can serve society by helping Muslims interpret Islamic principles as well.'[89] Sefati is of the opinion that issues peculiar to women, especially matters pertaining to 'purification' (*taharat*), must be interpreted by female religious experts for their female followers.[90]

Whatever the reasons for this scarcity, the lack of female *mujtahid* limits women's influence within the clerical hierarchy, and women's seminaries continue to serve as platforms for the spread of religiously relevant social participation, which will not, at least for now, weaken the male-centric patriarchal system in contemporary Iran. As a result, so far, the women's seminaries have served as a bulwark against the growing pressure exerted by secular feminists as well as Islamic feminists—most of them lay intellectuals and activists—who advocate gender equality through the reinterpretation of the sacred text (Ahmadi, 2006; Hoodfar and Sadr, 2009:29–30).

To assess the role played by the Shia women's madrasas in Pakistan, it is important to take into account the contextual difference between Iran and Pakistan. First, female school enrolment in Pakistan is much lower than that in Iran. For example, the average enrolment rate for females at the ninth and tenth grades is 14 per cent, but this percentage dropped to 8 per cent in rural areas in 2001–02 (Qureshi and Rarieya, 2007: 13).[91] Generally, the lack of schools in the neighborhood or a suitable transport system for female students impedes female enrolment in schools, especially in the rural areas. Moreover, the concept of the *parda*, which means the seclusion of women from men, is widely observed in Pakistan, and the *parda* is used as a pretext for restricting women from studying in schools[92] and working outside the home. Therefore, the priority for Pakistani women is to acquire the right to education. Second, there is a deep rift between the Westernized elite and the religious majority in Pakistan. The Westernized elite society follows the Western model of women's lifestyle and social participation, which is not tolerated by the religious majority.

To sum up, the seminary education is in fact a 'total social phenomenon,' since the Pakistani women try to address the social and traditional difficulties they face in their everyday life. Therefore, with regard to women's claims and aspirations, the seminaries in Pakistan play the same role as the public space in Iran. Curiously, these women are concerned not only about their own rights but also about the difficulties in their society with regard to the implementation of the Islamic ideals and principles. The way they evaluate the current problems faced by the Pakistani society reveals that women are becoming very active with a clear social consciousness and that they are assuming charge of the fate of both Islam and their national identity. With regard to this, one might gather three strong points from the life experiences of such women: first, although they are deeply attached to the traditional practice of *parda* and very critical of the Western way of life, they try to strike a compromise between Islam and their own traditions in order to prevent their seclusion and segregation; second, they criticize the traditional interpretation of Islam that restricts individual rights; and finally, they underscore the necessity of reforming Islam according to the developments in Iran.

In order to gain a better understanding of this situation, it is worth citing a few cases. In a rural area, a 19-year-old student said, 'A woman can still study while remaining within the Islamic limitations of the *parda*. The *parda* does not stop women from getting an education.' Another student believes that 'Islam gives a high status and importance to women, and if that status is fairly and honestly given to her, she would be able to work side-by-side with men in our society.' A 16-year-old first-year student from a town went further and said, 'Our society today is in need of another Imam Khomeini. Just as Imam Khomeini declared a *fatwa* in Iran and ordered everyone to follow the right path, we need the same kind of guidance.'[93]

Conclusion

The establishment and subsequent rise of the women's seminaries in post-revolutionary Iran have dramatically changed the traditional framework of religious education in Muslim society in general and in Shia areas in particular. Although these seminaries were an outcome of the political ambition of the State in Iran, women's seminaries now seem to be unstoppable. In other words, women were not only at the core of the bureaucratization and rationalization of religious education (Adelkhah, 1999a: Chapter 5), but they extended its scope and reinforced its potential. That might explain, at least partly, the emergence of women's issues as a growing challenge for politicians in Muslim societies that have to deal with both Islamic feminists and the new female *mujtahid* as incontestable authorities in a male-dominated sphere, that is, the religious seminaries. As previously mentioned, this evolution does not undermine the overall religious hierarchy; however, there is no doubt that it has the capacity to affect and shift the emphasis of current issues. Paradoxically, through the reinforcement of Islamic discourse and religious practices, we are witnessing unprecedented transformations in Islam and these are mainly focused around two complementary observations:

- Religion is becoming a dynamic tool for reinforcing the social and political participation of women in society; this might eventually limit the present clerical domination over women's affairs in general and women's religious affairs in particular.
- The proliferation of the concept of seminary-educated women managing their own space, educating their own students, and mobilizing their own audiences will bring about a 'fragmentation of authority' (Eickelman and Piscatori, 1996: 131) that will reinforce at least pluralism, if not a kind of democratization of the religious sphere, by enlarging the circle and allowing women within it.
- Although we need time to better evaluate the possibilities and limitations of the Iranian religious education model, it appears, notably through the developments in Pakistan, that its consequences can hardly be the monopoly of the State or the leaders that have taken the first initiative.

Notes

1 In Iran, the Shia Islamic seminary—and especially the seminary complex in Qom—is called 'hawza' or 'hawza-i ilmiyya.' Fischer defines the term as a centre of religious learning, composed usually of a group of madrasas (Fischer, 1980: 290). But in Pakistan, the word 'madrasa' is commonly used to refer to the seminary.
2 For instance, women had access to mosques for higher education in the time of the prophet (Alatiqi, 2009). Another example can be found in the Mamluk era (1250–1517) in Egypt (Berkey, 1992: chapter 6).
3 The Commission on National Education formulated the first significant educational policy in 1959, in which it recommended compulsory primary education for boys and girls and the provision of equal access to higher education, in general education, as well as professional colleges for women (Qureshi and Rarieya, 2007: 4).
4 The first-ever admission of women to the Tehran seminary for high school teachers (Daneshsara-i Ali) in 1935 encountered fierce clerical opposition and Tehran University admitted its first female students in 1940–1 (Menashri, 1992: 108).
5 For example, the Bint al-Huda seminary for non-Iranian female students and the Imam Khomeini seminary for non-Iranian male students were opened in Qom. Jamiat al-Zahra offers special courses for non-Iranian students.
6 Tabatabai, the head of Jamiat al-Zahra, explained that before the Islamic revolution, the women's seminary was called a maktab and generally, maktabs were established by unqualified persons and lacked supervision of marja and appropriate educational programs (Namih-i Jamia 1383\2004–5, No. 1). <http:/67.18.3.204\sections\mag\1\index1.htm> (accessed 25 May 2007).

7 Maktab-i Narjis was established in 1345\1966–7.
8 Maktab-i Tawhid was established in 1352\1973–4 by Ayatollah Qudsi, the founder of Haqqani seminary in Qom (Gulbarg, no. 32, Murdad, 1381\2002). <http://www.hawzah.net/Hawzah/Magazines/MagArt.aspx?id=46347> (accessed 21 February 2010).
9 A women's section was established in 1973; two years later, it had 150 students (Fisher, 1980: 84–85).
10 Maktab-i Fatima was established in 1346\1967 by the first female mujtahid, Nosrat Amin who was born in 1886 and died in 1983 (Huda, 1385\2006–7, 1 (1): 45).
11 Maktab-i Zahra was established in 1973 (Kamalkhani, 1998: 48).
12 Payam-i Hawza, no. 14, 1376 \1997. <http://www.hawzah.net/Per/Magazine/PH/014/ph01404.asp> (accessed 21 February 2010).
13 Ibid. Jamiat al-Zahra is run independently and publicizes its statistics separately from those issued by the Management Centre for Women's Seminaries. The number of non-Iranian students enrolled in Jamiat al-Zahra was 660 in 1377\1998–9. <http://iranwomen.org/zanan/charts/Education/seminary/eh3-1.htm> (accessed 29 July 2007). This number increased to 900 in 1385\2006-7. The students hail from 40 different countries. For details see Ayandi-i Rushan, 17 Ordibehesht 1385 (7 May 2006). <http://www.bfnews.ir/vdch.mn-t23nixftd2.html> (accessed 25 February 2010).
14 This information is from the home page of the Management Centre of Women's Seminary. News no. 150, 5 Ordibehest 1386 (25 April 2007) <http://www.kowsarnoor.net/> (accessed 10 March 2010).
15 The total number of students at government universities and higher education institutes in the academic year 1370\1991–2 was 344,045—of which 28.2 per cent were female students. The number of female enrolments reached 549,570 (as compared to the male enrolment figure of 469,410) in the academic year 1383–4 (2004–5), so 53.9 per cent of students were female. In the case of bachelor's degree courses, the percentage of female students in that year was 61.5 per cent. In addition, 529,993 female students and 568,498 male students were studying at the Islamic Azad University, a huge non-profit university with more than 300 campuses all over the country. These data are provided by the Statistical Centre of Iran (Statistical Centre of Iran 1383\2004–5: 655–656).
16 'Dastur al-amal-i ijra-i tasis-i madaras-i ilmiyya-i khaharan,' <http:/www.whc.ir/index.php?action=article&id=625&artlang=fa > (accessed 27 December 2007). The minimum staff is prescribed based on the number of students. For example, 18 staff members must be appointed for a seminary with 271–300 students.
17 According to the deputy of the Management Centre, as regards the ownership of the seminary, 84 of the 229 women's seminaries in the entire country are owned by waqf trusts, 55 are part of individual estates, 55 are owed by various institutions and 35 are rented (Rasa news agency, 14 Shahrivar 1386 \ 5 September 2007). See <http://www.rasanews.com/Negaresh_site/fullstory/?id=20511&Title=56> (accessed 18 December 2007).
18 In Iran, according to government policy, co-education is prohibited from the primary to the higher secondary levels, but colleges and universities are mostly co-educational.
19 Many seminary students informed me that in the seminaries, students form strong bonds and help each other master the texts, but this kind of co-operation cannot be found at the college and university levels.
20 The council was composed of nine members, namely, three representatives of Khomeini, three representatives of Gulpaygani, and the remaining three were from the Society for Seminary Teachers (Jamia-i Mudarrisin-i Qum) (Shirkhani, 1384: 44).
21 Makarem-Shirazi was assigned to the head of the high council of seminaries.
22 In the directory of the Qom seminary, these independent seminaries are categorized as 'free schools' (madares-i azad). On the other hand, the seminaries that have accepted

the supervision of the management centre are categorized as 'official schools' (madares-i rasmi), pp. 627, 629. Intisharat-i Markaz-i Mudiriyat-i Hawza-i Ilmiyya-i Qum, Rahnama-i Jamia-i Moassasat-i Farhangi-i Ostan-i Qum, 1380 \2001. Ziba Mir-Hosseini writes that 'the supporters of the old system ... fear that reform is bound to result in the loss of independence and freedom of belief and speech in the Hauzeh' (Mir-Hosseini, 1999: 17).

23 There are 55 examination centers all over the country, except for the Khorasan province, which is not covered by the Management Centre (Markaz-i Mudiriyat-i Hawzaha-i Ilmiyya-i Kharan 1383–4 \ 2004–5).

24 For details, please visit the home page of the Management Centre for Women's Seminaries: <http://www.kowsarnoor.net>. When Khomeini was asked, 'Can women attain the position of mujtahid?' he answered, 'It is possible for a woman to become a mujtahid; however, she cannot become a marja-i taqlid for others.' The Institute for Compilation and Publication of Imam Khomeini's Works, The Position of Women from the Viewpoint of Imam Khomeini, p. 44. <http://www.iranchamber.com/history/ rkhomeini/books/women_position_khomeini.pdf> (accessed 13 October 2009).

25 Payam-i Hawza, 1382\2004, no. 38. <http://www.hawzah.net/Hawzah/Magazines/ MagArt.aspx?id=44852> (accessed 30 August 2008).

26 The forerunner of this organization was called 'daftar-i tablighat-i imam' (Sakurai, 2004: 72–73). From 1979 to 1984, the office organized 9,081 women's religious gatherings and dispatched female preachers to conduct them (source: internal document of the Islamic Propagation Office of the Qom Seminaries).

27 This branch provided a one-year duration short program and a four-year duration long program. By 1992, 1,550 students were accepted at this branch (source: internal document of the Islamic Propagation Office of the Qom Seminaries).

28 This course has five majors, namely, the Quran, Islamic history, education, philosophy and Islamic law. Daftar-i Tablighat-i Islami Hawza-i Ilmiyya-i Qum, Mushakhkhasat-i Kolli: barnama va sarfasl-i dorus, 17 Dei 1377 (7 January 1999).

29 Daftar-i Tablighat-i Islami Hawza-i Ilmiyya-i Qum, Ittilaat-i Pazirish-i Kharan, 1378–9\ 1999–2000.

30 Payam-i Hawza, 1382\2004, no. 38. <http://www.hawzah.net/Hawzah/Magazines/ MagArt.aspx?id=44852> (accessed 30 August 2008).

31 These are religious centers dedicated to Hussein, the third Imam of the Shia.

32 Although the supreme leader Khamenei appoints the head of the centre and its education system and certification are verified by the Ministry of Science, Research and Technology, the centre remains an independent non-government university specializing in the education of non-Iranian students (Shenasan, 2007: 29–30). In order to propagate Shia education outside Iran, the Organization for schools and seminaries outside country (sazman-i madaris-i hawzaha-i kharij az kishvar) was established in 1370\1991 the organization currently supports approximately 150 schools, providing education to about 10,000 students in more than 60 countries (such as Britain, Indonesia, Russia and Ghana) (Ghiasi, 1383: 179).

33 The International Centre for Islamic Studies was reorganized again as al-Mustafa international university in 2008. For details, see <http://miu.ac.ir/>.

34 It is obligatory to study the Persian language before starting the study of seminary subjects.

35 The following is printed on the back cover of all the Persian language textbooks for non-Iranian students issued by the International Centre for Islamic Studies: 'The Persian language is the most effective medium for conveying the message of revolutionary Islam. The diffusion of the Persian language does not imply Iranian nationalism at all.'

36 In the early twentieth century, Najaf and Karbala in Iraq were truly the centers of Shiism. In 1937, Najaf had 8,000 students from all over the world, while Qom had only 1,000 students. However, this situation was completely reversed in the 1950s

(Nakash, 1994: 259). We cannot overlook the fact that there is a growing antipathy among non-Iranian Shia against the overwhelming influence of Persian-speaking Iranian clerics.

37   Among the 235 graduates, 112 were from Iraq, 59 were from Pakistan, 20 were from Afghanistan, 6 were from India and rest were from Nigeria, Thailand, Lebanon, Syria, Bangladesh, Myanmar, Tanzania, Mali, Congo, Indonesia, the US, Tajikistan and Iran. Huda, 1385\2006–7, vol. 1, no. 1, p. 56.

38   Hawzahnews, 8 Ordibehesht 1387 (27 April 2008). <http://www.hawzahnews.com/printpage.aspx?dataid=4950> (accessed 4 June 2008).

39   Ibid.

40   According to the account of the principal of the Bint al-Huda, its students organized about 500 propagation programs in 400 cities in the last academic year (source: Hawzahnews, 19 Murdad 1387 (9 August 2008). <http://www.hawzahnews.com/printpage.aspx?dataid=6376> (accessed 14 August 2008).

41   Huda, 1385\2006–7, vol. 1, no. 1, p. 41.

42   According to the directory of Shia madrasas in Pakistan, the women's madrasa founded by her father is named Jamiat al-Zahra, and it was established in 1995. Three out of five teachers at this seminary have graduated from major Iranian women's seminaries, namely, Maktab-i Narjis, Bint al-Huda and Jamiat al-Zahra (Kazmi, 2004: 619).

43   According to the note under Article 1210 of the civil code of Iran, the age of puberty for girls is nine lunar years (Taleghany, 1995). This ceremony was initiated in Iranian society in the early 1990s and was popularized through official channels such as TV and school programs. For details, see Adelkhah (1999a: 120).

44   Huda, 1386\2007–8, vol. 2, no. 4, p. 61.

45   Jamiat al-Zahra accepts foreign students not through the International Centre for Islamic Studies but through its own channels (Prospectus for Full- and Part-time Entry for Overseas Students 2006–7: 6).

46   Ayanda-i Rushan, 17 Ordibehesht 1385 (7 May 2006), op. cit.

47   These include the days between 12 and 22 Bahman in the Iranian calendar. On 12 Bahman, Khomeini returned to Iran from France after 15 years of absence, and 22 Bahman is the day of victory for the Islamic revolution.

48   Nama-i Jamia, Ordibehesht 1384\2005, no. 8, <http://67.18.3.204/sections/mag/8/index8.htm> (accessed 25 February 2010).

49   For details see <http://www.m-narjes.org> (accessed 25 February 2010).

50   One of the Afghan students I met at Maktab-i Narjis in 1999 told me that she was a war refugee who came to Iran with her family. Due to her inadequate educational record, she could not apply to a government school in Iran; however, the Maktab-i Narjis gave her the opportunity to stay in its dormitory and continue her studies. When I visited a women's madrasa in Lahore in 2007, I found that two of its teachers had graduated from Maktab-i Narjis.

51   There are four Sunni boards, namely, Wafaq al-Madaris al-Arabia (Hanafi, Deobandi, founded in 1959); Tanzim al-Madaris (Hanafi, Barelvi, founded in 1960); Wafaq al-Madaris al-Salafiya (Ahl al-Hadith, founded in 1955); and Rabita al-Madaris al-Islamiya (Jamaat Islami, founded 1983). The board for Shias is called Wafaq al-Madaris al-Shia and was established in 1959 (Institute of Policy Studies, 2002: 19–20).

52   Out of the 2,861 madrasas, 1,840 belong to the Deobandi sub-sect; 717 to the Barelvi; 161 to the Ahl al-Hadith; and 96 to the other sects and sub-sects (Institute of Policy Studies, 2002: 26).

53   From among these 9,880 madrasas, 7,000 were Deobandi, 1,585 were Barelvi, 367 were Ahl-e Hadith and 500 were Jamaat-i Islami (Riaz, 2005: 18).

54   Among the 84 women's madrasas in 2004, 55 were situated in the Punjab province, 11 were in Sindh, 9 were in Gilgit-Baltistan formerly known as the Northern Areas, 3

were in Kashmir, 2 were in the North-West Frontier Province (NWFP) and 1 was in Islamabad and the Federally Administered Tribal Areas (FATA) (Kazmi 2004).

55 The Zakat and Ushr Regulation was issued in June 1980. Originally, this regulation was intended to allow indiscriminate deductions from any account, including those of the Shias, non-Muslims and non-Pakistanis (Malik, 1998: 102).

56 The Shia believe that the zakat should be paid on a voluntary basis and that it should be paid to the marja-i taqlid, not to the state (Ahmed, 1987: 281).

57 To be eligible for receiving zakat, the madrasa had to be registered as a society and present accounts showing an appropriate use of the funds (Malik, 1998: 144).

58 Although the Shia are exempted from the compulsory collection of zakat, the Ministry of Religious Affairs grants Shia madrasas part of the zakat proceeds (Malik, 1998: 143).

59 Due to strong resistance from the clerics, the Zia government failed to modernize their curriculum (Malik, 1998: 133–139).

60 Having a BA or MA degree is the basic requirement for obtaining a post in government organizations (Malik, 1998: 141).

61 According to the official data for 1995, 2,010 new madrasas have been registered since 1979, and the total number of registered madrasas at present has reached 3,906 (International Crisis Group, 2002: 9).

62 The Hazaras are mostly Shia, who are believed to have adopted Shiism at the time of Shah Abbas Safavid (1589–1629) (Mousavi, 1998: 73–74).

63 Before the 1979 revolution, seminaries in Najaf, Iraq were the most popular destinations for Pakistani Shia. Therefore, the elder Pakistani clerics mostly received their advanced study at Najaf.

64 Since the number of Pakistani students increased in Qom, the seminaries started restricting the entry of Pakistani students in order to secure the diversity of non-Iranian students in Qom. In the case of female students, Iran currently invites about ten female students per year, on the basis of the graduation examination conducted by the Shia Madrasa Board in Lahore. In 2005 and 2006, the selection was finalized through personal interviews conducted with the candidates in Lahore.

65 Abou Zahab introduced this madrasa as 'the girls' section in the Jamiat al-Muntazar' (Abou Zahab, 2008: 132).

66 It was founded in 1954 and presently has 31 affiliated madrasas in Pakistan, Iran, the US and England. Madrasa al-Zahra is one of these affiliated madrasas. For details, please visit the madrasa's home page at <http://www.jmuntazar.org/English.htm> (accessed 22 February 2010).

67 The properties and buildings of the madrasas and their hostels were originally called 'Baqiyyat al-Allah,' owned by two Shia clerics who had studied at Qom. They started the men's and women's seminaries after returning to Lahore; however, they were unable to continue their project due to financial difficulties. I obtained this information on visiting Baqiyyat al-Allah and Madrasa al-Zahra in 2005 and 2006.

68 Idara Minhaj al-Husayn was founded in 1990 and currently runs both men's and women's madrasas. For details, please visit its home page at <http://minhaj-ul-hussain.com> (accessed 22 February 2010).

69 He explained that he was granted the use of khums for the madrasa by Sistani and other leading mujtahids.

70 A full-time female teacher with an MA degree (14 years of study) teaches secular subjects to students preparing for the FA (12 years of study) examination at this seminary.

71 She was still in her 20s when I met her in 2006 and had been educated in Pakistan.

72 BBC News, 1 April 2005 <http://news.bbc.co.uk> (accessed 22 February 2010).

73 The qualifications for acceptance into Sakina bin al-Husayn are apparently different from those of the other three madrasas, which follow the Iranian seminary model more directly.

74 According to Tariq Rahman, the refutation of other sects has always been part of religious education in Pakistan. Therefore, preparing students to defend Shiism is regarded as an important course of study (Rahman, 2008).
75 From the prospectus of the Sakina bint al-Husayn seminary.
76 I first visited four madrasas in September 2005 and revisited them in September 2006 to distribute questionnaires and collect them (165 in number) with the consent of the Shia Madrasa Board and the principals of each madrasa.
77 See <http://stats.uis.unesco.org> (accessed 22 February 2010). In Pakistan, the net enrolment of girls in primary schools was 57 per cent; in secondary schools, 26 per cent; and in tertiary education, 4 per cent in 2000.
78 One who recites the tragedy of the Karbala at women's gatherings.
79 Motahhari wrote that Islam 'has observed the principle of equality between man and woman, but it is opposed to the uniformity of their rights.' The English translation of Morteza Motahhari's work, Woman and Her Rights, can be obtained from <http://www.al-islam.org/WomanRights/> (accessed 20 February 2010).
80 Motahhari's most important text on the gender issue is entitled System of Women's Right in Islam, and Javadi Amoli's book on the same issue is entitled Women in the Mirror of Glory and Beauty (Mir-Hosseini, 1999: 19, 83–84).
81 The Urdu translation of his book is taught at Shia women's seminaries in Pakistan.
82 The Office of Research and Study of Women's Issues was established in 1377 (1998–9).
83 Daftar-i Mutaliat va Tahqiqat-i Zanan, Markaz-i Mudiriyat-i Hawza-i Ilmiyya-i Khaharan, Rayhana, p. 1.
84 For instance, Motahhari argues that 'it is essential that the position of woman should be reviewed, and the abundant rights which Islam has granted her and which throughout history have been denied to her, should be restored to her,' (Mutahheri, 1992:72).
85 Intisharat-i Markaz-i Mudiriyat-i Hawza-i Ilmiyya-i Qum, Rahnama-i Jamia-i Muassasat-i Farhangi-i Ustan-i Qum, 1380 (2001), pp. 662–663.
86 Level 3 is offered only at a few seminaries such as Jamiat al-Zahra and Maktab-i Narjis. Maktab-i Narjis started a Level 3 course in 2007. <http://www.hawzahnews. com> 27 Bahman 1386 (16 February 2008). <http://www.hawzahnews.com/showdata. aspx?dataid=4113> (accessed 25 February 2010).
87 Nosrat Amin was born in Isfahan in 1886 and passed away in 1983. She is regarded as the first female mujtahid (Iran Daily, 18 October 2004). Zohreh Sefati was born in Abadan. In 1970, she moved to Qom to study and became a renowned female mujtahid (Iran Daily, 15 January 2007).
88 According to Sefati, 'A number of renowned Islamic scholars believe Islam does not ban mujtahid women from growing to be sources of emulation' (Iran Daily, 15 January 2007).
89 Iran Daily, 9 October 2006.
90 Payam-i Hawza 1376\1997, no. 14. op. cit.
91 Compared to the female enrolment figures for Pakistan and Iran based on the statistics taken by UNESCO, the gross percentage of enrolment into secondary education in Iran is 76 per cent, while that in Pakistan is 26 per cent. < http://stats.uis.unesco.org> (accessed 1 December 2009).
92 The highest dropout rate for girls occurs at the stages of transition from lower to upper primary (class 3) and from primary to secondary school in Pakistan (Qureshi and Rarieya, 2007: 13).
93 These women's voices are all based on their essay written in the last part of the questionnaires distributed in September 2006. For details see, note 76.

4 Contested notions of being 'Muslim'

Madrasas, ulama and the authenticity of Islamic schooling in Bangladesh

Humayun Kabir

The theoretical complexity of combining diversified facets of Islam into a 'single entity called "Islam"' (Graham, 1993: 495) lies in the challenge of blending the theological and contextual differentiation within Islam (Eickelman, 1982: 1). In that sense, the study of madrasa, the major religious institution playing the guardian's role in 'cultural reproduction and identity formation' in the Muslim world (Metcalf, 2007: 104), faces the same challenge: how particular doctrinal inclinations and differentiation within the realm of the madrasas may be perpetuated in a certain historical and social context and conjoin each other, which would eventually lead to the creation of a wider context for Muslim cultural tradition. This study attempts to decipher the internal worlds of differentiation of the madrasas and the mechanism by which the differentiated worlds of madrasas interplay and connect with the external worlds of social space. Prima facie I try to illuminate the distinct functionality of the madrasas of Bangladesh by situating them in a broader South Asian context and suggest that internal motivations and divisions within Islam have important implications for understanding madrasas and their custodians—ulama, as Zaman (2002) dubbed—in contemporary Bangladesh. I argue that madrasas in Bangladesh are primarily concerned with the construction and reconstruction of Muslim cultural identity; however, the process of formation of such identity is not linear, but marked by a complex 'web of interlocutors' in which the madrasas propagate particular interpretative tenets of Islamic precepts, notions and ideas of being Muslim while their custodians contest for their authority by pursuing their own pedagogical methodology and by placing their voices in different madrasa-related religious forums and spheres (Taylor, 1989: 36). Such plural forms of contestations and notions are functional in Bangladesh in relation to the tradition of Islam, a tradition that is inherently 'discursive.'[1]

Historians and other scholars documented the internal differentiation of madrasas in South Asia in terms of sectarian, 'quasi-sectarian'[2] or *maslaki*[3] differentiation (e.g. Metcalf, 1982; Zaman, 1998; Nasr, 2000b; Alam, 2008a, 2008b; Sanyal, 2008). Scholars explicate that the doctrinal differentiation of Islamic precepts leads to the formation of Muslim identity in a contested array of space within madrasas (e.g. Alam, 2008a, 2008b; Sanyal, 2008). However, the contestation is not merely marked by an interpretative differentiation of Islam (*maslak*), but rather by many other denominations and the forces of modernization. The challenges and forces of modernity certainly severely impinge on the religious institutions and their protagonists (Zaman, 2002: 1); at the same time, however, they facilitate the contestation within their internal and external worlds. Such contestation is also conspicuous in many Islamic forums and movements. Ahmad (2005, 2008) shows us how Jamaat-i Islam and its founder faced the challenges for a 'total revolutionary reforms' and moderation of the movement in a changing context of modernity and transnational interactivity. I contend that it is important to view madrasas' functionality in relation to the changing circumstances in which they are embedded. In this study, I attempt to depict that the contestation involving madrasas and their custodians in Bangladesh is argumentative and discursive in nature, where many facets of modernity pose challenges and in turn facilitate the varied responses to the challenges.[4]

The study of madrasa in Bangladesh has been overlooked in the field of Islamic studies, although such studies are consequential.[5] Madrasas' specific social and religious role in the Bangladeshi context cannot be properly understood if not situated in the wider social and historical circumstances of South Asia, which Bangladesh simultaneously shares and differs from. Cornell's (1998) study is herein exemplary with reference to the manner in which he interrogates the specific meaning of Moroccan sainthood in a wider social and historical context which certainly differs from the other realms of Islamic mysticism. 'The study of sainthood must reconcile both social and doctrinal perspectives if it is to have any lasting value' (Cornell, 1998: 272). Even though the study of the madrasa cannot be equated with that of sainthood, what Cornell (1998) explicates is useful for our purpose to reveal how both the doctrinal and social aspects of madrasas are operative in relation to the formation and reformation of Muslim cultural identity in a specific social circumstance. The aim of this study, therefore, is not only to elucidate the contestation of madrasas and ulama in terms of their ideological or doctrinal differentiation but also in terms of their contestation for gaining control over religious spheres, pedagogical superiority and religious authority.

The thesis of this chapter is informed by ethnographic fieldwork conducted in several phases in the Brahmanbaria municipal area, on the east-central district town of Bangladesh, a territory of 30.82 square kilometers (see Figure 4.1). My discussion is not based on the analysis of a particular madrasa in this area; rather, it is grounded in the analysis of different madrasas and their custodians, and therefore, I refer to various madrasas at several points in my discussion.

Muslim selfhood, identity and madrasa

The 'sources of self' (Taylor, 1989) for being a proper Muslim lie not in the sources of Islamic tradition but in how such tradition is translated into institutionalized practices in the everyday lives of Muslims in a particular context 'into which Muslims are inducted *as* Muslim' (Asad, 1986: 23; emphasis original).[6] Various institutional sources such as *maktab* (elementary Islamic schooling), madrasas and mosques provide a primary induction into how to emulate Islamic practices

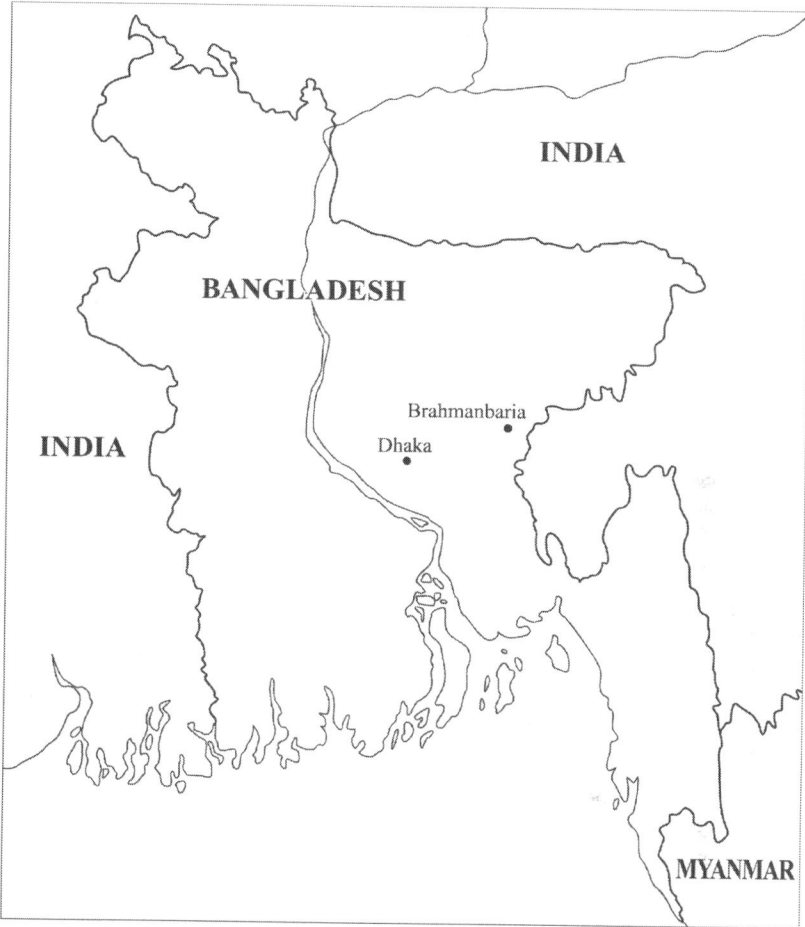

Figure 4.1 Map of Bangladesh

in order to be a proper Muslim in Bangladesh. In that sense, Islamic schooling has a profound role in constructing Muslim selfhood in Bangladesh. Such institutionalizing endeavors are often confounded, however, by the question of which practices are authentically 'Islamic' since Islam in Bangladesh is historically configured by two major trends: reformist-revivalist and syncretistic tradition.[7] Because of these contradictory facets of Islamic tradition embedded in the history of Islam which is further intertwined with the contemporary societal changes brought about by modernization,[8] the Muslim identity in Bangladesh becomes a matter of ambiguity and tensions where many individuals are just culturally

Muslims,[9] or where many of them associate their identity with 'Bengali-ness' and others with 'Muslim-ness.'[10] Though madrasas, in a general sense, advocate an identity associated with 'Muslim-ness' by indoctrinating Islamic practices and a sense of consciousness of Muslim selfhood, the process of formation of Muslim selfhood is highly debatable and contestable even within madrasas affiliated with different *maslaki* orientations or interpretative modes of differentiation of Islamic precepts, as I depict in the latter part of this chapter. The conceptualization of Muslim selfhood as envisaged in this chapter is tantamount to Bilgrami's (1992: 824) contention that Muslims' selfhood, even devout Muslims' selfhood, is highly 'differentiated internally into a number of, in principle, negotiable detailed commitments.' By the same token I conceptualize that the selfhood produced through madrasa schooling, mostly by the ulama, is differentiated within a negotiable space of interpretation of Islamic commitments and convictions.

Merry's (2007: 74–75) work also facilitates the understanding of how the madrasa functions for the formation of Muslim cultural identity which 'is always relational and comparative to others' in 'a coherent sense of self *within* a particular cultural matrix' (emphasis original). She considers the madrasas' role in Muslim cultural coherence, in the context of some Western countries where Muslims are immigrant and minor in comparison with dominant Western values and schooling, as a prerequisite for the formation of Muslim cultural identity.

Cultural coherence points to an important aim in the process of passing on deeply held commitments, values, and beliefs that are necessary for sustaining identity formation and psychological health. Cultural coherence can, and often does, encompass religious identity; either way, it does refer to the shaping of one's identity by a particular group. To speak of cultural coherence, then, is to refer to the shaping of one's identity by a particular group (Merry, 2007: 77).

However, Merry does not consider how internal tensions and conflict within Islam shape the cultural coherence in relation to Muslim identity and how it is differentiated from one group to another and from one context to another. Although his analysis provides a primary ground for understanding madrasas in relation to Muslim cultural identity, for the concept of identity, I rely more on the Holland *et al.* conceptualization (1998: 270): 'Identity is one way of naming the dense interconnections between the intimate and public venues of social practice' in which our selves and sets of actions are organized and being organized over the history of personal selfhood and social collectivities.

Identity is a concept that figuratively combines the intimate or personal world with the collective space of cultural forms and social relations. It is a key means through which people care about and care for what is going on around them. They are important bases from which people create new activities, new worlds, and new ways of being (Holland *et al.*, 1998: 5).

The conception of identity allows us to interrogate the Muslim self, which the madrasas pursue in different contexts and different situations. It is seemingly applicable to understanding how the madrasa and the ulama are contesting for a cultural identity that configures with a newly 'figured world' in a social terrain in which they face challenges from various corners such as modernization or globalization as well as from different denominations of their own religion. Further such a 'figured world' of the ulama is 'a socially and culturally constructed realm of interpretation in which particular characters and actors are recognized, significance is assigned to certain acts, and particular outcomes are valued over others' (Holland *et al.*, 1998: 52). To understand how the *maslaki* differentiation of madrasas engenders a differentiation of interpretation by which particular practices are valued over others for being a 'proper' Muslim, we need to consider the broader context of madrasas and their affinity to particular doctrinal interpretations and motivations.

Internal reasons of differentiation within madrasas: South Asian context

Interpretation is necessitated within Islam since it is a religion that is founded on the scriptural tradition. The 'ethics of disagreement in Islam' in terms of juristic methods including the prophetic tradition (*hadith*) and intellectual reasoning (*ijtihad*) can be traced back to the early period of Islam (al-Alawi 1935). Such traditions of interpretative differentiation have led to the emergence of sectarian, 'quasi-sectarian' and different denominational groups' (*maslaki*) orientation among the ulama and madrasas in South Asia (Table 4.1). Interestingly, in the nineteenth century, all the sectarian and *maslaki* offshoots such as Deoband, Ahl-i Hadith, Barelvi, Nadwah and Ahmadiyya originated in the northern part of India; these later proliferated all over South Asia (Metcalf, 1982: 266). Madrasas in Pakistan and India are divided by such sectarian and *maslaki* differentiation (Malik, 1999: 124; Alam, 2008a, 2008b).

Of all sectarian and *maslaki* orientation, 'Deobandi Islam' gained momentum in South Asian history (Haroon, 2008). Deobandi thought is founded on *Ahl-i*

Table 4.1 Unfolding the school of thought of madrasas in Sunni Islam in terms of *maslaki* differentiations in South Asia

Maslaki division	Sources of religious authority and interpretation	Motivation
Deobandi	Quran, Sunnah and four *majhab*, especially Hanafi school; writing of several Deobandi *ulama*	Individual reform and piety
Barelvi	Quran, Sunnah and four *majhab*; writings of Ahmad Riza Khan (d. 1921)	Intercession and extra devotion to the Prophet
Ahl-e Hadith	Quran and Sunnah eschewing classical *majhab*	Direct access to the Quran and Sunnah
Jamaat-e Islami	Quran, Sunnah and four *majhab*; writings of Saiyid Abul Ala Maududi (d. 1979)	Implementation of *shari'a* law
Nadwatul Ulama	Quran, Sunnah and four *majhab*	Integration of all variants of *maslak*

Source: Field survey in Brahmanbaria municipality, March 2007

Sunnat wal-Jamaat,[11] an allegiance to the Sunni Muslims which literally means upholders of Prophetic tradition, and on the jurisprudential method '*Hanafiat*,'[12] and conforms in thought to 'Wallliullahian' (Deoband homepage, 2007).[13] Though its teaching of Islamic content largely springs from *dars-i nizami*, the first structured form of its madrasa curriculum was devised by Mulla Nizam al-din Sahalawi (d.1748) in the eighteenth century;[14] later, its reform initiative underwent transformation of the *nizami* curriculum towards a greater focus on *hadith*-based teaching, and a shift from 'rational sciences' to 'reveal sciences.'[15] As historian Robinson (2000: 105) contends, Deoband's *hadith*-based, that is, revealed knowledge based reform can be seen as 'a shift in traditional Islamic knowledge away from the rational towards the revealed sciences, and a more general shift in the sources of inspiration away from the Iranian lands toward the Arab lands.'

In contrast, the Barelvi, which is associated with the notion of its founder, Ahmad Riza Khan (1856–1921) of Barevli, India, and his movement *Ahl-i Sunnat wal Jamaat*, believes on intercession and prefers a ritualized form of devotion to the prophet and to other holy men of Islam (Zaman, 2002: 11).[16] The Barelvis believe that Muhammad is not a 'role model' only; rather, he is a man made of *nur* (light of Allah) who had no shadow. They also profess Muhammad as a possessor of the knowledge of the unseen (*ilm-i ghayb*), who is always *hazir u nazir* (Ar. *hadir wa-nazir*), a precept that asserts that the Prophet is able to be present at the same time in different places (Sanyal, 1998: 641–642; Alam, 2008a: 12). For the Deobandis, the Prophet is a human being who possesses knowledge to the extent given to him by Allah. For them, considering Muhammad as possessor of the knowledge of the unseen (*ilm-i ghayb*) is polytheism (*shirk*) since only Allah is omnipotent and thus able to possess such knowledge.

The Ahl-i Hadith, also a movement of the late nineteenth century, differs on the legitimacy of four classic juristic methods, unlike Deoband. They prefer a direct access to the Quran and the prophetic tradition (*hadith*)—a view that Deobandi ulama disparaged for the heavy responsibility it places on individual Muslims, which might cause discord over textual interpretations.[17] The Nadwatul Ulama has endeavoured to integrate all variant doctrinal interpretations, though it has failed to do so.[18] Whereas in terms of the sources of religious authority, Jamaat-i Islam shares many aspects of Deoband and Ahl-i Hadith by accepting the Quran and Sunna as sources of Sharia and the four classical mediaeval law schools, its view on implementing Sharia law is unlike that of Deoband and Ahl-i Hadith; these focus mainly on religious reform at the individual level.[19] On the other hand, the entire *maslaki* group within the Sunni sect and the Shia community are strongly antithetical to the Ahmadi tenets of Islam which deny the finality of Prophethood of Muhammad and accept the prophecy of Mirza Ghulam Ahmad (d.1908) (Zaman, 2002: 11).[20]

Madrasas in Brahmanbaria, Bangladesh

Brahmanbaria is one of the oldest towns to have received municipal status in 1869 during the British colonial period. At that time, it was under the control of the district of Tripura which is now a part of India. Brahmanbaria became a district in 1984. The district town is situated on the bank of the river Titas. The population of the town is 131,334, out of which the males represent 51.34 per cent of the population and the females, 48.66 per cent. The literacy rate among the towns' people is 52.3 per cent, which suggests that a preponderant number of people still lack access to formal education (Banglapedia, 2003: 273). Probably, 'Brahmanbaria' derives from Brahman, Hindu priests, though this has not been historically authenticated. The proportion of the Hindu religious community in the district is 9.07 per cent as compared with the Muslim population, which constitutes 90.73 per cent, while Buddhists constitute 0.05, Christians, 0.04 and others, 0.11 per cent (Banglapedia, 2003: 273).

Form and structure of madrasa schooling

The entire madrasa schooling in Bangladesh is broadly categorized in terms of government recognition into two types: Aliya and Quomi (also known as *kharizia*, and Arabic *qawmi*) madrasas (see Table 4.2). Aliya madrasas are those that are either fully government or government-registered madrasas operating under the prescription and supervision of the Bangladesh Madrasa Education Board, an autonomous body of the Ministry of Education. These madrasas represent the historical legacy of the British-patronized Aliya madrasa, that is, the Calcutta Aliya Madrasa established in 1780,[21] a portion of which was later shifted to Dhaka in 1947 (Ali, 1983: 160). On the other hand, Quomi madrasas are exclusively private having their funding from the local community, religious alms (*zakat*) and endowments (*waqf*), but seldom from expatriate Bangladeshis.

Table 4.2 Types of madrasas in Bahmanbaria by management and level of schooling

By management	Government registered/government-aided		Private/independent
	Aliya madrasa		Quomi madrasa
Pre-primary (2–3 years)	–	Maktab/Nurani	Maktab Furqania/Nurani
Primary (1–5 years)	Ebtedayee	Ebtedayee	Ebtedayee
Secondary (6–12 years	Dakhil Madrasa Alim Madrasa	Dakhil madrasa Alim madrasa	Cadet Madrasa Islamia/Uloom Madrasa
Tertiary (12–16 years)	Fazil Madrasa Kamil Madrasa	Fazil Madrasa Kamil Madrasa	Jamia Madrasa
Specialized (3–5 years)	–	–	Darul Quran Madrasa Hafizia Madrasa Qiratia Madrasa

The Brahmanbaria municipal area consists of 12 wards and almost every ward has a madrasa.[22] *Maktab, nurani* and *furqania* madrasas provide the pre-primary level of Islamic schooling and the primary objective of these schools is to introduce the rudiments of Islam and to acquaint the children with the sacred Quran. There are 58,124 such institutions in the country and many of these are attached to mosques or higher madrasas (BEPS, 2004: 8). *Ebtedayee* represents the institutional level of primary schooling both for Aliya and Quomi madrasas. The Aliya madrasas maintain a grade-based system of schooling, and hence, the naming of such madrasas denotes the level of grade or degrees up to which the madrasa imparts instruction such as *Dakhil* (10th grade), *Alim* (12th grade), *Fazil* (14th grade) and *Kamil* (16th grade).

In contrast, Quomi madrasas follow subject-based rather than grade-based schooling. The naming of Quomi madrasas, therefore, is determined by their level of subject-based schooling and teaching specialization. For instance, Darul Quran and Hafizia madrasas are concerned with the production of scholars who 'embody' the Quran through memorization 'as a point of reference, a compass' for moral and spiritual guidance (Boyle, 2006: 491–492; 2004: 134). On the other hand, the Qiratia madrasa, the name of which derives from *Qiraat*, literally meaning the proper reading and recitation method, is named for its specialization in teaching proper Quranic enunciation. The secondary level of Quomi madrasas such as 'Islamia' and 'Ulum' madrasas focuses on subject-based teaching at varying degrees of schooling periods. These madrasas also use 'Jamia' as part of their names, though 'Jamia' refers only to those madrasas which impart all the *kitabs*, the texts at *kitabkhana* (division of text) up to the highest level of the Quomi madrasas—Daura-i Hadith or Takmil-i Hadith.

In many cases, the 'Jamia' madrasas also interchangeably use the terms 'Islamia' and 'Ulum' as part of their names. *Suba-i ifta*, a department of practical lessons for issuing religious verdicts (*fatwa*), is often established in these madrasas to cater to the students who obtain the highest degree of the Quomi madrasas. Although these features are characteristics of many Quomi madrasas in Brahmanbaria and all over the country as well, the emergence of a 'cadet' madrasa at the secondary level is a recent manifestation of the ulama's endeavour to orchestrate modern subject knowledge with Islamic religious lessons and sophisticated disciplinary practice for students. The central objective of these madrasas is to attract the guardians of the pupils by asserting that their pedagogical method is tantamount to that of the Cadet Colleges, one of the elitist categories of general schooling maintained by the armed forces.[23]

On the other hand, the emergence of independent girls' Quomi madrasas in Brahmanbaria is a recent phenomenon. The first Quomi girls' madrasa, Islamia Balika (Girls') Madrasa, emerged in 1988, followed by Nadiatul Quran Kendrio Mohila Madrasa in 1993 and Al-Batul Mohila Madrasa in 1997. Out of a total of eight girls' Quomi madrasas (Table 4.3), six were founded between 2000 and 2008. These madrasas challenge the 'secondary status of all women' in Islam where Islamic schooling is predominantly associated with males (Messick, 1988: 647–648).

Within the scope of this chapter, it suffices to say that the nascent girls' Quomi madrasas are engendered in a symbiotic social and economic matrix, for which the founders of these madrasas found their motivation in most cases. The ulama establish such madrasas as a way of earning their livelihoods; the learners are taught, housed and provided with meals usually on the same premises as the founder's home, in exchange for a monthly fee. Because of these institutions' flexible, loose and open system of student recruitment and shortened course-curriculum,[24] considerable numbers of students—including those who have crossed the standard age limit for or discontinued the study in public schooling—attend these madrasas as a means of securing marriage prospects and gaining empowerment in familial and social space.

Distribution of madrasa types and students

Until June 2006 there were 15,941 Aliya madrasas in Bangladesh; of these 6,711 were *Ebtedayee* madrasas, 6,745 *Dakhil*, 1,246 *Alim*, 1,062 *Fazil* and 177 *Kamil*.[25] In contrast it is not certain how many Quomi madrasas are currently operating in contemporary Bangladesh since no efforts have been made to monitor these madrasas. According to one source, there are more than 20,000 Quomi madrasas across the country and the number of students in these madrasas is not less than three million (*Prothom Alo* 2006).

The Brahmanbaria municipal area has 13 primary schools, seven high schools, two colleges and two educational institutes.[26] At the same time, there are 36 madrasas, two of which are government registered, that is Aliya, and the remaining 34 are Quomi madrasas at different levels, suggesting that madrasas constitute a substantial part of schooling options in Brahmanbaria. At the national level, Aliya madrasas constitute 27.61 per cent of all post-primary educational institutions in comparison with general educational institutions which constitute 62.98 per cent (BANBEIS, 2006: 25). In terms of enrolment rates, madrasa students (students of Aliya madrasas only) comprise 16.32 per cent of all post-primary general schools at the national level (BANBEIS, 2006: 26). As the case of Brahmanbaria suggests, the contribution of madrasa schooling in the entire education sector in Bangladesh would undoubtedly be higher if the number of Quomi madrasas and their students were statistically considered at official level.

According to the estimation of 30 out of 36 madrasas, the total number of students in Brahmanbaria is 5,880 (Table 4.3). Of these, the Aliya madrasas have

Table 4.3 Distribution of madrasas and students by management and gender in Brahmanbaria

Distribution of madrasas						Distribution of students		
By management		By gender				By gender		
Aliya	Quomi	Boys	Coeducation	Girls	Total	Boys	Girls	Total
2	34	23	5	8	36	4040	1840	5880

1,135 students while the remainder attend the Quomi madrasas. In contrast, in the Brahmanbaria sub-district (Upazilla), the municipal and its contiguous areas comprising 495.85 sq km, there are 59 post-primary schools and 17 Aliya madrasas in which the total numbers of students studying are 29,373 and 3,597 respectively.[27] Even though the Brahmanbaria municipality is a smaller geographical territory, 30.82 sq km, as noted earlier, the preponderant number of Quomi students suggests the significant contribution of these madrasas in educating the pupils alongside general schools in Brahmanbaria. However, to address the question why these madrasas are gaining desirability as a social choice of educating Muslim pupils in Brahmanbaria we need to consider the aspects of the ulama who, equipped with certain religious techniques and tactics, try to ensure their existence as well as that of their primary institution—the madrasa—in association with which they became ulama. Apart from this, madrasa education might have a positive correlation to the sociology of employment in Bangladesh, which is predicated on an inordinate rate of unemployment, nepotism and politicization of employment. In many cases, the articulation of certain discourses by the ulama—which allege that public schooling is a machinery for the production of immoral values and its pedagogical process is inimical to being a proper 'Muslim'—also influences many people who deem education as the functional base of moral construction and identity formation; thus, they choose madrasa schooling as an alternative.

How have madrasas evolved? Authorizing social and religious space

How madrasas evolved even after the introduction of Western-style schooling is a crucial question. Some observers might contend that poverty is a primary cause of the evolvement of Muslim religious education. Some might also argue that the evolvement of madrasas is the result of the failure of public schools to accommodate a mounting number of Muslim pupils. Irrespective of the degree of influence such factors have, on the basis of the Brahmanbaria case, I suggest that the transformation of madrasas is associated with the venture to expand the authorizing social and religious space, where the madrasa functions as a 'space of authoring' in which the ulama maintain the discourses of Islam in regard to the changes and challenges they receive.[28] Madrasa as an authorizing social and religious space is created for the ulama, and very often, by the ulama.

Creating avenues of social and religious space

The expansion of avenues of social and religious space as developed by the ulama is the result of a widened conception of knowledge about Islam (*din*). Islamic education became devalued in the colonial period because Western-style education was more closely associated with social advancement in the colonial era. The historical legacy in contemporary Bangladesh is such that numerous Islamic scholars, mostly madrasa graduates, find their knowledge to be as less applicable and useful in many arenas of public life. This has led them to recreate their own avenues of social and religious space; the evolvement of the madrasa is one of many such avenues created mostly by madrasa-educated persons or the ulama.

In most cases, the social functions of Islamic-learned persons trained in religious educational institutions are restricted to the religious domain. They earn their livelihood in religiously workable jobs such as preacher, prayer leader at mosques, performer of certain religious rites and madrasa teachers. Their engagement with other arenas of public life is coterminous not only because of their limited adaptability but also because of the limited applicability of Islamic knowledge to public life, where adaptability is achieved through the acquisition of modern disciplinary knowledge. For example, there is no official recognition of the madrasas and their education is not certified. Quomi madrasas and the certification they offer are officially unrecognized, while the degrees at Bachelors and Masters levels of Aliya madrasas are yet to be fully recognized in Bangladesh.[29] The students who pass out from Quomi madrasas are educated Muslims but without formal recognition. Therefore, they are not eligible for any public or even private job regulated by the government rules. As such, the students have very limited options for making a livelihood. The ulama establish madrasas as a way of creating avenues of social and religious space where they can apply their religious knowledge of Islam (*din*), maintain their livelihood and establish an ongoing social interaction with the community, a space in which their voices can be heard. After my first field visit to Brahmanbaria in 2004, with every consecutive visit in 2005, 2007 and 2008, I found the establishment of new Quomi madrasas, a total of eight madrasas within four years. Most of the founders of the newly established madrasas assert that they establish the madrasa to spread knowledge on Islam (*ilm*), which they deem as an obligation for them, who bear such knowledge. However my field observation suggests that religious commitment is not the cardinal cause of evolving madrasas. By establishing a madrasa, in reality, they can on the one hand arrange their livelihood and on the other create a space for authoring, a context of identity in which they can negotiate their social identity through continued interaction with the community, sometimes by mastering social and religious networking in the locality and beyond.

Social and religious networking

In the contemporary Muslim world, networking has significant implications for understanding Muslim history, politics, movements and aspects of 'mobilized Islam' (Cooke and Lawrence, 2005; Wickham, 2002; Wiktorowicz, 2004). By the same token, networking is also important in understanding how the ulama create social and religious space. In the realm of a networked world, the ulama invite and communicate with ordinary Muslims, socially and politically influential persons and philanthropists, and hence proceed to founding madrasas, sometimes with new pedagogical methods and ideas. There are plenty of examples in Brahmanbaria where the evolvement of a madrasa is a result of orchestration of such social and religious networking. Consider the following background to the establishment of a girls' madrasa, Al-Batul Mohila Madrasa, in 1997.

We, some Islamic learned persons [Maulana Abdus Sattar, Maulana Mahfuzul Hasan who is now the director, Hafez Maulana Zalal-ul-Islam], discussed with one another the necessity of a girl's madrasa in Brahmanbaria town. We also discussed the need for one with a physician [Dr. Zahirul Haq], who is a generous donor. We mentioned that he had some lands at Collegepara and we were planning to establish a girl's madrasa and therefore we were seeking his opinion. He donated four decimal [a unit of land area approximately equal to 1/100 acre or 40.46 square meters]. We invited Harun Islamabadi [an eminent Islamic learned person from Chittagong district, who is the brother-in-law of Maulana Zalal-ul-Islam], who is also a noble donor, to come here and see the land and its location. He appreciated the location and suggested that we establish a madrasa. He also helped to secure financial support. With his funds, we began to construct the madrasa, beginning with a five-storey building. Initially, we began to build the first floor and launched the madrasa at the house of the physician. The purpose of the initiative was to educate women in Islam, since the very beginning of a child's education starts with the mother.[30]

Although religious motivation might have some causal effect on the establishment of a madrasa, it is not the foremost reason. Rather, the cause is the social context in which the ulama have limited life choices. All the founder members of Al-Batul Mohila Madrasa are Islamic-educated persons from Quomi madrasas. Their individual networked worlds, both within and beyond their locality, serve as a useful means for founding a madrasa. The contact between the founding members of ulama of Al-Batul Madrasa and Maulana Harun Islamabadi, who was titled 'Islamabadi'[31] (devotee of Islam) for his continuous economic and moral contribution to Islam—and who is credited and much revered among the Quomi ulama circle in Bangladesh for leading one of the country's biggest and oldest Quomi madrasas at Patia in Chittagong district—is an example of how individual networking functions beyond a particular locality. The name of Harun Islamabadi, as mentioned on madrasa billboards and in other campaign materials, as the leading founder of the madrasa denotes how the ulama of Al-Batul Madrasa try to get authorization from a religious authority of the Quomi ulama circle in the country. Associating itself with the name of such a religious authority on the one hand increases the status and prestige of a madrasa and on the other facilitates the opportunity to gain pedagogical authenticity and authority from others in the Quomi ulama circle. The networked world of ulama, as the case of Al-Batul Mohila Madrasa demonstrates, is not restricted internally; many 'Muslim modernists'[32] are included in this circle, such as the physician, who like the ulama, patronized such schooling not merely out of religious commitment but to gain a higher social status in the locality since the giving of donations for educational and religious purposes is hitherto revered and admired.

Occasionally, personal interest and affiliation with particular religious groups could inspire the foundation of madrasas through religious networking, as suggested by the case of Darul Ajkar Giasul Uloom Madrasa in Brahmanbaria.

The founder of the madrasa is Sufi Giasuddin Khan of Datiara, Brahmanbaria. He is the district representative of a Sufi clan called *furfura pir*[33] (spiritual preceptor). On the occasion of a visit of his spiritual guide—*furfura pir*—in 1990, he arranged a public religious gathering (*mahfil*). After the gathering, the chief spiritual guide visited his house and encouraged him to establish a mosque in his locality. Inspired by his spiritual preceptor (*pir*), he decided to donate five decimal lands for building a mosque in his locality. Afterwards, again inspired by his spiritual guide, he established a madrasa in 1991 in the same place where he founded the mosque. The madrasa was named after him. When he established the madrasa, his Sufi master also allowed him to practice different forms of Islamic healing such as amulets (*tabiz*[34] and *maduli*[35]) and sacred water (*pani-pora*[36]) as remedies for those who are sick or affected by evil spirits. His Sufi master suggested that out of the amount of gift (*hadia*) he earned through this practice he should spend half for maintenance of the madrasa and the other half for maintenance of his family.[37] When I made a follow-up visit on him in 2008, I learnt that he had founded another madrasa in the same locality, a girls' madrasa named the Fatima (R) Mohila madrasa. He explained that the reason for setting up the madrasa was to educate women in *din* just as males were educated: 'My *furfura pir* told me that we teach the male students, not the female. If we don't teach the females also we would not be able to make any progress in Islam. So the objective of establishing this girls' madrasa is to teach Islam to the females. We should teach Islam to both the male and female.'[38] The establishment of both these madrasas by Sufi Giasuddin sheds light on how religious networking and individual interest contribute to the evolution of madrasa schooling. Since Sufi Giasuddin was the founder of two madrasas, his identity has been transformed from an ordinary disciple of a spiritual preceptor to that of a promoter of Islamic education.

Interpretative contestation within madrasas: Who are proper Muslims?

What are the beliefs of a proper Muslim? The answer to the question varies with the internal differentiation of interpretations and with the *maslaki* orientation of Islam in some madrasas in Brahmanbaria. In this section, I will draw a comparative illustration of two madrasas—the Jamia Islamia Yunusia Madrasa (hereinafter YM), the biggest Quomi madrasa, and the Darus Sunna Kamil Madrasa (hereinafter DSM), the biggest Aliya madrasa in Brahamanbaria—showing how their *maslaki* orientation of Islam differ on the question of being an 'authentic' Muslim.

YM can be considered emblematic of the local version of Deoband in Bangladesh, which is indoctrinated with 'Deobandi Islam.' The madrasa was established in 1914 by a Deobandi *alim* (Islamic scholar), Maulana Abu Taher Muhammad Yunus, after whom the madrasa was named. He came from India to dissuade 'Qadiani' confusion (*fetna*)—a Muslim religious offshoot anathematized by mainstream Muslim for their belief in the prophecy of Mirza Ghulam Ahmad (d.1908) after Muhammad— in Brahmanbaria.[39] All the *muhtamims*, the directors of the madrasa, were graduates of Deoband. The eligibility and responsibility of the directors (*muhtamim*) outlined in a booklet of the madrasa notes that the director is the custodian of the madrasa and Islam, and he is required to be a follower of the Hanafi school of law (*majhab*) and must follow the accord of the Deobandi ulama, depicting YM's concern for sustaining 'Deobandi Islam' down to this day.[40] Being founded and promoted by a number of Deobandi scholars from the early twentieth century, YM became a local version of the Deoband madrasa in Bangladesh which remains committed to its patron—Deoband.

On the other hand, DSM which is located some three kilometres away from YM at Vadugarh in the Brahmanbaria municipal area was established in 1964 by a group of ulama. One of the oldest mosques—Sahi Masjid—founded in 1663 during the Mughal period (1526–1858) is adjacent to the madrasa premises. The *khatib* (religious leader) of that mosque and the local municipal commissioner were the leading founders of this madrasa. Though it is an Aliya madrasa maintained and supervised by the government, some of the ulama serving as teachers in this madrasa have a close *maslaki* affiliation with Barelvi. They are indoctrinated with the theological precept of Ahmad Riza Khan (d.1921) of Bareilly and his movement—*ahl-i sunnat wal jamaat*, which places emphasis on intercession and Muhammad's life in a ritualized form of devotion, a stance which is antithetical to the ulama of YM, as it is to their patron Deoband. Though the ulama of YM, like Deoband, claim that their creed (*aqida*) is also based on the followers of the people of the prophetic tradition (*ahl-i sunnat wal jamaat*), the interpretative differentiation on the status of the Prophet markedly differs between the ulama of YM and those of DSM, while each asserts that its understanding of the Prophet is 'authentic' and in accordance with the scriptural guidance of Islam. The following assertion depicts the position of the ulama of DSM who are opposed to the theological precept of YM.

> The Deobandi creed (*aqida*) is based on Muhammad bin Abdul Wahab of Arabia ... They are not the true followers of the people of the prophetic tradition (*ahl-i sunna wal jamaat*) ... Our creed is founded on that belief that Rasul's [the Prophet] position is just after Allah. And so do we believe. There are some other rules of guidance (*masla*) that differentiate between us and those [Deobandi followers]. For instance, they believe Rasul as a person who is made of mud but we believe he is a man made of light (*nur*). They negate the concept of spiritual preceptor (*pir*). They also believe that Allah's holy men (*wali*) cannot help us and after their death they don't have any power. But we believe that even after death we can seek help from them; they can mediate for us with Allah. Rasul is the messenger of *gaeb* [Ar. *ghayib*, unseen] ... Our creed is Allah teaches Rasul the complete knowledge of the sky (*asman*) and the earth (*jamin*). He knows the knowledge of *gaeb*.[41]

The ulama associated with YM are strongly against such a doctrine. They assert that considering the prophet as a possessor of the knowledge of the unseen is unauthentic, according to the Quran and the prophetic tradition (*hadith*).

Allah observes what you and I are talking about, thinking and doing. As Muslims we usually believe that. What you bear in your mind and what you are supposed to say a few minutes later is known to Allah. And they (Barelvi) believe that it is known to the Prophet also. This is the difference (between us and them). It is the difference similar to the distance between land and sky ... They believe that if we do something in the name of our Prophet he is able to be present with us. Islam does not hold such belief and thought. Concrete evidence from the Quran and the prophetic tradition rules out such belief.[42]

Although the ulama of both madrasas—YM and DSM—assert that their creed (*aqida*) is based on the Quran, the prophetic tradition, the Hanafi school of jurisprudence and the path of the followers of the prophetic tradition (*ahl-i Sunna wal Jamaat*),[43] some aspects of doctrinal differentiation lead these ulama to a contesting situation where both sides claim that their doctrinal stances are 'true.' The ulama of YM contemplate that it is their religious duty to protect the Muslim from any sinful innovation (*bidat*). In the preamble of a booklet on *Bidati* (those responsible for sinful innovation), Maulana Mufti Mobarak Ullah, the deputy Islamic jurist-consultant (*naib-i mufti*) and scholar of prophetic tradition (*muhaddith*) of YM stated that a group of people in the country calling themselves devotees of the prophet (*asiki rasul*) are breaching the 'true *iman* (faith on God) and the creed' of common Muslims and are encouraging common Muslim people to perform polytheism (*shirk*) by misusing the name of Sunni (Kasemi, 2005). Though Maulana Mubarak Ullah does not refer specifically to those who are breaching the 'true' Islam, he certainly points his finger at the Barelvi followers. Citing several Quranic injunctions, prophetic tradition and jurisprudential interpretation, the booklet rules out all the doctrinal tenets of Barelvi followers. Referring to the Deobandi ulama, the booklet nullifies the notion of professing Muhammad as a possessor of the knowledge of unseen and *hazir u nazir*—the two principle theological precepts of Barelvi tradition. It reasons that the ulama who believe in such theological precepts are engaged in *shirk*, that is, associating Muhammad as the partner of Allah. This doctrinal interpretative contestation, therefore, is an example of understanding how the Deobandi ulama associated with a particular madrasa, in this case the YM, differentiate themselves from other denominational thought held by other ulama in the same locality by a process of 'othering' another doctrinal precept and its followers as if the (other) interpretation is 'unauthentic.' For the Barelvi, the same process occurs in reverse. Thus, madrasas are the functional bases for transmitting a group of ulama's denominational orientation and its creed in which the conceptualization and formation of Muslim identity is always contestable and debatable.

Contestation for pedagogical and religious authority

The differentiation of madrasas is not only restricted to different denominational orientations but also to diverse pedagogical and institutional approaches. Ulama have their own reasons with regard to 'positionality'[44] where they have the opportunity to cultivate their religious authority in their own domain of social and religious spaces with a plurality of notions, ideas and pedagogical conceptions of Islamic education.

Pedagogical contestation within madrasas

The primary pedagogical contestation within madrasas in Bangladesh is the difference between Aliya and Quomi. Each claims that their pedagogical method is the correct one. The Quomi madrasas' ulama argue that the religious education imparted in the Aliya madrasa is heavily burdened with modern disciplinary subjects, and hence is remote from a 'proper' Islamic education. On the other hand, the ulama of Aliya consider Quomi pedagogy as 'inferior' to the Aliya system because of their rigidity in maintaining a 'traditional' Islamic pedagogical learning system. Consider the following assertion of a teacher of the Aliya madrasa.

> A Quomi madrasa is not better than an Aliya madrasa since the Quomi madrasa students' learning is one-sided; they know nothing about the other side [i.e. modern general education]. We allow the students who passed grade eight in a Quomi madrasa to be admitted to grade four in the Aliya madrasa. We allow the students who completed *Daura-i Hadith* in the Quomi system to be admitted to grade eight in the Aliya madrasa. They study the same Arabic text here that they studied before [in Quomi madrasa] but the difference is that they used to study in Urdu while we teach the same in Bengali.[45]

The ulama of the Aliya madrasas differ markedly from the Quomi ulama on the issue of Urdu and Persian lessons in madrasas. They argue that Urdu and Persian lessons are not necessary and should be substituted by Bengali. On the contrary, the Quomi ulama favor Urdu and Persian teaching in addition to Bengali. They contend that since in the past many seminal literary works on various aspects of Islam and its interpretation were written either in Urdu or Persian by many noble Islamic scholars, there is no choice but to study these languages. This pedagogical differentiation leads the ulama of both types of madrasas to a debate; the ulama of Aliya madrasas contend that the Quomi madrasas' ulama claim their pedagogy to be 'perfect' simply because of their inclusion of Urdu and Persian lessons, although there is no significant difference between the Aliya and Quomi madrasas in the teaching of the Quran, the prophetic tradition and fundamental tenets of Islamic knowledge.

> But now we don't need Urdu in Bangladesh and it is applicable in some parts of Pakistan. Persian is needed only if you go to Iran; otherwise nowhere else in the world is Persian necessary. I often suggest to the Quomi ulama that they could change their Urdu and Persian lessons. What is the necessity of these languages? Is Urdu necessary for studying three *kitab* (texts) to bother the students? We rejected Urdu. It is fully abolished. Persian is also rejected. It is just an optional subject. So far as I know no one studies

Persian and in reality it is not necessary. Instead of Persian, one studies political science. Instead of Urdu, we teach social studies, political science, and psychology.[46]

The preference for sustaining the Urdu and Persian languages is intricately intertwined with the question of authorizing space for many Quomi ulama. Neither Urdu nor Persian is taught in any other educational institutions as they are taught from the very beginning of school life in Quomi madrasas in Bangladesh. Many Quomi madrasa ulama are still the bearers of these languages. If lessons in these languages are abolished, the 'space of authoring' of such ulama would diminish. In that sense, the preference for Urdu and Persian lessons in the madrasa is the expression of the ulamas' struggle to maintain their authorizing space where they can cultivate and practice these languages in relation to Islamic knowledge.

Institutional differentiation of madrasas

The ulama compete within different institutional nexuses of madrasas. They have complex power relations and their 'positionality.' The case of the Bangladesh Jamiatul Madarisin, an association for Aliya madrasa teachers, located in the capital city, is here illustrative. The organization was established in 1937 with a view to developing madrasa education and tackling the problems and challenges the madrasas and their ulama face in modern times.[47] Today, it is a government-approved organization with a large complex of mosque and office premises and a network of offices throughout the entire country.[48] Though it is an association of more than 200,000 teachers who work in Aliya madrasas, it also functions as a public religious sphere where the voices of ulama are to be heard regarding the diverse aspects of Islamic subjectivities; an endeavor for reconciliation of differentiation within ulama circles. For instance, in an organizational meeting, the ulama from all over the country made a declaration that recognizes differentiation within the ulama. According to the clauses of the declaration, all the *pir-mashayikh* (generally referred to as ulama; *mashayikh* pl. of *sheikh*, title of Sufi master or Muslim descended from the Companions) should work together with a view to spreading and implementing Islam for the sake of fostering greater interest in Islam; any law that goes against the tenet of the Quran and the role model of the prophet must be defended; Islamic scholars (*alim*, sing. of ulama) should avoid taking an oppositional stance with each other; and action should be taken against those ulama who brand many Islamic practices, such as observing the night of forgiveness (*laylat-ul barat*), the night of ascent of the prophet to Allah (*laylat-ul miraj*), the day of mourning the slaying of the prophet's grandson in Shia Islam (*ashura*), the birth anniversary of the prophet (*id-i miladunnabi*), visiting grave-shrines (*majar*) of the holy men in Islam (*wali*), as sinful innovation (*bidat*).[49] The ulama of the organization are also concerned with the 'propagation' of media, which are breaching the 'authentic' creed (*aqida*) of Islam and hence have argued for the establishment of Islamic TV in aid of the ulama (*Inqilab*, ud).[50] Even though the organization's primary concern is to unify the ulama, it generated further fissures, with the establishment of the Madrasa Sikhsok Parishad (Association for Madrasa Teachers) in 2006 which opposed the Jamiatul Madarisin on the grounds that it primarily fails to address the original purpose of the organization, that of serving the group's vested interests. The important facet of the newly established organization is that it was formed with the political leaders of Jamaat-i Islami,[51] an action unacceptable to the present ulama of Jamiatul Madrisin who oppose any political influence on their organization.

> Our Jamiatul Madarisin is an apolitical organization. Jamaat-i Islam wants to use our teachers politically. We are against it. We, the madrasa teachers, have some differences with regard to the creed in Islam (*aqida*) with Jamaat-i Islami. In reality Jamaat-i Islami is a cadre-based organization. They operate according to their ideology and their operation is not limited, whether it is an Aliya or a Quomi madrasa. Especially, the ulama of Aliya have been speaking up against Jamaat since the British and Pakistan period. Here, a number of Islamic learned men and scholars differ with some writings of Maududi.[52]

The scope of this section does not allow for the discussion of the complex political differentiation within the ulama, but it is evident enough here to argue that the differentiation associated with Jamiatul Madarisin is the manifestation of how the ulama compete for their influence in the public religious sphere with different techniques of knowledge and power.

On the other hand, the institutional nexus of the Quomi madrasas also have important facets of differentiation. For instance, Bangladesh Befaqul Madarisil Arabia (Bangladesh Quomi Madrasa Education Board), which is known as the 'Befaq Board,' and which was founded in 1978 by a group of ulama, is trying to integrate all variants of Quomi madrasas within a common framework of schooling methodology, but they have failed to do so because of disavowal by different factions of the ulama within the Quomi madrasa. Nearly 2,000 madrasas are affiliated with the board, leaving a preponderant number of Quomi madrasas all over the country outside of its jurisdiction.[53] Many ulama prefer an individual authorizing space where they will have the autonomy of their own religious authority, maintaining the distinctiveness of their own madrasa. This position has led to the emergence of several Quomi madrasa boards, often centered on one madrasa founded by a local eminent Islamic scholar.[54] Such individually controlled madrasas assert their distinctiveness that differentiates them from others and, hence, prefer not to conform within a system. To substantiate this assertion the case of the Nurani and Nadiatul Quran system of madrasa schooling, both of which were innovated by an individual Islamic scholar, is illustrative here. Nurani refers to a particular system of primary level Islamic schooling, three years in tenure, which aims to produce 'proper' Muslim individuals from childhood by teaching lessons on basic Islamic rituals as well as 65 prophetic traditions (*hadith*) and 66 Quranic passages. Maulana Qari Belayet Hosan is credited for his innovation of the system. This system of madrasa schooling has since proliferated all over the country. Nearly 10,000 branches have a central board—Nurani Talimul Quran

Board—in Dhaka.[56] On the other hand, like Nurani, the aim of Nadiatul Quran madrasa is to spread Quranic lessons into every Muslim house in order to produce 'proper' Muslims. Maulana Abdul Ohab, a Deobandi *alim* of Brahmanbaria, is credited for the proliferation of the Nadia system of madrasa schooling, of which there are nearly 10,000 branches, all over the country. The central board of these madrasas, Nadiatul Quran Board, is situated at the house of Maulana Abdul Ohab at Bhuiyapara in the Brahmanbaria municipal area.[57] Both the Nurani and Nadia madrasas claim their system of madrasa schooling is distinct and righteous for the production of 'proper' Muslims and therefore are belligerent in their opposition to submitting to the oversight of the Befaq Board. This difference not only manifests the differentiation of madrasas' institutions but also suggests how the ulama compete for their influence and authority in their own authorizing space.

The madrasa as a site for reconstructing Muslim cultural identity?

In many Western societies, the emergence and maintenance of Islamic education are associated with the preference of parents for their children to be attached to their Muslim cultural tradition, by which they can distinguish their identity in the multicultural societies where they live (Merry, 2007). Is the same assumption applicable in the context of Muslim societies, where madrasas function not only to teach Islamic religious knowledge but also to produce a cultural identity of being Muslim? Contemporary Muslim societies in the world are facing rapid changes through the process of globalization, 'Westernization,' modern mass education, new communication technologies, and above all, the threatening pressure of global culture. Since the cultural identity of being Muslim is associated with these complex changes, very often compounded, many Muslims consider the madrasa as an alternative way of nurturing their cultural tradition, one that connects them to an ideal past and Islamic role model (Graham, 1993: 522). This process of connection or the process of identification as being Muslim is neither uninventive nor unchanged, as suggested here; rather, it is constantly adaptive within the changing facets of their society and among madrasas and the ulama as well.

Although Islamic education is the doorway to being Muslim, in many cases the ulama also regard modern education as a pathway to compete with the modern world. As the principal of the Brahmanbaria Cadet Madrasa said:

> I have two identities. First, I am a human being and then I am a Muslim. To lead life as a human being in the world, I need to acquire necessary knowledge both for myself and for the country. To lead my life as a Muslim, I need Islamic education also … Religion shows the path. No one can define the destiny of life without religion. I am a Muslim and I feel the necessity for both worldly education and education after this world. My Hereafter (*akhirat*) will depend on how I am leading my life in this world. This world (*duniya*) is the working field of Hereafter (*akhirat*) … Thus, without this world Hereafter

has no meaning ... If Islam is claimed to be the most superior religion, how will the superiority come? Will it come by religion only? No. We have to achieve superiority in religion, science, and in all other fields. Then, we can be considered as one of the best nations in the world.[57]

During my fieldwork, I observed that many madrasas, particularly the Quomi ones, maintain strict discipline among students. Such discipline is closely associated with how madrasas shape the Muslim identity; by encouraging students to follow an Islamic etiquette and manner, that is, *adab* as well as by teaching them Islamic practice and doctrinal precepts. Maintaining such etiquette by madrasa students, in many cases, is obligatory. For instance, in YM, all the students before their enrolment are required to sign a paper outlining the disciplinary rules. According to this paper, all students should do their everyday activities in accordance with God's command and the role model of the prophet. They are required to abide by maintaining the attire and the haircut of the prophet (*Sunnati*-dress and *Sunnati*-haircut), reciting the Quran, performing prayer every day and so on. They are not allowed to smoke and to move around without prior consent.[58] In most cases students of Quomi madrasas follow an Islamic etiquette and manner, and many ulama deem it as the first and foremost identity marker of being a 'proper' Muslim. In contrast, most of the Aliya madrasas are not of the seminary type like their Quomi counterparts where the students attend the school from outside. In that sense, the Aliya madrasas are not able to maintain strict discipline like the Quomi or to impose Islamic etiquette and manners on their students due to which the ulama of the Quomi madrasas claim that their method of teaching is more 'authentic' than that of Aliya madrasas in terms of promoting a sense of Muslim identity among their learners. At the same time, the Aliya madrasa students' conceptualization of Muslim selfhood has been intermingled because of the intense focus on modern education, which leads the ulama of Quomi madrasas to censure the Aliya madrasas as teaching and promoting an 'improper' Islamic identity. In response to such allegations, the ulama of the Aliya madrasas have their own arguments.

> It is true that there are some differences regarding Islamic etiquette (*akhlakh*) between them [Quomi] and us. The reason is that our system is different. After graduation in Dakhil from an Aliya madrasa, students enter college. But the students of Quomi cannot enter any other institution even when they graduate with the highest degree. For students admitted here, the dress and etiquette of the prophet (*sunnati lebas*) is mandatory. But after graduation we cannot control what they will wear. We advise them to follow the dress and etiquette of the prophet. They [Quomi ulama] try to claim their system is a more righteous Islamic education ... The point is they are also spreading Islam and so are we.[59]

Most of the Aliya madrasa ulama also contend that since their students are embracing modern education, they tend to wear 'modern dress' which does not necessarily mean that they are not observing the basic religious obligations as individuals. One Islamic scholar exemplifies that his son is studying for an MA in Political Science at Dhaka University after his *Kamil* graduation from an Aliya madrasa, and he has a daughter pursuing a Master of Business Administration after her *Dakhil* graduation. Though his son and daughter often wear 'modern dress,' they do not leave Islamic practices or stray from religious obligations. In this sense, he argues, Aliya students are also maintaining 'proper' Islamic good deeds-etiquette (*amal-akhlakh*).[60] The ulama's contesting notions on how madrasas can produce a 'proper' Muslim selfhood through Islamic education and training Islamic manner and etiquette (*adab*), again, suggest that the concept of Muslim identity within the madrasas and within the ulama circle is marked by plural forms of argument and contention—that is refashioning with the changing facets of society.

Conclusion

In this chapter, I have sought to illuminate how madrasas and their custodians are fraught with competing doctrinal orientations to Islam, ideas, conceptions and contentions. Considering the case of the Brahmanbaria municipality, this study explicates that the madrasas in contemporary Bangladesh share historically the different interpretative traditions, that is, *maslaki* traditions of Sunni Islam, originating in nineteenth and twentieth century South Asia. In varied circumstances, the contestation among different madrasa systems is not enlivened by the inclination to different Islamic denominational orientations and the manner in which such orientations are accentuated within the realm of madrasas. The contestation is conjoined with the techniques of social contention by which certain theological interpretations of Islam struggle for social legitimization in the sphere of Muslim cultural tradition. In that sense, the madrasas' functionality in Bangladesh is not only delimited to its existence as a social or spiritual entity which provides education with religious morality to the Muslims (Bano, 2007); rather, it is a primary site for facilitating and generating the internal reasoning, debates and contestation within Islam in a discursive manner wherein both religious and social issues intricately interplay in refashioning the larger context of Muslim cultural tradition. What follows from this is that madrasas promotes certain denominational aspects of Islam (such as Deobandi, Barelvi) as a way of guiding Muslim identity. I have shown in the above discussion that for many religious and learned Muslims or in a more generic sense—ulama—madrasas are those places where they can resuscitate the ways of being 'Muslim,' even though being a proper 'Muslim' is equivocal and contentious in terms of doctrinal inclination, social and behavioral etiquette. In equating Islamic religious education with the necessity of forming Muslim selfhood and identity, both the custodians of state-approved (Aliya) and non-state (Quomi) madrasas disparage each other on the question of pedagogical methodology that is germane to the process of constructing virtuous and devout Muslims. What follows from this, as I have argued, is that pedagogical exclusivity is not only associated ineluctably with the process of formation of 'proper' Muslim selfhood. It also seemingly associated to the other techniques of power—such as the ulama's individual fame and scholarly religious authority, social and religious networking and the discursive nature of madrasa-related religious forums. These techniques generate the contestation with regard to the formation of Muslim selfhood and simultaneously function as facilitators for securing the authorizing realm of social and religious space for many madrasa custodians. Through this contestation certain discourses of being 'Muslim' are not only given more weight over others but also permit the madrasa-educated Muslims in Bangladesh to relocate their social existence using their religious dexterity that is undervalued in the public space.

Notes

1 The use of the notion of 'discursive' for understanding Islamic tradition in academic scholarship can be traced back to Marshall Hodgson's seminal work Venture of Islam (1974). Eickelman (1982: 12) also pursued the utility of thinking Islam as discursive: 'What is "traditional" in Islam is necessarily subject to ongoing debate and interpretation.' Asad (1986: 14) reiterated: 'An Islamic discursive tradition is simply a tradition of Muslim discourse that addresses itself to conceptions of the Islamic past and future, with reference to a particular Islamic practice in the present.'

2 The term 'quasi-sectarian' refers to the doctrinal differentiation and interpretation of certain Islamic precepts within a Muslim sect such as Sunni. This is used by Metcalf (1982: 264).

3 Alam (2008a) prefers the use of the word maslaki instead of sectarian commonly to denote such differences. According to Messick (2005), 'maslak' can be understood as an 'interpretative community,' the interpretation of which is founded on interpretative worlds by 'othering' other interpretative communities in Islam (cf. Alam, 2008a: 3, n.5). Like Alam I also prefer maslaki since it rightly denotes the interpretative differentiation even within a particular sect like Sunni or Shia.

4 Huq's (2008) explication is illustrative here to understand how the women of the leading female Islamist organization in Bangladesh are facing global cultural challenges as well as other challenges of modernity in their everyday lives and how they are propounded through Quranic reading circles to renew their 'belief' with a view to fending off such challenges.

5 Eaton (1994), Roy (1983), Ahmed (1996/1981), Ahmed (1996), Uddin (2006) are some noted academic works on Islam in Bangladesh.

6 Asad (1986: 24) defines 'A practice is Islamic because it is authorized by the discursive traditions of Islam, and is so taught to Muslims—whether by an alim, a khatib, a Sufi shaykh, or an untutored parent.'

7 For historical account of such trends in Bangladesh see Ahmed (1988) and Roy (1983).

8 See Eickelman (1992), Eickelman and Anderson (2003/1999) and Robinson (1993) on how mass higher education and modern technology facilitate the transformation of Muslim societies.

9 By 'culturally Muslim' I mean those Muslims in Bangladesh who are not regular in practicing Islamic practices such as daily prayers and Ramadan. These Muslims occasionally perform Friday's congregational prayer and attend certain Muslim festivals such as id-ul fitr and id-ul-azha.

10 Raju (2008: 125–126) contends that the identity of Muslims in Bangladesh is imbued with two contradictory facets: a 'cultural-nationalist' approach which prioritizes Bengalis' indigenous cultural practices and considers Islam as alien, and a 'pro-

Islamic' approach which considers Islam as part of the indigenous culture. According to Raju, within the backdrop of skirmishes the identity of 'Bengali-ness' and 'Muslim-ness' was always in motion. The notion of 'Muslim-ness' was a result of a growing communal consciousness among Bengali Muslim peoples that emerged in the wake of the nineteenth and twentieth century's Islamic revivalist movement and on the backdrop of the formation of communal ideology between Hindu and Muslim. On the other hand, the notion of 'Bengali-ness' rooted with its ethno-linguistic identity had emerged particularly after the Bengali language movement in 1952 in Bangladesh against the Pakistani rulers' decision to make Urdu a state language for both East (then Bangladesh) and West Pakistan. On the formation of a communal ideology in twentieth-century Bengal, see Datta (1999), and for how a sense of 'Muslim-ness' and 'Bengali-ness' influence the conflict of Bengali and Bangladeshi nationalism, see Uddin (2006: 117–153)

11 Ahlus-Sunna wal-Jamaah denotes 'a highly emotive emic identity marker, which in normative etic discourse means nothing more than a label to denote allegiance to the Sunni or dominant grouping of Muslims' (Geaves 2005: 2).

12 Hanafiate refers to the Sunni majhab, a system or school of Islamic jurisprudence, ascribed to Abu-Hanifah (699–767 CE) (Hodgson, 1974: 514).

13 Shah Waliullah (1703–62) was a leading ulama of Delhi who laid emphasis on studying 'transmitted science' (manqulat) rather than 'rational science' (maqulat). He popularized the six canonical texts that are sihah sitta of Prophetic tradition in the Indian subcontinent (Sikand 2005: 48–49). On his life and influence on the Deoband Madrasa, see Metcalf (1982: 35–43) and Faruqi (1963: 135–136).

14 On dars-i nizami curriculum, see Robinson (2001: 48–51).

15 From its medieval heritage, Islamic education is bifurcated in manqulat/naqli (transmitted) and maqulat/aqli (rational) sciences. Transmitted or revealed knowledge refers to the knowledge of God and His messenger which is unchangeable such as Quran and the prophetic tradition, whereas rational knowledge denotes those branches of knowledge which are based on human intellect that is changeable. See Metcalf (1982: 19) and Nasr (1987: 126).

16 For discussion on the life of Ahmad Riza Khan and his movement, see Sanyal (1996, 1998) and Metcalf (1982: 296–314).

17 There is no significant academic work that illustrates a detailed account of the Ahl-i Hadith movement. See a prima facie discussion in Metcalf (1982: 268–296).

18 On Nadwatul Ulama, see Metcalf (1982: 335–347) and Hartung (2006: 135–157).

19 For how Jamaat-i Islami understands Islam, see the writings of its founder Mawdudi (1988); also see Nasr (1994).

20 Ahmadiyya Muslims consider Prophet Muhammad as a law-bearing prophet (Shariati nabi) while accepting Mirza Ghulam Ahmad as 'zilli nabi', i.e. 'shadow prophet', who promotes the messages of Muhammad. For fuller discussion, see Friedmann (2003).

21 For how the British patronized the establishment of Calcutta Aliya madrasa, see the 'Minute by Warren Hastings, governor-general of Fort William (Calcutta) in Bengal' in Lynn Zastoupil and Martin Moir (1999: 74–75).

22 Ward is the smallest administrative unit of a municipality which is composed with several para or moholla, a cluster of homesteads.

23 Cadet Colleges are considered one of the most important seats of general schooling in terms of their academic performance and sophisticated disciplinary practices of schooling. The prime objectives of these colleges are to produce prospective skilled army officers and hence the colleges are directly maintained by armed forces. The first Cadet College was established in 1958 at Faujdarhat in Chittagong district by the then Pakistan government. At present there are 12 Cadet Colleges in different regions of Bangladesh.

24 In these madrasas the course duration of Daura-i Hadith, the highest degree, is for eight years while it is 15–16 years in their counterpart boys' Quomi madrasas. The custodians of these madrasas contend that if the female students cross their puberty period they could get married and hence would not be able to study further. Thus they shorten the duration of lessons in order to provide the advance religious education to the female students within a short time, particularly before their marriage.

25 These data were provided by an officer of Madrasa Education Board, Dhaka in February 2007.

26 According to the lists provided by the municipal office of Brahmanbaria, March 2008.

27 According to the information provided by the Upazilla office of Brahmanbaria, September 2004.

28 The term 'space of authoring' is one aspect of changing identity of human agency in the sense that Holland *et al.* (1998) argued. 'Space of authoring' refers to the 'answerability' of the world where 'authorship is not a choice—but the form of the answer' and 'a matter of orchestration:' of arranging identifiable social discourses/practices that are one's resources (which Bakhtin glossed as 'voices') in order to craft a response in a time and space defined by others' standpoints in activity, that is in a social field conceived as the ground of responsiveness (Holland *et al.* 1998: 272). In concordance with the meaning I view madrasa as a 'space of authoring' for ulama where their 'voices' are to be heard and where their responses are to be perceptible as form of answer resulting from the social field grounded on multiplied and multifaceted aspects of responsiveness. In that sense the evolvement of madrasa means the creation of social and religious space for ulama and by ulama as 'space of authoring.'

29 Dakhil, equivalent to Secondary School Certificate (SSC) and Alim, equivalent to Higher Secondary School Certificate of general schools, degrees of Aliya madrasa had been recognized officially in 1985 and 1987 respectively. The other two degrees, Fazil as equivalent to Bachelor level and Kamil as equivalent to Master level, are to be recognized as the government promised by amending two necessary laws—Islamic University Act, 1980 (Act XXXVII of 1980) and Madrasah Education Ordinance, 1978 (Ord. No. IX of 1978) (Bangladesh Gazette, 2006a, 2006b). On the other hand, though the government vouched for recognizing the Quomi system of education by establishing a separate board of Quomi madrasa, it is still uncertain.

30 Interview of Maulana Abdus Sattar, founding member and teacher of Al-Batul Mohila Madrasa, Brahmanbaria, March 25, 2008.

31 'Islamabadi' as a title usually awarded to show respect to individual alim or even to other individual Muslim by his followers and subordinates or by other ulama or by local people for their donations and other contributions to Islamic institutions like mosque, madrasa, etc.

32 Zaman (2005: 82) defines 'Muslim modernist' as 'those who have been educated in modern Western (or Westernized) institutions of learning and have sought to rethink or adapt Muslim practices, institutions, and discourses in light both of what they take to be "true" Islam—as opposed to how the Islamic tradition has evolved in history—and of how they see the challenges and opportunities of modernity.'

33 Furfura is the name of a clan of spiritual preceptors originating from the village of Furfura in Hooghly district in West Bengal, India. The clan is popularly known as furfura sharif, which has networked disciples in almost every district in Bangladesh. They had a central office at Mirpur in Dhaka. Details about furfura are unknown due to the paucity of any academic work on it.

34 An amulet, which contains some sacred text or incantation for the cure of illness or to scare away evil spirits.

35 Also a kind of amulet similar to tabiz.

36 Pani refers to water and pora to utterance. It is a form of Islamic healing where Islamic preceptors utter some sacred passage onto water which is given as remedy for curing illness or evil spirits.

37 Interview with Sufi Giasuddin Khan, September 2004.

38 Interview with Sufi Giasuddin Khan, March 24, 2008.

39 According to the recorded interview of Mufti Nurullah, now the muhtamim, director of the madrasa, September 2004, and conversations with several other ulama in the town.

40 Nesabnama of YM, a booklet written in Urdu, where curriculum and duties and responsibilities of the directors and teachers are stated.

41 Recorded interview of Md. Abdul Matin, Vice-Principal, Vadugarh Darus Sunna Kamil Madrasa, March 30, 2008.

42 Recorded interview of Imam and teacher of YM, March 7, 2007.

43 Ahl-i Sunnat wal Jamaat, Bangladesh, situated in Dhaka, is the central organization of Barelvi ulama of Bangladesh, though for the Deobandis so far there is no such central organization.

44 According to Holland *et al.* (1998: 271) 'positionality' is a context of identity which refers to 'the "hereness" and "thereness" of people; it is inextricably linked to power, status, and rank.' In the modern era peoples' identities, as Holland *et al.* (1998) suggests, are not fixed with particular social and cultural worlds, rather with different contexts of 'figured worlds'. In that sense 'positionality' denotes how the people connect with their changing 'figured worlds.' I use the term in a similar sense to denote how the ulama configure their status of religious authority with positing different 'positionality' in a 'figured' Muslim cultural and social world that is refashioning.

45 Interview with Md. Jalaluddin, teacher of Brahmanbaria Islamia Dakhil Madrasa, September 2004.

46 Interview with Maulana Shibbir Ahmad Momtaji, Secretary-General of Jamiatul Madarisin Bangladesh, national association for Aliya Madrasa teachers, Dhaka, March 20, 2008.

47 For instance, this organization is demanding the official recognition of Fazil (Bachelor) and Kamil (Master) degrees. It is also demanding a fully fledged government facility for all Aliya madrasas like other public schools, and for establishment of an Independent Public Islamic and Arabic University.

48 The government gives the land on which the organization is situated. The complex of the mosque is funded by the government of Iraq from a religious endowment (waqf) fund of the Sufi master Abdul Quadir Jilani. According to the interview with Maulana Shibbir Ahmad Momtaji, Secretary-General, Bangladesh Jamiatul Madarisin, Dhaka, March 20, 2008.

49 Laylat-ul barat refers to the auspicious night of 15 Shaban, the Arabic month. This night is observed largely by many pious Muslims in South Asia, though it is alien to many Arabic Muslim people. Some ulama claim that the celebration of this night is bidah (reprehensible innovation). Laylat-ul miraj refers to the night of Ascent, the 27th day of Rajab month of Arabic, when Prophet Muhammad undertook a journey to Allah. Ashura is the 10th day of Muharram, which is commemorated by the Shia as a day of remembering and mourning the martyrdom of the grandson of the Prophet, Husayn ibn Ali. Id-i miladunnabi refers to the day when the Prophet was born and died, 12th Rabiul Awal. Ulama are diverse in their opinion on the authenticity of celebrating the day.

50 One of the popular daily newspapers in Bangladesh Dainik Inqilab, a pro-Islamic newspaper, is believed to have been established by Jamiatul Madarisin. The founder editor of the daily Maulana, Abdul Mannan, was also the founder member of the organization. His son A.M.M. Bahauddin is the current President of the organization.

51 For instance, the current President of Madrasa Sikhsak Parishad is Maulana Delwar Hosain Saydee, an Islamic preacher and former parliament member of Jamaat-i Islami, Bangladesh. The Vice-President of the organization is Muhammad Kamaruzzaman, assistant secretary-general of Jamaat.

52 Interview with Maulana Shibbir Ahmad Momtaji, Secretary-General, Bangladesh Jamiatul Madarisin, Dhaka, March 20, 2008.

53 Interview with Maulana Abdul Jabbar, Secretary-General, Bangladesh Quomi Madrasa Board, March 24, 2007.

54 According to estimates there are at least 13 such individual alim controlled boards, which are scattered in different regions of the country (Prothom Alo 2006).

55 Interview with Maulana Qari Faizullah, director, Nurani Talimul Quran Board, Dhaka, March 31, 2008. The board also supervises annual examination in all the Nurani branches of madrasas. It also provides training to the unemployed madrasa educated students who seek teaching jobs in Nurani madrasas. There are two kinds of training for the prospective teachers—Arabic course training for two months and English course training for one month. During the field visit I found some hundreds of students having their training.

56 Interview with a teacher of Nadiatul Quran Central Madrasa, Brahmanbaria, March 25, 2008. The founder of the Nadia board also established the Nadia Publishing house in Dhaka which published popular Islamic texts for pre-primary and primary level madrasa pupils such as nadia kayeda, a booklet on introducing Arabic alphabets, nadia ampara, a booklet on selected Quranic verses, the Quran etc.

57 Interview with Mobarak Hossan Akand, Principal, Brahmanbaria Cadet Madrasa, March 24, 2008.

58 The conditions required to be followed by the students of Jamia Islamia Yunusia Madrasa, a handout written in Bengali and collected from the madrasa.

59 Interview with Md. Abu Taher, Super (head teacher), Brahmanbaria Islamia Dakhil Madrasa, March 23, 2008.

60 Interview with Maulana Shibbir Ahmad Momtaji, Secretary-General, Bangladesh Jamiatul Madarisin, Dhaka, March 20, 2008; the allegation of Quomi ulamas is based on the conversation with different ulama of Quomi madrasas in Brahmanbaria.

5 Islamic education in China

Triple discrimination and the challenge of Hui women's madrasas

Masumi Matsumoto and Atsuko Shimbo

No country has experienced changes as dramatic as China has throughout the last three decades. The World Bank predicts that by 2030, China will be the world's most prosperous country in terms of its gross domestic product (GDP) and foreign currency reserves. These new economic dynamics have deeply affected the lifestyle of China's Muslims, whose population reached 21 million in 2007. The development of western consumerism, the rise in literacy, and increasing contact with Muslim countries has brought about new ethno-religious consciousness and socio-political claims.

Western scholars who have studied Muslim minorities in China have focused mainly on the Turkish-speaking Uyghur, most of whom are settled in Xinjiang, because of their political grievances and the government's use of coercion against them. It is not our intention to downplay the State's repression of any ethnic and religious group in China, but the Uyghurs' plight is not representative of all Chinese Muslim communities. Other Muslim minorities have tried alternative survival tactics to get themselves integrated or recognized in Chinese society; one such group is the Hui.

The Hui, estimated at around 9.8 million in the 2000 census (Zhongguo Renmin Gongheguo Guojia Tongjiju, 2008: 87), comprises almost half of the Chinese Islamic community but a mere 0.75 per cent of the total Chinese population. Religious claims have allowed them to enlarge their social autonomy and address issues such as marginality, inequality, and the acknowledgment of their ethnic identity, while contributing to better national integration. The Hui have been influenced by an Islamic awakening, or revival, the subject of this chapter. We focus especially on the development of Islamic education for Hui women. The expansion of educational opportunities in both Islamic and secular subjects for Hui women has contributed to lessening women's marginalization in both the Hui and Chinese communities in three spheres: economic underdevelopment, ethnic intolerance and neglect, and gender discrimination. Although the struggle against discrimination seems to reinforce religious particularities, it does not necessary lead to a strict and exclusivist Islamization of education. Most often, women simply intend to make strategic use of both their Chinese and Islamic legal statuses for their benefit.

While our respective fieldwork studies have broadly dealt with the marginalization of Hui women in Chinese society, our special focus is Islamic education and the hybridizing process involving the secular and authoritarian state on the one hand and the religious claims involving Islamic identity on the other. This dynamic tension is at the basis Hui distinctiveness and educational dynamics.

The Hui community and the establishment of an educational system

The most populous of the ten national Muslim groups in China, the Hui claim to be descendants of Central Asian and Middle Eastern Muslim traders, soldiers, bureaucrats, sailors, and engineers. According to historians (Ma Shinian, 1988: 224–227; Qiu Shusen, 1996: 7–31; Li Xinghua *et al.*, 1998: 3–50), the first Muslim traders came to China during the Tang Dynasty (618–907) and settled in the coastal cities and Chang'an, the capital city at that time. The Yuan dynasty (1271–1368), known as the Mongolian era, saw the massive immigration of Muslims from Central Asia who married native Chinese women. Their descendants were the Hui, who were conferred Chinese nationality in 1936. The Hui eventually stopped using their mother tongues—Persian, Turkish, or Arabic—and adopted Chinese for everyday conversations since the Ming era (1368–1644), partly because of their intermarriage with the local Chinese and partly because of the pressure to assimilate into Chinese society. However, they maintained their native languages to teach the Islamic faith up to the end of the Qing era (1911), while upholding their religious faith and observing Islamic practices in their everyday life. Their pious lifestyle remained unchanged even in the wake of the profound modifications wrought by the twentieth century. For instance, 94.7 per cent of the Hui who live in the poor mountainous region of southern Ningxia fast during Ramadan, 69.2 per cent offer daily prayers, and 46.8 per cent (72.7 per cent of the women) are taught religion at home (Wang Zhengming and Tao Hong, 2003: 147).

Hui communities can be found mainly in the impoverished northwestern provinces of China: the Ningxia Hui Autonomous Region, Gansu, Inner Mongolia, and Qinghai (see Figure 5.1). Although the group's largest concentration is in Ningxia—about 1/3 of the area's population[1]—significant numbers of Hui live in Gansu, Qinghai, and Xinjiang in China's northwest; Beijing, Hebei, Henan, and Shandong in the centre; and Yunnan in the southwest.

Through their involvement in the nationalist movement, Hui religious and ethnic leaders were able to obtain a very special status in 1936: China's Communist authorities recognized the Hui as a national minority (Matsumoto, 1999: 215–216). As such, they became entitled to religious freedom and equality with other nationalities. However, ethnic discrimination remains deeply entrenched among ordinary Chinese and the Chinese Communist Party (CCP), which continues to repress religious leaders and their activities. Up to now, therefore, the two national principles of ethnic equality and religious freedom have remained nominal. The

Figure 5.1 Map of China

communist regime, which promotes atheistic socialism, discourages people from wearing religiously symbolic attire in public, such as veils or Muslim caps. In particular, party cadres are prohibited from performing any kind of religious practices in public. Moreover, religious associations in China are kept under CCP's surveillance and inspection. All clerics must obtain approval from the CCP and are obliged to preach to their congregations the importance of patriotism and the legitimacy of the Communist party's governance.

Thus the Hui are marginalized both as a religious minority in secular communist China and as an economically disadvantaged people, doomed to live in very impoverished areas. One must add gender discrimination, which has long been forgotten or neglected in the context of the male-dominated Han and Hui societies. Thus, Hui women have been forced to live under strict patriarchal control. The status of rural Hui women resembled that of Han women until about 1949. They were compelled to have their feet bound and were not allowed to study or go out of their homes. Women were valued for hard domestic work, chastity, obedience as daughters-in-law, and good mothers to their sons (Harris, 1947). Even after the revolution in 1949, the Hui in Ningxia lagged in literacy compared with the rest of the Chinese ethnicities, and Hui girls fared worse than Hui boys. Many families could not afford textbooks and other school expenses, which sometimes exceed a quarter of their annual income (Shimbo, 1995). Other serious obstacles included the 'feudal' idea of the predominance of men over women; the lack of female teachers; the secular and Marxist educational system wherein girls and boys were supposed to attend the same class; an early marriage for girls (generally 15–17 years old); and the belief that education would pull girls away from Islam. Until the Compulsory Education Act was promulgated in 1986, the majority of Hui girls, notably those living in Ningxia, remained illiterate.

Hui modern education in Ningxia during the first half of the twentieth century

Modern western-style education was introduced in China at the end of the Qing Dynasty, but its development in the Ningxia region did not follow the same path as in other regions. Hui education mainly took the form of religious education at madrasas[2] from the early Qing era (1644–1911) until around the beginning of the twentieth century.

During the Republican period (1912–1949), which was characterized by the promotion of modernity, ethno-consciousness, and nationalism, a few male religious and other local leaders in the region began to note the importance of female education in increasing the ethno-religious strength of their community. They established a few female madrasas to promote Arabic literacy and Islamic education. These exceptional female madrasas, located in Gansu, Ningxia, and Yunnan taught not only elementary Arabic but also elementary Chinese writing to Hui girls (Laycock n.d.; Pictures of Pickens Collection 1934–35; Yao Jide, 2005: 96–97). Generally known as *nüxue*s,[3] these female madrasas became the prototypes of women's Islamic schooling in contemporary China. However, in spite of the dramatic efforts of some Muslim intellectuals to promote the education of Hui girls, the number of *nüxue* remained low because of the lack of funds and the parents' unwillingness to educate their daughters. Thus, there were few educated Muslim girls in the Northwest. Nevertheless, education became the main concern of Muslim *ahong*s (religious authorities) and local Hui political leaders. They established modern schools that taught both Chinese and Arabic.

For example, Su Le (1868–1950) belonged to the gentry and was a successful entrepreneur at Weizhou in Tongxin County, Ningxia. He studied Chinese classic literature in preparation for the imperial examination and graduated from the Advanced Elementary School, a public school for boys in Pingyuan County, in 1906. Su Le was one of the founders of the Weizhou Islamic Girls School in 1905 as an extension to a mosque. *Ahong*s were in charge of teaching Arabic at that time. The Weizhou Islamic Girls School changed its name to Weizhou Girls Normal School in 1933. Although this was a public school, the Qur'an and religious doctrine were taught alongside Chinese and mathematics. In 1939, the school's name was once more changed to the Weizhou Girls Junior Elementary School (Li Xinghua, 2008: 73–88; Li Zongdao and Wang Kelin, 2000: 62–64; Tongxinxian jiaoyuzhi bianzuan xiaozu/Tongxinxian jiaoyuju, 1991: 139).

After the revolution of 1949, the government adopted various measures to boost public education in the Ningxia region to promote national integration; the establishment of Hui ethnic elementary schools was one such measure. Hui elementary schools were public schools, and Muslim children obtained scholarships in a government drive to encourage schooling. There were 28 lower Hui primary schools (one was exclusively for girls) and three complete elementary schools in 1954. Although the ratio of girls' enrolment remained very low, the school attendance rate of Hui children gradually increased (Ding Guoyong, 1993: 269–270).

The paradoxical impact of the cultural revolution

The Anti-Rightist Campaign in 1957, the Anti-Religion Movement triggered by the Tibet Uprising in 1958, and the anti-religious Cultural Revolution (1966–1976) severely crippled the educational conditions in the Ningxia region. All religious activities, including schools and classes run by *ahong*s, were banned, and countless *ahong*s and madrasa students were persecuted and exiled to the countryside for compulsory work. Many did not survive the rigors of starvation and violence. Religious books and writings, including the Qur'an and *hadith*s' collections, were burned or thrown away, and many mosques were destroyed. Some Muslims were even forced to feed pigs—animals that Muslims shun. Men were prohibited from growing beards, and women from wearing veils (Ma Lan, 2001: 29–31). The government banned practically everything related to religion and ethnicity, trampling over Muslim pride and social relations. During this period, private lay and religious schools established and run by local Hui leaders were forced to either close down or transform themselves into secular public schools in which Arabic was no longer taught.

At the end of the Cultural Revolution, the ban on religion was lifted gradually, spurring an unprecedented educational reassertion in Muslim areas. Religious and political Hui leaders not only reopened the girls' madrasas, built exclusively for Islamic education, but also invested in the establishment of girls' public schools. In contrast to madrasas, these new girls' public schools developed both secular and religious curricula and promoted national identity, loyalty to the party, coeducation, and gender equality. The government was also eager to develop public schools in the region in order to promote national integration, and the *ahong*s had to bear this in mind while promoting their own Islamic agenda. Secular schooling contributed to the integration of Muslim women, raising their visibility and acceptability in the public sphere and giving them access to job opportunities. Simultaneously, this situation contributed to enlarging debates on Hui identity and its stance on modern education and women's economic autonomy.

Educational development after the Cultural Revolution

The expanded role of Hui leaders

Until the end of the 1980s, the number of enrolled Hui girls remained low compared with their male counterparts, but quickly increased afterwards (Ningxia nütong jiaoyu yanjiu ketizu, 1995: 56–95; Ningxia Jiaoyu Kexue Yanjiusuo, 2001; Zhouwei, 1997: 291–292). *Ahong*s and local Hui leaders exerted notable efforts to improve girls' school enrolment in Ningxia, building schools and promoting female education. Together with the government, they established public schools to improve the educational standards of Hui while striving to make both secular and religious education coexist in order to preserve religion and ethnic identity. The experience of three secular public schools founded in cooperation with *ahong*s and local Hui leaders shows how this process worked.

The Weizhou Girls Junior Elementary School in Tongxin County, converted into a co-ed school in 1953, was re-established in 1985. Ma Xinlan, the granddaughter of Su Le (one of the school's founders, as mentioned earlier), was its new principal (Ding Guoyong, 1992: 134–140). Taking advantage of their social prestige, liberal *ahong*s and Hui leaders advocated the importance of girls' education at Islamic festivals and other gatherings (Ma Xinlan, 1995: 18–32). Their zealous persuasion had a powerful impact on the Hui, who had believed that public school education would weaken the girls' Islamic faith. In order to sweep away parents' fears, the curriculum was designed to meet the demands of devout Muslims who wished to make their daughters learn basic Arabic greetings and phrases.

*Ahong*s and teachers compiled a document called 'Two Hundred Famous Phrases in Arabic,'[4] which was used by female *ahong*s in teaching students welcoming words and songs in Arabic. The textbook included the Arabic alphabet, Arabic expressions of greeting, time, the four seasons, family, the history of Ningxia, the general characteristics of the Hui ethnic group, religious beliefs, and excerpts from the Qur'an. The appendix contained tape recording of songs to welcome guests. Each lesson introduced particular contents, such as 'Today's words of wisdom,' 'Seeking knowledge is a Muslim's mission,' 'Seek knowledge even unto China' (*hadith*) and 'Time is money' (Ningxia jiaokesuo guojia nütong jiaoyu yanjiu ketizu, 1992: 3–42). Parents welcomed these efforts, which emphasized respect for the Islamic culture, and began to send their children to the school willingly. Meanwhile, educators saw to it that what was learned at school was useful for daily life and provided guidance for career choices. Vocational and technical training, such as sewing, embroidery, knitting, vegetable cultivation, and other practical courses, were included in the school's curriculum.

In the 1990s, several public schools in the most disadvantaged north-western regions received subsidies from the United Nations Educational, Scientific and Cultural Organization (UNESCO), various non-governmental organizations (NGOs), and other benefactors, as the establishment of gender equality and penetration of secularism was a goal shared by the government and the said international organizations (Li Xiaojiang, 2005; Aaftaab, 2005: 47–51, 57–60). The Weizhou Hui Girls Elementary School was a pilot project of UNESCO, and it affected eight other schools (Ningxia nütong jiaoyu yanjiu ketizu, 1995: 56–95; Xibu sishengqu nütong jiaoyu yanjiu zonghe ketizu, 1999: 29–36, 109), all of which participated in a girls' education project sponsored by the Ningxia Institute of Educational Science from 1992 to 1995. Under the project, the schools' curricula were redesigned to value Islamic culture as UNESCO was stressing respect for ethnic minorities.

A second institution, the Shizi-shan-zhuang Elementary School in Xiji County, was established by Ma Jiafu in 1980, at the end of the Cultural Revolution. He had been arrested in 1958 at the age of 23 and was released in 1980. Ma Jiafu, an *ahong* in the Xiji, used the money he received from the government as compensation for his imprisonment to get the school started. Shizi-shan-zhuang was a public school, and the government shouldered the operating costs. The school also participated in the experimental project of the Ningxia Institute of Educational Science, which included Arabic lessons in the curriculum. The concept, which was very popular among students, increased enrolment.

A third school, the Hairu Girls Junior High School, handles secondary education. It was established in Tongxin County in 1986 by Hong Weizong, the Vice Chairman of the Tongxin County Committee of the Chinese People's Political Consultative Conference (CPPCC) (Mei jie 1999: 268–274). Hong Weizong was a religious leader—a *murshid* (*jiaozhu* in Chinese)—of Hongmen Menhuan (Sufi Order), who was banned during the Cultural Revolution. He was well aware of the obstacles encountered by teenage Muslim girls who wanted to continue studying after elementary school. In particular, co-ed boarding schools posed insurmountable problems. To help Hui girls overcome these difficulties, he founded the Hairu Girls Junior High School, an exclusive boarding school for girls. The start of the school's operation was most timely; the rising number of Hui girls graduating from elementary schools increased the demand for secondary education. The school also offered disadvantaged Hui girls the chance to continue studying by providing them grants and free textbooks and exempting them from various required fees.

As a secular public school, the Hairu Girls Junior High School offered no Arabic classes, but the founder made sure that religious education was not completely eliminated. The school taught Islamic wisdom to both Hui and Han students. The school also edited an extracurricular textbook on the history of the Hui and their heroes, such as Zheng He, who had travelled to the Arab countries up to the Somali coast in the Ming era, and Ma Benzhai, who had fought in the Anti-Japanese War. In teaching students the history, culture, and religion of the Hui, the textbook contributed to reinforcing their identity and promoting mutual understanding between the Hui and the Han. Vocational and technical training in sewing, embroidery, knitting, vegetable cultivation, and other practical courses was part of the school's curriculum. Many graduates of Hairu went on to state-founded secular normal schools or vocational schools for teacher training and eventually became secular elementary school teachers. The roster of graduates shows that 92 students entered the school in 1986 and graduated in 1989; 22 became teachers at secular public schools (Hiaru Nüzi Zhongxue, 1996: 1–81).

In this respect and although the girls' schools founded by *ahong*s and *murshid*s were successful at promoting education—basic literacy as well as Islamic teachings—they encountered a different challenge in the 1990s: the growing number of Hui girls enrolled in secular public schools towards the end of the 1980s.

Faced with the rising popularity of public schools among Hui girls, the schools that had participated in the project sponsored by the Ningxia Institute of Educational Science decided to remove Arabic classes from their curricula. One possible reason for the drastic turnaround was government's pressure to increase the percentage of students proceeding to junior high school. In China, the government runs all schools, even those built by private individuals or NGOs. In other words, even when the private sector supplies large initial investments to build the facilities, the government pays for the teachers' salaries and overhead costs and ultimately, defines the curriculum. As a result, the schools built by religious leaders for promoting education without sacrificing religious identity were eventually transformed into government schools that served its policy: national integration and secularization.

Because of the growing number of elementary school students wanting to enrol in junior high schools, parents welcomed the shift in the schools' curricula. They actually asked for a more ambitious learning agenda instead of basic education and emphasis on Islamic knowledge. Their motivations were pragmatic. For instance, the headmaster of an elementary school that used to teach Arabic told us, 'Studying Arabic takes time away from preparing for the junior high school entrance examinations.' In general, Hui pupils have no one in their families to help them with their studies as most parents are illiterate or semiliterate; therefore, schools play an especially important role in children's education.[5] The Shizi-shan-zhuang Elementary School established by Ma Jiafu *ahong* does not teach Arabic any more 'because there is no Arabic teacher.'[6] The Weizhou Girls Elementary School still offers Arabic classes, but only as an extracurricular activity.[7] In order to meet the changing demands of the authorities and parents, Arabic classes were abolished and the curriculum was revised to fit in with national curriculum standards. In sum, the schools established by the religious leaders were obliged to spend more time on general subjects at the expense of Islamic teachings.

Adapting to the development of China's market economy, Hui students also had to compete with their Han peers in school entrance examinations, an equivalent of the *Keju* test (the imperial examination in ancient China). Because those who couldn't keep up fell by the wayside, Hui girls were forced to conform to the secular national requirements. Moreover, girls' schools had to go co-ed in accordance with the government policy of state schooling and gender equality. One of them was the Hairu Girls Junior High School, which went co-ed in 2002. According to government officials, 'Since there are both men and women in society, it is not good for women's development to educate girls separately from boys.' Yet, it seems that the primary purpose of making the Hairu Girls Junior

High School co-ed was to increase the admissions to senior high schools and colleges among its graduates (2005 survey).

To sum up, after the Cultural Revolution, *ahong*s and local Hui leaders were actively involved in founding schools and promoting Hui girls' education without sacrificing religious identity. However, bowing to the pressure from the government and the Hui community, they gradually converted their schools into secular public schools to raise their educational standards. Eventually, Islamic teaching was dropped from the curriculum and the exclusive girls' schools became coeducational.

The expansion of secular schools for Hui girls

In the past, most parents considered girls' education a waste of time because, once married, a daughter became part of her husband's family. They also believed that public school education was anti-religious, as it weakened Islamic values. However, when confronted by the new socio-economic demands, parents re-evaluated the economic advantage of secular public school education and changed their attitude towards it. Today, the first choice of most Hui girls and their parents is a public school, even if they know that the values taught at the secular public school are incongruous with Islamic values. The chief reason is economics. Education increases the girls' job options, improves their social mobility, and creates better marriage opportunities.

Teaching has been one of the most popular careers for young educated Hui women. Girls who are successful in their education at public schools are often eager to become teachers. A public school teacher earns a monthly salary and is even allowed to register as an urban resident. More importantly, the teaching profession is not regarded as against Islamic values. In addition, the Hui believe that a female teacher makes a better wife because she is a specialist in children's education. Therefore, becoming a teacher enhances the possibilities for young Hui women to find husbands with respectable social status, such as doctors and government employees.

A change in Hui perceptions of secular education opened the floodgates for public education among Hui girls. However, it was government initiative that produced the most important and influential measures; the Compulsory Education Act of 1986 and the Education Act of 1995 inspired students to attend secular government schools (Cui Xiangsu and Lao Kaisheng, 1995: 20). The Compulsory Education Act requires all children to complete nine years of schooling; Article 8 mandates the separation of education and religion. In 2006, the Compulsory Education Act was amended to eliminate all charges for textbooks and miscellaneous fees, dramatically reducing the dropout rate. Even the poorest Hui girls could now finish elementary and junior high school.

Faith and career in a secular society

Though some Hui women are aware of certain points of conflict between Islamic values and secular public education—specifically, the ban on religious education—they have nevertheless chosen to teach in public schools. In the past, the shortage of female teachers had been one of the major obstacles to female education in the Hui region. As a result, since the mid-1980s, teacher training for Hui females has been promoted in Ningxia by the government. We conducted a survey of 123 female Muslim students trained as secular public school teachers at the Guyuan Normal School for Nationalities. This school provided upper secondary level education and aimed at training teachers for primary schools in Ningxia in the years 1995, 1996, and 1997. Most of the students were born between 1978 and 1980. It was in 1978 that the Reform and Open Policy started. The life course of those students has been synchronized with the progress of China's market economy. By 2008, almost all of them had become state schoolteachers in the southern region of Ningxia.

The Guyuan Normal School for Nationalities adopts a standard national curriculum that includes politics, Chinese, mathematics, calligraphy, music, speech training for teachers, psychology, painting, physics, chemistry, and basic linguistics. It should be noted that 'politics' includes philosophical education based on Marxism-Leninism and Maoism.

Female Hui teachers impart to their students what they learned at the normal school. What they teach follows the standard national curriculum, wherein anything related to the Han culture is the exemplar. Other regional or ethnic cultures are not taken into consideration. Portraits of Mao Zedong, Marx, Engels, Lenin, and Stalin are hung on the walls of rural elementary schools. Motivated by communist ideology, public education is aimed at cultivating loyalty to the communist regime. It could be said that the Hui are now almost fully integrated into the Han culture.

Some female Hui teachers are members of the Chinese Communist Party. They say, 'I will constantly strive for girls' education because I was educated and developed under the good policy of the Party.' They claim that 'villagers have an old-fashioned mindset' and 'believe that girls will be exposed to bad influences if they go to school.' Thus, these female teachers believe that it is their mission to eliminate these narrow-minded notions and 'sow the seed of love in poor villages.'[8]

Detached from their Islamic traditions, more and more female Hui teachers have achieved professional success. The absence of religious practices in their daily lives has blurred the distinction between them and female Han teachers. The only religious custom Hui teachers have preserved is the Islamic dietary prohibition on eating pork. Female Hui teachers know about Islam but exhibit no interest in it. They do not read the Qur'an or go to mosques, although they attend Islamic events and festivals. They do not pray at home or fast during the month of Ramadan. They show no interest in female madrasas (*nüxue*) and the students enrolled there. They talk about their fathers' visits to Mecca but seem to think that religion is for old people only and has nothing to do with them.

In sum, female Hui teachers seem to have lost touch with Islamic traditions, and many of them no longer care about practicing religion in a social context. For example, when summer training workshops were held in Yinchuan for female teachers working in the mountainous areas in South Ningxia in August 2002 and again in August 2004,[9] it was observed that an increasing number of teachers were fashion-conscious and wore accessories like necklaces and earrings. Of the 120 participants in the 2004 training, 64 were married Hui women, only 13 of whom (20 per cent) wore cups—the symbol of Hui women's marital status. Instead of cups, some donned half-sleeved blouses and skirts with permed hair. Traditionally, Hui women do not express their opinions before a large group of people, but these teachers did so without hesitation in front of government officials. It seems that the Hui have gradually assimilated the Han code of conduct and values. They build their careers on their secular education by concentrating on professional pursuits.

Among the Hui, giving up one's faith and blending into the host society is not on everyone's agenda. Nonetheless, some female Hui teachers value their Muslim identity. Dejected about being isolated from their religion, a few teachers decide to shift to other jobs. For example, a Hui woman (Ms. M), who used to work as a Chinese teacher at a junior high school after graduating from Ningxia University, began to feel that she was gradually getting separated from her religious beliefs. Consequently, she quit the post to work as an interpreter at an Arab–Chinese trading company in Yiwu, Zhejiang Province, where her family had moved. Ms. M, wearing a veil, told us, 'Working as an interpreter is tough, but I am satisfied with the job. All of my colleagues and friends are pious Muslims. It keeps me closer to my religious beliefs.'[10]

After retirement, many Hui cadres make the pilgrimage to Mecca, as did Mr. M, an official who founded the Xingyuan Women's Islamic School (madrasa or *nüxue*). It is possible, therefore, that female Hui teachers at secular schools will revert to being pious Muslims after retiring.

Far from being a simple case of conflict between Muslim and secular identities, debates on modern education have uncovered deeper concerns of Chinese society: state control versus the autonomy of private institutions, local/ethnic affiliation vs. national acceptance, and eventually, marginalization vs. better social and national integration. In the last part of this chapter, we will discuss the extent to which madrasa development is related to overcoming marginality.

Nüxue: Women's madrasas in China

The new female madrasas

State education is exclusively secular, so religious leaders see a need for Islamic teaching. Many devote themselves to running *nüxue*—private organizations that promote Arabic literacy and Islamic education for women (Jashock and Shui, 2000). These institutions have avoided government control and for this reason their numbers are increasing. Established mainly by *ahong*s (religious authorities), retired party cadres, or Muslim community leaders in the 1980s and 1990s, *nüxue* used to pursue a variety of goals, including the elimination of women's illiteracy, bottom-up Islamic education. They also advocated late marriage. Many contemporary *nüxue* originated in small Arabic study classes for girls and illiterate older women; several of these classes subsequently expanded into schools with high-quality equipment and facilities. The number of such schools and classes is growing yearly, although no official statistics to verify their growth are available.

In general, *nüxue* curricula include the Arabic language, the Qur'an, *hadith*, *kalam*, and morality. For example, Hong Yang, the *murshid* (religious leader) and son of Hong Weizong that we discussed earlier, is venturing into new *nüxue*, such as the Beidasi Women's School and the Haiyuan Women's School for the training of female *ahong*s. He shoulders the teachers' salaries and operational costs, thereby staying independent of governmental control.[11] *Nüxue* teachers emphasize the acquisition of religious knowledge and moral values. The curricula also include Chinese literacy, general knowledge (e.g., computer science), and occasionally, crafts (e.g., sewing). In general, a part of the schools' expenses—teachers' salaries and school equipment—is covered by endowments and donations from religious leaders and other Muslims, and tuition fees. *Nüxue* do not receive any government aid, although many students are exempted from paying tuition or are charged minimal tuition. Almost all students and teachers come from the Hui, Uyghur, and Salar ethnicities.[12] Some *nüxue* also accept a small number of non-Muslim students who wish to learn Arabic. The courses usually span two to four years. However, few students complete the four-year course because of economic difficulties, lack of motivation, and family pressure to get married.

In the 1980s and 1990s, *nüxue* accepted students who had dropped out from public schools or were home-schooled. For this study, we constituted a sample of female students, girls aged 7 to 12, and teachers from three *nüxue* in Weizhou (Ningxia) in 1999 (Matsumoto 2001). In Linxia (Gansu), the first *nüxue* opened as an Arabic class in the early 1980s. Twenty-five years later, the school had developed into the prestigious Linxia Zhong-A Nüxiao (the Linxia Muslim Women's School) with more than 600 students, and is now nationally renowned (Ma Qiang, 2003). Since Linxia—called the 'Little Mecca of China'—is the centre of Islamic culture in China, girls who study there are bestowed with prestige. The number of students that the *nüxue* could accommodate is more than in other areas.[13] The school's success has far exceeded the expectations of its founders.

Since 2000, due to the rise in enrolment at public elementary schools, the role of *nüxue* in providing supplemental education has diminished, except in the most deprived regions of China. Most *nüxue* have become vocational schools for training Arabic interpreters and *nüxue* teachers, with 60–70 per cent of the students undergoing nine years of compulsory schooling. Some of the students have failed high school or university entrance exams. *Nüxue* graduates pursue various careers. Most choose to become teachers in *nüxue* or in Muslim kindergartens, female clerics (*nüahong*), or Arabic interpreters. Some go abroad for further studies, whereas others work as clerks or senior managers; and a few become housewives.

According to our survey sample, 80 per cent of the students in Ningxia and Gansu and 50 per cent in Yunnan wished to pursue a religion-related career, such as teacher, *nüahong*, or *tabligh* (those who engage in the propagation of the faith). Only 3.5 per cent of the students from Ningxia and none from Gansu, Qinghai, and Yunnan wanted to be soldiers or police officers. More than 80 per cent wanted to go abroad on pilgrimage, especially to Mecca and Medina. Some wished to study in Islamic countries such as Malaysia and Pakistan, while others wanted to visit 'advanced' countries, such as Singapore, Japan, and Korea. Few girls expressed a wish to go to the US or Europe.

Strengthening adherence to Islam

The *nüxue* experience helps women develop self-esteem and enables them to choose a career. Girls who become teachers or *nüahong* improve their status and gain greater respect from their community. Female interpreters enjoy several economic advantages, as there is considerable demand for Arabic interpreters in the coastal cities (Tsukamoto 2006). For example, there are 20,000–30,000 migrant Muslims from the Northwest who reside in Yiwu and Guangzhou, which are world-famous wholesale trade centers. In these cities, several interpreters have established lucrative trading companies, and the success stories of poor *nüxue* graduates are well known. In a sense, *nüxue* help Muslim girls achieve their potential by strengthening their religious moorings, which complements the Maoist emphasis on the importance of careers for women.

Nüxue teachers and students insist that, while pursuing economic independence, the younger generation must resist atheism, materialism, and nihilism—the alleged results of an expanding market-economy. This is evident in their answers to questions regarding the differences between public schools and *nüxue*. They view secular public schools as places of corruption, competitiveness, individuality, and fear; and *nüxue*, as places of fairness, cleanness, sisterhood, mutual assistance, and security. *Nüxue* also teach calmness of mind, politeness, self-reliance, self-control, enrichment of mind, and the woman's way of life.

The 'new' and modern Islamic views on gender held by China's Muslim society highlight the right of women to education, freedom of marriage, to buy and sell assets, and to work. At the same time, these views underscore the perceived biological and psychological differences between men and women, and gender separation. In this context, they draw attention to a mother's supposedly primordial and essential role: an educator. Female education is seen as crucial in the reformation of a polluted and contradictory world. A woman is taught to be a 'wise mother and good wife' in order to assure the equality of the two genders in front of Allah on the premise of the division of gender roles. The catchphrase 'wise wife and good mother' was popular in China during the Republican era—when female education was seen as a pivotal element in a productive nation's rejuvenation, a key to regaining national strength—but seemingly slid into oblivion after 1949.

After 60 years, the catchphrase reappeared in the context of Islamic revival in China's Muslim community. The discourse on the division of the genders was again strongly supported by the newly imported 'modern' theory on Islamic women. Authors like the Egyptian Sayyed Qutub, insist on the inherent biological and psychological difference between men and women.[14] In the 1990s, apparently eager to learn the authentic and popular views on Islam outside China, Muslim women in *nüxue* expended great efforts to translate the 'new' writings on Islamism from Arabic to Chinese and circulate them among Chinese Muslims.

Some Muslim women, following 'modern' Islamic interpretation, believe that women can realize submission to Allah through marriage (Wadud, 2006: 121, 161). They assert that the woman's role as spiritual educator of her family and female students should be prioritized over social labor and secular self-realization. This leads us to the question of how women in *nüxue* rationalize the contradictions between such a doctrine, their faith, and future careers.

Today, the young girls' desire to learn Arabic and Islam can be attributed to an increasing awareness of their ethnic identity. A considerable number of the Hui have realized that even though they obtained the status of a specific group of Islamic faith, their religion, history, and traditions will remain neglected and marginalized in the Han-dominated secular public sphere. Thus, ashamed of their lack of Islamic knowledge, they have decided to attend *nüxue*.

Almost all *nüxue* students wear veils. According to the sample's survey, 73 per cent of students started to wear veils after their admission to the *nüxue*. Covering their head and wearing an Islamic dress are new practices for them. Another name for Islam in China is *qingzhen* or 'pure and true,' which represents the essence of Allah. Wearing a veil, they explain, makes them experience a real spiritual change and leads them from confusion and impureness to pureness and piety. In Chinese society, women with veils are often disdained or cast curious looks. In fact, veiling in public is banned. In this context, the veil becomes an icon of their pride in being 'new' Muslim women (Khadija, 1994; Ahmed, 1992: 164). Women's Islamic attire has multiple connotations, such as the expression of Islamic values and subtle resistance to the male-dominated existing order (El-Guindi, 1999: 177–185) or, in China, to the secular and Marxist CCP. Veils also imply a spiritual independence and solidarity with the weak (Wang Jianxin, 2001: 233–234).

Religious education and spiritual hijra

As a consequence of the development policy for the greater Northwest initiated in 2000, the flow of immigrants and money into the region has accelerated. In some *nüxue* in Linxia (Gansu), more than 80 per cent of the students stay in dormitories. Some, learning about the *nüxue* by word of mouth, come from distant parts of China. The highway route and the development of bus services have made it possible for girls to travel independently. Migrant workers—from the Northwest to the coastal region—send money to their parents in their hometown, and a part of this money is given as *sadaqa* to the mosques that govern *nüxue* for further development.[15]

China is not an Islamic country. In countries such as Malaysia and Saudi Arabia, the status of women is stipulated by Islamic family law, which is not always beneficial to women. However, in China, Muslim women are protected by national family laws that promote gender equality. If China applied Islamic family laws and criminal laws, permitted polygamy, and legitimized domestic violence towards wives in its predominantly Muslim regions—as is the case in some Muslim countries—Chinese Muslim women would probably strongly protest against them. In China, Muslim women are pleased to follow the Islamic ideals of equality between men and women and take advantage of both the Chinese laws or their knowledge of Islam.

After graduating from *nüxue*, most Muslim girls obtain employment. Moreover, even after marrying and having children, they may wish to continue to work. Based on their 'mission' to convey the Islamic spirit, exercises, and ethics, *nüxue* graduates aspire to the duality of being educators of their children or husbands at home and teachers and role models for Muslim girls in society.

Their way of life is a far cry from the one propagated by the conservative division of gender roles, which turns a blind eye to women's ignorance and stresses absolute submission to the husband. It is also different from the Maoist and Western feminist calls for absolute 'masculine' gender equality, which supports equal opportunities for women and men, including the right to serve in the military. *Nüxue* women are aware of the fragility of their social status, and they thus strive for religious self-formation and self-esteem in order to change the situation from within the framework of Islam. In this context, *nüxue* can be assessed as a safety net, channel for communication, human network, and sisterhood, which provides women with the power to confront difficulties on their own.

Muslim women are at the forefront of Islamic feminism in China. Mir-Hosseini from Iran defines feminism as 'women's awareness of discrimination in family and in society' and 'actions to improve their life and change the situation' (Mir-Hosseini, 1999: 40). *Nüxue* women represent such feminism. Their Islamic faith and knowledge enable them to convey alternative values: 'non-masculine' gender equality that appreciates women's biological characteristics as given by Allah, criticism of traditional and oppressive patriarchy, and fierce competitiveness. At the same time, *nüxue* women understand the meaning of piety and modesty.

Although they provide opportunities that benefit Muslim girls, *nüxue* face various structural and societal problems. A *nüxue* is often not recognized as a valid academic institution. Moreover, in China, religious study tends to be regarded with prejudice by the majority of the population. All Chinese universities are secular, and while the knowledge of English is compulsory for taking exams, the knowledge of Arabic is not always appreciated in the academic-career based society. Some *nüxue* prohibit girls from having mobile telephones, accessing the Internet, and even watching television. In fact, some *nüxue* ban all men, including male religious leaders (*ahongs*), from their premises. Thus, educated in a purified culture and an ascetic atmosphere, many feel that female students may not have the opportunity to develop their critical thinking skills.

Moreover, a *nüxue*'s typical admonition, 'Being a responsible mother is superior to all other social responsibilities,' might be regarded as irrational by teenagers who wish to pursue a career and are still too young to seriously think of raising children. Additionally, it is likely that government inspection and censorship will become stricter because the religion-centered curriculum of a *nüxue* does not include Marxist and Deng Xiaoping indoctrination.

Having being deprived of education and social participation for a long time, Muslim women in China have currently pinned their hopes on *nüxue*. To avoid becoming entangled in the trap of male-centered Islamism, Muslim women must closely monitor the management and curricula of the *nüxue* and extend their willingness to work in the society and virtues to the public sphere.

Conclusion

In this chapter, we have examined the ideals and realities of two types of schooling in contemporary China available to Hui women. One is secular public schooling and the other is *nüxue*, or Islamic religious, schooling. We described attempts made by the *ahong*s and Hui leaders to promote Islamic and secular education for Hui girls since the early twentieth century and at the beginning of the People's Republic of China. We also pointed out the partnership between *ahong*s and local Hui leaders in building public girls' schools in cooperation with the government after the Cultural Revolution ended. During this period, the CCP attempted to send Muslim girls to public schools, where religion-related matters were excluded from the curriculum. Helped along by the increase in the Party's administrative and monetary power, the vast majority of Hui girls now attend secular public schools.

It is crucial to understand how the spread of state schooling institutions changed the Hui girls who had lived in deprived conditions. State schooling enhanced their literacy and created new opportunities for them. Some became teachers at secular schools, able to support themselves and their families financially. Accordingly, their social status rose and they earned the respect of their community. In fact, they have become annoyed by the mental conflicts between their 'Muslimness' and secular identity.

On the other hand, the *nüxue*, established by religious authorities and local Hui leaders in the 1980s and 1990s as a supplementary educational institution, enabled illiterate or semiliterate girls to acquire Islamic knowledge, following a 30-year religious hiatus in the wake of the revolution of 1949. However, since the ratio of girls enrolled in secular public schools has reached almost 100 per cent since 2000, it would appear that the role of *nüxue* as providers of supplementary education has ended. The secular political power's victory over religious authorities in China is unequivocal.

However, *nüxue* have survived thanks to the options they offer to those who wish to continue their studies after the nine-year compulsory secular education— studying the essence of Islam and the *raison d'être* of their status as Hui and learning Arabic, which is believed to be the sacred language of Allah. Thus, *nüxue* serve as a safety net for poor and marginalized Muslim women and double as vocational training schools. At the same time, *nüxue* provide girls with a novel gender view that denies the official 'masculine' gender equality, which only aims to create excessive competition without imposing any conditions. The 'new' gender view stresses the 'wise wife and good mother' role in order to train women to be good educators of the next generation and to convey Allah's messages to human beings. After understanding this new interpretation, they realize Allah's will in bestowing womanhood upon them and thus take pride in their womanhood. In sum, *nüxue* empower Muslim women by encouraging them to build self-esteem and achieve self-affirmation.

The above-mentioned gender views on 'essentialism,' 'motherhood,' and 'womanhood' were the only means by which Hui women could re-evaluate and reform their fragile status. Such essentialism can be considered the strategy of the weak. Presently, the majority of the Han population is still dubious about the Hui because of their religion and their alleged relationship with Chinese separatists and Islamic extremists.

Given these circumstances, Muslim women in China have adopted Islamic feminism based on essentialism in an attempt to eliminate discrimination towards women and resist the patriarchy system. However, this requires that they retreat from the excessive competition prevailing in the current environment. Nonetheless, even though Islamic feminism appears to be different from Western feminism, previously muted voices for emancipation and development have prevailed, and Muslim women throughout China have been increasingly enthusiastic and active in this regard for a long time now. They believe that the contemporary *nüxue* education provides them with opportunities for emancipation. Their Islamic faith and piety make them feel empowered and contribute to their self-esteem. In defining feminism, we should not forget to take into account these women's struggle for a better life and their utilization of the biological attributes of a woman in achieving that goal.

Notes

1 The total population of Ningxia is 6,102,518, of whom 2,182,260 or 35.76 per cent are Hui (Ningxia Huizu Tongjiju, Guojia Tongjiju Ningxia Diaochadui, 2008: 79). They are concentrated in the Huangtu Plateau region in southern Ningxia, including counties such as Guyuan, Xiji, Haiyuan, Tongxin, and Jingyuan.
2 Madrasas are schools where Hui and other Muslim nationalities are taught Islamic knowledge, particularly Arabic and the Qur'an, usually in addition to other secular education.
3 *Zhong-A nüxiao*, *Zhong-A nüxue*, and Islamic *nüxiao* are other names of female madrasas. *Nüxue* means 'female school.'
4 Hajj Yusuf, Liu Jinglong, who was the vice president of the Ningxia Islamic Association, edited this text.
5 Shimbo's survey in Ningxia, 15 September 2002.
6 Shimbo's survey in Ningxia, 15 March 2000.
7 Shimbo and Matsumoto's survey in Ningxia, 2 September 2007.
8 Shimbo's survey in Ningxia, 20 August 2004.

9 The ten-day workshops were organized by the Ningxia Educational Agency, the Soong Ching Ling Foundation of China, and the Soong Ching Ling Foundation of Japan. The aim was to train female teachers in the rural area of Ningxia to develop an understanding of the curricular reforms, as well as to improve their teaching and computer skills. About 120 female Hui teachers attended the workshops (Shimbo, 2007: 1–10).

10 Shimbo and Matsumoto's Survey at Yiwu, 25 December 2007.

11 Shimbo and Matsumoto's survey at Ningxia, 2 September 2005 and 4 September 2007.

12 Some *nüxue* accept Uyghur students from Xinjiang, where the establishment of Arabic classes or mosques is under strict control. Some pious parents wish to send their children to Islamic schools in Ningxia and Gansu. In this sense, a *nüxue* has become a place in which to foster Muslim consciousness beyond the boundaries of ethnicity.

13 Shimbo and Matsumoto's interview with the principals (Ma Xiulan, Ma Chunxiang and Wang Zhongyi) of three *nüxue* in Linxia, 12 September 2006, 5 and 6 September 2007.

14 His book, Jahiliyya of the Twentieth Century (*Jahiliyat al-qarn al-`ishrin*), was translated into Chinese in the middle of the 1990s. Other very important books are those of Wahhabi Sulaiman, an Albanian Wahhabi Islamist, *Muslim Women* (n.d.) which were also translated in the mid-1990s by Ma Xiulan, the principal of the Linxia Muslim Women's School that was discussed in this chapter.

15 Shimbo and Matsumoto's Interview with Ms. Ma Xinlan, the principal of the Weizhou Huizu Women's Elementary School, 2 September 2007.

6 Religious dependency in Afghanistan

Shia madrasas as a religious mode of social assertion?

Fariba Adelkhah

Spaces devoted to religious observance—mosques, madrasa and pilgrimage sites—have become major phenomena in our societies. They are diversifying and multiplying; they are also being updated, being made bigger and more in tune with modern tastes. With the help of demographic growth, the faithful are frequenting them in their millions. They sometimes provide shelter to politicians, and can in such cases be taken by storm, occupied or even destroyed, either by dissidents or believers from other faiths, or by the security forces.[1]

Accordingly, religious spaces are not homogenous, instead they constitute a likely field for social and political interests to grow and clash. This is not to deny their role in religious engagement, with its specificity or autonomous nature.

The debates, tensions and conflicts crystallized by the religious arena call into play not only its relations with the outside world, notably the West, to such an extent that some intellectuals forecast an inevitable 'clash of civilisation' (Badie, 1987; Lewis, 1988),[2] but also, and perhaps primarily, relations between Muslim believers themselves, besides the not so contemporary conflict between lay and religious intellectuals.[3] In this way, and although religion is undergoing massive changes in all its main institutions, madrasa are usually considered these days as entirely unyielding institutions, impervious to any kind of communication with the outside world, whereas they have always been in touch with modernity or the West—at least through schooling. In fact, the madrasa, as they can be observed today, are the fruit of both colonial times (and the para-colonial period in the case of Iran, Afghanistan and Iraq), to the extent that they simultaneously resisted and collaborated with colonial authorities (Sikand, 2005: 81, chap.3; Malik, 2008),[4] and of the Islamic awakening/resurgence notably in the years 1980–2000. They have always offered an opportunity for trans-ethnic or trans-national relationships by accepting students and scholars from different areas (Berkey, 2003: 208). They are therefore not the embodiment of a timeless or centuries-long tradition, but rather of the political and religious change of which they are part (Zaman, 2002). In particular, they contribute to the redefinition of what is or is not religious, the delimitation of what one could, in reference to Bourdieu, call the '*problématique légitime du religieux*,' or as it is called by Dale Eickelman (1979), 'the political economy of the meaning,' which is not an essence but is historically constructed (Bowen, 2003). For instance, the veil, the proscription of interest-paying loans and teaching, particularly of girls, only became relevant religious topics in the twentieth century, in a context characterized by social transformation in Muslim societies.

This chapter, a study of Shia madrasa in post-2001 Afghanistan based primarily on a field trip carried out in 2007, obviously does not pretend to cover the entire breadth of these changes (and exchanges). The Shia minority represented from 10 to 20 per cent of a total population of about 30 million Afghans. According to Shia sources, this percentage could range from 25 to 30 per cent![5] This study will leave aside the question of theology, its variations and its pundits, the *ulama*, to focus on the context of religious practices by which madrasa develop, without however postulating that these three pillars (theology, *ulama* and madrasa) do not influence each other. It is intended to put the internal logic prevailing in Afghan society into the context of that society's regional and international environment in order to question the claims, aspirations, mobilization, and, last of all, the social dynamics that subsume the madrasa and their emergence as a key provider of education in Afghanistan. Madrasa give rise to impassioned feelings and political confrontation. Their evolution follows the twin dynamics that Georges Balandier (1974) termed 'outside' and 'inside,' in a neo-Leachian perspective. Indeed, madrasa, as crossroads where diverse social groups engage one with another—by dint of the educational services they provide—structure networks that allow intellectuals from a given area to interact with others outside.

The need to stress this point is heightened by the fact that the denunciation or the legitimization of religious schools easily puts on the margin 'insider' debates and conflicts opposing local religious authorities and secular intellectuals. That said, today's discussions on the clash of civilizations curiously echo those that accompanied the emergence of secular schools in Muslim countries in the nineteenth and twentieth centuries, depending on the country, at a time when clerics did not have any outsider rivals in the field of knowledge and when literacy was in any event only embryonic and obviously unequally shared. While Muslim intellectuals, religious or lay, insist on the diversity and openness of Islamic education as a religious experience, echoing classic work in the social sciences, it must be borne in mind that a powerful current of ideas, with its roots in lay and public teaching, was quick to seize on the madrasas' obscurantism and has unceasingly cast itself as a rival to or opponent of clerical institutions.[6] The picture becomes even more complicated if one adds the fury of clergies, with their load of fatwas, condemnations and even executions of lay intellectuals for the sake of protecting Islam. The most telling example is the attempt made to assassinate the great historian Ahmad Kasravi by Navvab Safavi, a cleric, in Iran in the spring of 1945.[7] In the other side of the border, in Afghanistan, in recent years, one could also cite charges brought against Ayatollah Mohammad Mohagheghnasab, a Shia cleric, in 2005, for having shown disrespect for Islam by questioning whether it was right to stone adulterous women or put thieves and apostates to death, or those made in 2003 against Mir Hossein Mahdavi, a journalist, after he wrote 'Religious fascism,' an article in which he criticized clerical institutions.[8] The complex nature of these debates should put some perspective on the inability of people to hear each other on the clash of civilizations. It is true that religious-inspired violence, through fatwas, was already a notable feature of Muslim societies, even before it moved outside the Muslim world and became the issue it is today. A case in point is the confrontation with the Bahai movement, which called for equal rights and education for men and women as early as the mid-nineteenth century. It is important to observe both these types of violence, in that they are so closely entwined and prolong international conflicts and might even strengthen the conflict between religious and lay people, in particular around the question of schooling. If we limit ourselves to the nineteenth and twentieth centuries, violence in the Muslim world comes across as being the result of pressure, either from Western military occupation, or from the centralization of the states themselves and their heightening compromising with European imperialism. The vigor of the resistance to Western intrusion has often drawn a veil over the violence used against some parts of Islamic societies, in the upheaval provoked by the new context. However, violence has not been the only response in the Muslim world to this change, namely modern education. There has also been a series of social and political innovations that have limited the scope of violence and brought about not only the collaboration between religious and modern education, which was later termed, in the Islamic Republic, the 'union between hawza and university,' but also the formation of hybrid intellectual groups following the two curricula, who later become known as 'Islamic intellectuals,' 'Muslim intellectuals,' or even 'Islamists' and are nowadays the most important component of the reformist movement (Kepel and Richard, 1990; Zeghal, 2008). In Iran, the best known among these intellectuals were Jala Al-e Ahmad, Mehdi Bazargan, Ali Shariati, Abdolkarim Soroush, Reza Davari, and Mostafa Malekian, who followed the teachings of great clerics including Allameh Tabatabai, Ayatollah Taleghani and Ayatollah Jafari. Modern education was initially called the 'sciences of the day' (ulum-i ruz),[9] as opposed to the religious sciences, which were considered part of the classical sciences. Therefore, it was not necessarily thought to be antagonistic to the religious sciences, but to complement them. As of the 1950s and 60s, whatsoever against the repressive environment that came in the wake of the coup against Mohammad Mosaddegh, or because of rivalry with the modern intellectuals,[10] lay religious people and clerics took the initiative of founding schools devoted to 'sciences of the day' (ulum-i ruz). The most renowned of these private educational institutions in Iran were *Kamal* (lit. Perfection, founded by Yadollah Sahabi, an eminent leader of the National Liberation Movement, who later became an advisor to Mehdi Bazargan, the head of the provisional government in 1979), *Din-u Danish* (lit. Religion and Science, founded by Ayatollah Beheshti, who was later the founder of the Islamic Republic Party in 1979), *Alavi* (lit. related to Imam Ali, founded by allama Karbasian, Ayatollah Boroujerdi's student), *Mufid* (founded by Ayatollah Moussavi Ardebili in memory of Sheikh Mufid (c.948–1022 CE)) and *Rifah* (lit. welfare, founded under Hachemi Rafsandjani's advice), which was attended by a large number of the leaders of the 1979 Revolution, and hence the leaders of the Islamic Republic. Some of them also taught in their youth, including Ayatollah Beheshti, Hojjatoleslam

Bahonar, Ayatollah Motahhari, Aallameh Mohammad Taghi Jafari and the very conservative Ayatollah Mesbah Yazdi.[11] Symbolically, Ayatollah Khomeini took up residence in a girls' school, Rifah, for few days when he returned to Tehran on 1 February 1979, before settling at Alavi's School for security reasons.[12] This belief in a positive interplay between religious and lay education also exists in Afghanistan in that sense that Islamists have recruited in governmental schools and universities during the 1970s (Roy, 1985: 97), and, since 2001, madrasa are taking charge of building governmental schools to provide an equivalent to the necessary diploma to enter the University.

In any event, it is very important that we not get bogged down in the debate surrounding the supposed link between madrasa and violence, if only because most of the students who attend them, even Deobandis, do not resort to violence and because the Islamic school field is not synonymous with war, even holy war. Without citing the wealth of literature dealing with trends in madrasa, we would stress two findings that should help measure both the madrasas' complexity and vitality. On the one hand, they emphasize relationships—areas in which they compete and areas in which they complement each other—between religious schools and lay teaching. On the other hand, they show that religious teaching has responded in various ways to lay teaching, not only from one country to another, but also within a given country, within clerical institutions or between urban and rural areas.[13] It is not possible to stick simply with the 'reactive' view, namely the madrasas' 'response' to public schools. It would be more precise to speak of a 'configuration' (Elias, 1978) between them. Their links have changed depending on the time and the context. If religious and public schools need to be seen in the same light, this does not mean that they are identical and that they are not charting their own specific course. Similarly, the question of modernization cannot be brought down to the abstract question of its acceptance or rejection. It involves a contingent situation in which the plans in terms of which players define themselves, attitudes brought about by social change, the restructuring of hierarchies, the levels at which decisions are taken are multiple and to a great extent unforeseeable. What goes pompously by the name of modernity is no more than the result of such shake-ups.

It may be interesting here to draw a parallel with Catholic schools in western France, as brilliantly analyzed by historian Michel Lagrée, although naturally we would not imply that the reality of Shia madrasa can be compared to Catholic education in France. In order to meet the ideological and political challenge of the 1789 Revolution, the Church built a very dense school network that borrowed the teaching methods of the new public schools. Gradually, the school movement gave birth to new social institutions, ranging from the union of the Christian Youth Workers Movement (*Jeunesse Ouvrière Chrétienne*) to the Christian Agricultural Youth association (*Jeunesse Agricole Chrétienne*), the Seamen's Education Movement, a very strong Catholic press and an active business movement. In the end these institutions pushed rural areas that were generally considered conservative to the left of the political spectrum (Lagrée, 1992). This is not to suggest that the madrasa are helping convert Afghanistan to social democracy.

But the example of Brittany reminds us that God has indeed moved in mysterious ways throughout history and that religious movements are at the same time social movements, and must be studied as such. The logic of the connections between religions and politics is often paradoxical. For instance, Ernst Troeltsch, commenting on Max Weber, said that Protestantism encouraged capitalism 'in spite of itself and without knowing it' (Troeltsch, 1912).

In Afghanistan, Islamic teaching has also been combined with social, economic and cultural development, particularly with the development of modern schools in the twentieth century as well as with other transformations that are no less important: war, migration and the economic changes that accompany them, such as remittances, growth in the informal markets for goods and financial services, and even the increase in opium farming and the laundering of revenues derived from it. At the same time, it should be noted that the timeline favored by the Afghans themselves does not necessarily coincide with that used in the social sciences: for instance, the first rupture, for the madrasa, probably came as early as 1973, with Dawoud's coup against the reigning monarch,[14] five years before the communist coup against the regime in 1978, and the Soviet invasion which apparently did not interfere with religious observance by Shias. The period of the Jihad 'commanders,' after the Russian withdrawal, appears to have left more lasting scars than the Taliban regime, which it is generally agreed re-established a form of civil calm that was good for trade.

Even more fundamentally, madrasa have provided a melting pot. Granted, Shia madrasa foster a critical view of the 'West,' a term that in Afghanistan's historical context encompasses Russia via communism and the Soviet occupation, of sectarian pluralism in that Shiism is a minority in the country, of tradition or social conservatism; at the same time, they are tributary, through emigration, to the temporality of Dubai and its prosperity. Simultaneously, madrasa also contribute to the emergence or the re-establishment of a feeling of national belonging independent of ethnic or tribal descent. The religious reference comes across as a factor of de-ethnicization and de-tribalization. At the same time, religious practices have a complex relationship with ethnicity, tribalism and localism: for instance, they can foster the desire for autonomy and broaden the scope for political negotiation of the Shia Hazaras with respect to the Afghan state.[15] In this context, the religious convictions that the madrasa carry and dispense, and the ethical discussions that they foster, bring about a social confidence that helps to legitimize change and innovation. However, and as we expand on below, this social confidence does not come automatically. It should be built or built again as it is the outcome of complex interactions between the historical background of religious ideas/thoughts, the intermediaries or ulama and Muslim intellectuals, and the material means that support their influence. For instance the relations that Shia Afghan madrasa maintain with their Iranian counterparts, for historical as well as geographical reasons, play a crucial role and help place them, and legitimize them, in the national context. But schools are nothing these days without rational management and important financial support, which should be provided from different social groups. Therefore Afghan Shiism, which was entirely dependent on Iran's religious historical experience, is today as much dependent on former jihadists, who now make up the majority of religious school managers, and on migrants because of the important financial resources they remit. At different times these three features, as elaborated below, may be the conditions for success of madrasa that in turn provide in this case the political autonomy of Shia, notably Hazara, not only inside Afghan society but also toward his Iranian brothers. In that sense the Afghan historical dependence on Iran constitutes a strong political resource to make up for the Hazaras' inequality with the Afghan political system, dominated by the Sunnis, or, more exactly, the Pashtuns. Reciprocally, the Hazaras' inclusion in the Afghan political landscape allows them to distance themselves from Iran and the vilayat-i faqih's model. However, while keeping at bay the vilayat-i faqih concept, or partly because of that, Afghans like Imam Khomeini, endorse the pre-eminence of politics on religion, a stance that is neither proper to Iran, nor Islamic movements in the Arab world, as Olivier Roy underlined (1995: 101–105; 2002: 36).[16] This is the context that ensures the viability of the affirmation of Shiism in contemporary Afghanistan.

The madrasa are pivotal to this assertion. They respond to a need for religious expression. They fulfill an educative function that public schools are unable to fulfill. They embody a model of cultural, social and economic modernization that has notched up at least a few successes in neighboring Iran, where numbers of Shia Afghans have spent time over recent decades. They open the doors to global knowledge, starting with English and computers. They give women the opportunity to make something of themselves.

Pioneer Shia!

It is impossible to dissociate the place occupied by Shiism and Shia religious teaching in contemporary Afghanistan from Afghanis' representation of history. It gives rise to often-passionate accounts in which Shia Afghans willingly paint themselves as the victims. It is important to bear in mind the anachronistic nature of this view, if only because the distinction between Shia and Sunni Islam in its current configuration cannot be analyzed without reference to the formation of the nation-state, the crystallization of national consciences, and the institutionalization of the religious arena, notably the madrasa. Even today, overlaps are a lot more frequent than one may think, in ritual practice as well as in dogma. For instance, it is not uncommon to see sanctuaries frequented by the faithful of different denominations, such as those of Imam Reza in Mashhad, in Iran's Khorasan Province, or Sayda Zaynab in Syria. Despite the strongly held belief in Iran that Jamal al-Din al-Afghani was Shia, no one really knows whether he was Shia or Sunni;[17] similarly, the Saudis cannot really deny that Muhammad Ibn Abd ul-Wahhab, the founder of Wahhabism, was a regular attendee of Shia religious centers such as those in Najaf and Ispahan (Shoushtari, 1363/1984: 477). Even today, Afghan ulamas, in their desire to promote if not 'union' (*vahdat*), but at least 'rapprochement' (*taqrib*) and 'brotherhood' (*ukhuvvat*) between Muslim denominations, via the Council of Brotherhood,[18] focus paradoxically on looking for what differentiates them, following the traditional metaphor of the tree and its branches: the most important thing is the trunk, it being understood that each branch can be different, some longer or thicker, some with more or fewer flowers. It makes sense that an Ayatollah, Mohammad Assef Mohseni, should cite only the practice of temporary marriages as a factor that set the Shias apart from the Sunnis even though he is naturally aware of other differentiating factors that are not questions of law, but have to do with the convictions of the faithful as to the Prophet's descendants or their own experience. In truth, this in no way reduces the depth of the miscomprehension, animosity, or even conflict between people, nor the Shia claim (echoed by the Sunnis) to be the 'true defenders of tradition' (*sunnat*), to quote the title of a book written by a Paris-based Tunisian author, Tidjani Tunissi (1383/2004), published in Qom and widely circulated in Afghanistan. But this brings us into the realm of what Freud termed the 'narcissism of minor differences,' historically constructed and, today, deconstructed by a reformist movement committed to contextualizing the divine word as it was taught by a man, the Prophet. Included in this movement in Iran are Abdolkarim Soroush, a secular intellectual, as well as Mojtahed Shabestari and Mohsen Kadivar, two clerics. Mohammad Mohagheghnasab is the main representative of this current in Afghanistan. In this respect one should not take too literally the discussion on Shiism: those who, in Afghanistan, cite distinctive or identifying factors in support of this claim do so less for reasons of religious hermeneutics or new well-argued speeches than because they are just repeating the same arguments as in the past.

Moreover, the history of Shiism in Afghanistan cannot be separated from a broader history of Islam, from the succession of kingdoms and empires in the region—especially the Moghol Emire, the Safavid domination over Herat and Kandahar into the eighteenth century and the rivalry between that dynasty and the Ottoman Empire—and from the imperial expansion of England and Russia, and then of the Soviet Union. We obviously cannot encompass this complex history in this chapter, but we will identify the stories to which it gave birth among Shia, and notably among the Hazara.

The most important point to note is the confusion that now exists between Shiism and the Hazara people, or the parallel that is drawn between them, and the fact that this association confirms the Hazaras' feeling that they have been marginalized and victimized in Afghan society. So while the Hazara people may all be Shia,[19] it cannot be said that all Afghan Shia are Hazara nor that they have been persecuted. Also, the Qizilbash are Shia people according to common belief. There are also Pashtun Shia, just as there are Shia among the Sadat and Bayat peoples, and even among the Tajik (the Ismaili are also considered to be Shia, but stigmatized by the Twelvers, and surprisingly they are not considered Muslim by the Sunni). It should be remembered that the guards of the royal palace were Qizilbash. The basis for this parallel between Shiism and 'Hazarism' is the political, ethnic and agrarian conflict that prompted King Abdulrahman (1891–93) to chase the Hazara off their land in order to give it to the Pashtun tribes, bringing their rebellion to an end in a bloodbath and forcing them into exile or to emigrate due to their so-called Iranian origins, during the formation and centralization of the monarchy under the auspices of the British Raj (Kakar, 1979). This was followed by a dolorist narrative surrounding the 'genocide' of the Shia and the persecution of the Hazara, in the context or rivalry between the Afghani monarchy, supported by Britain, and the Qajar, gradually pushed out of Afghanistan, and then the context of contemporary ethno-nationalism which came to the fore between the two World Wars in Afghanistan, as in Iran and Turkey.[20]

The sources vary as to the date at which the Hazara people converted to Islam. Three historically distinct moments are generally cited. Some say that Shia Afghans converted when Islam first penetrated the region, through Herat, by bowing before Ali as Caliph (35–40 AH).[21] Others date their conversion to the thirteenth century, under the Mongol empire of the Ilkhanate and the persecution of the Sadat, the Prophet's descendants, in the Khorasan Province and their exile to Afghanistan, in the region of Ghowr, the contemporary Hazarajat. The predominant view is that the conversion to Shiism coincided, as it did for Iran, with the foundation of the Safavid Empire, in the sixteenth century, which expanded its sovereignty to Kandahar.[22] Sayed Askar Mousavi (1985) suggests that these three moments should be seen together and that they are not mutually exclusive. He does, however, stress that Afghanistan was the land of asylum of Shia persecuted in Iran, particularly at the outset of the Abbasid Caliphate, in the eighth century. In his view, this means that Shiism in Afghanistan can be traced back to a period before the Ilkhanate and the Safavid and that the refuge of the Sadat in Afghanistan suggests the presence of other faithful. Whatever the truth may be, all these authors agree that the Hazara and the Shia should be seen in the same light and that the marginalization of the Hazara people in Afghanistan's political history should be interpreted as the expression of the religious domination of the Pashtun tribes, Sunni by a large majority. The Dawoud government and the revolutionary period prior to the Soviet intervention in 1979 were too brief to usher in any real or lasting change in the position of the Hazara and/or the Shia. In contrast, the anti-Soviet Jihad drew the Shia—mainly the Hazara—into the resistance and into the national political landscape.

According to various testimonies, it was not until the 1940s, when Seyed Mir Ali Ahmad Hojjat (1268–1353/1889–1974) was elevated to the rank of Ayatollah[23] and built a *hoseynieh* in Chindawul, in the outskirts, at that time, of Kabul, and rehabilitated an old mosque, Ghazi Chehab, that the Shia call to prayer was made for the first time and that the denomination came out of its *taqiya* (dissimulation) and Shia practices began to express themselves openly.[24] Since this time, the celebration of Nawruz, in Ziyarat-i Sakhi, a sanctuary dedicated to the Imam Ali located in Ali Abad, in the Kabul suburbs, gives Shia their main cause to pray in public, their hands open, prostrating with their foreheads touching a small earth stone from Karbala (Safdari, 1384/2006 :74–75; Muassisih-i amuzishi-i imam Khomeini, 1980/2001: 63–66). Even today, Shia remember a time when they were obliged to camouflage their funerals and renounce public mourning processions, during which they would have had to recite the call to prayer in accordance with the customs of their denomination.[25] Expressions such as 'Hazara

sitizi' (Hazara phobia) and 'Shia kushi' (genocide of the Shia) spring to the
or the pens of Afghans when they want to express the sentiment of frustration and
marginalization felt by the Shia. Since the overthrow of the Taliban regime, the
Shias have seen an improvement in their political and legal situation. Contrary
to the 1964 Constitution, the 2003 Constitution gives Shia the right to be elected
president and, since 2009, will allow the use of Jafari fiqh for questions relative
to personal law (ahwal-I shakhsiyya),[26] as long as all parties are Shia—but not for
business, commercial or penal law.

A revolution in education (1979–2007)

It is against this historical backdrop and in the light of this dual marginalization,
ethnic and denominational, that the growth of Shia religious schools in Afghanistan
should be seen. In the last thirty years, this growth has been marked by the
conjunction of three events, all different in nature but in fact closely bound together:
the Jihad against Soviet occupation and the subsequent civil war; emigration to
Iran, Pakistan, the Gulf States or the West; and the Islamic Revolution in Iran
in 1979. In 2001, a fourth event added itself to this list: the US intervention,
which in theory at least put an end to ethnic or denominational discrimination.
Sticking to the period prior to this, religious authorities of all denominations were
active against the Soviet Union and participated in the resistance by encouraging
the faithful answer the call to fight. They also obtained financial and logistic
support from other Muslim countries, including Pakistan, Saudi Arabia and Iran,
and from various autonomous Muslim political bodies in these countries as well
as in Algeria, Egypt and Palestine. A new social category, that of Jihad fighter,
gradually emerged. This category partially transcended ethnic or denominational
consciences and represented in a sense a generational phenomenon, even though
the Jihad brought together fighters of different ages and prompted criticism or
even hostility among the younger generation, which accuse the Jihad fighters of
having blood on their hands and of having enriched themselves at the expense of
the Afghan population with the war and foreign aid. (However the Modjahedins
are still the majority of the new Parliament elected in September 2010).

Forced emigration left Afghan refugees with three options: camps in Pakistan;
the most accessible economic opportunity, specifically in Iran or the Gulf States;
or the traditional path out of the country, namely religious instruction in Mashhad
or Qom. Lastly, the fact that the resistance and this wave of emigration coincided
with the founding of the Islamic Republic and the development of religious
schools in Iran made Persian-speaking and Shia Afghanis the prime beneficiaries
or the natural users—at least until 2003, when Teheran implemented a more or
less coercive policy of sending Afghani refugees or immigrants home (Adelkhah
and Olszweska, 2007)—of the culture and institutions for promoting faith that
sprang up there. These three moments allowed Afghan Shiism to return to its
historical roots, and also to foster its singularity in a paradoxical manner, marking
its contemporary destiny: dependence on Iran but also a trend towards autonomy
in relation to Iran; reinforcement of localism and specificity under the guise of

religious claims; and the defense of Afghan nationalism. The following pages try to shed light on the ambivalent trend of the religious school in Afghanistan. While they much imitate them in many regards concerning Islamic education and curriculum, Afghans also claim that they are by essence different from Iranian and do not for instance have to follow the concept of vilayat-faqih. This description indeed confirms the point made by Sabrina Mervin (2008) when she stressed that Iran is still a very effective test case for the Shiite world, though they do not obey and follow the same rules and regulations.

Shiite religious education in Afghanistan is dispensed in a variety of institutions: mosques, hoseynieh, madrasa, maktab, hawza, zeynabieh, markaz, universities, and in one case, in a private house which is the property of the founders, a couple (the establishment is associated primarily with Ms Shahin's name). There are 17 main institutions in Kabul, half of which were founded after the fall of the Taliban[27] (see Figure 6.1). These institutions were created by religious authorities, both clerical and lay. Political authorities, and particularly, Senator Ghorbanali Erfani, a member of parliament, have recently taken the initiative of establishing religious institutions in Dashti Barchi, a poor area in order to aid in their development, notably the west of Kabul which shelters predominantly Shia neighborhoods. Afghan emigrants (principally those living in Iran, Pakistan and Australia) are also keen to build up religious centers, which are managed remotely, both through intermediaries and thanks to modern telecommunications and/or regular trips.

For instance, Mohammad Javad Rajabzadeh and Ms Hemmati set up the Quran wa Itrat, Scientific and Cultural Institute, initially in Mashhad, in 1990, originally reserved exclusively for Hazara. They took it to Herat in 1992 after the victory of the Mudjahidin but in the face of the difficulties they encountered, they quickly put the Herat branch on ice before reactivating it in 2004 after the Taliban regime was overturned. The Institute has four departments: a religious school for men, Madrasa Ilmiyya-i Baqyyatalla; a religious school for women, Hawza-i Ilmiyya-i Itratiyyih; the Koran school; and the local school, which is not for profit, even though it is compulsory to pay school fees. Two thousand people are enrolled at the Institute. Similarly, hojjatoleslam Mohammad Hossein Jafari, who spends part of the year in Mashhad, opened the Maktab Nargues in Kabul, which has two branches, one in Mazar-i Sharif (Maktab-i al-Zahra) and another in Kondouz (Maktab-i Hazrat-i Khadijah)[28]. After immigrating to Iran, where he founded his first school, Madrasa Ghaed, in the Silo quarter in Mashhad, before being opened to all Afghans, Ayatollah Sajedi subsequently went to live in New Jersey, in the United States, at the request of the local Afghani community, after first leaving the management of his school in Mashhad to his brother. Once firmly ensconced in the United States, he opened a Zeynabieh in Karta-i Char, in the Shia area of Kabul. As for Chindawul's Hoseynieh, it was re-established by the nephew of Ayatollah Hojjat, who lives in Australia. More broadly speaking, the role of the World Centre for Islamic Sciences in Qom deserves to be emphasized. Most of the founders or managers of these institutions passed through this Centre. The list includes Mr Rajabzadeh, Ms Hemmati, Mr Jafari and Mr Rezazadeh, the manager of the Koran teaching schools at the Quran wa Itrat Institute.

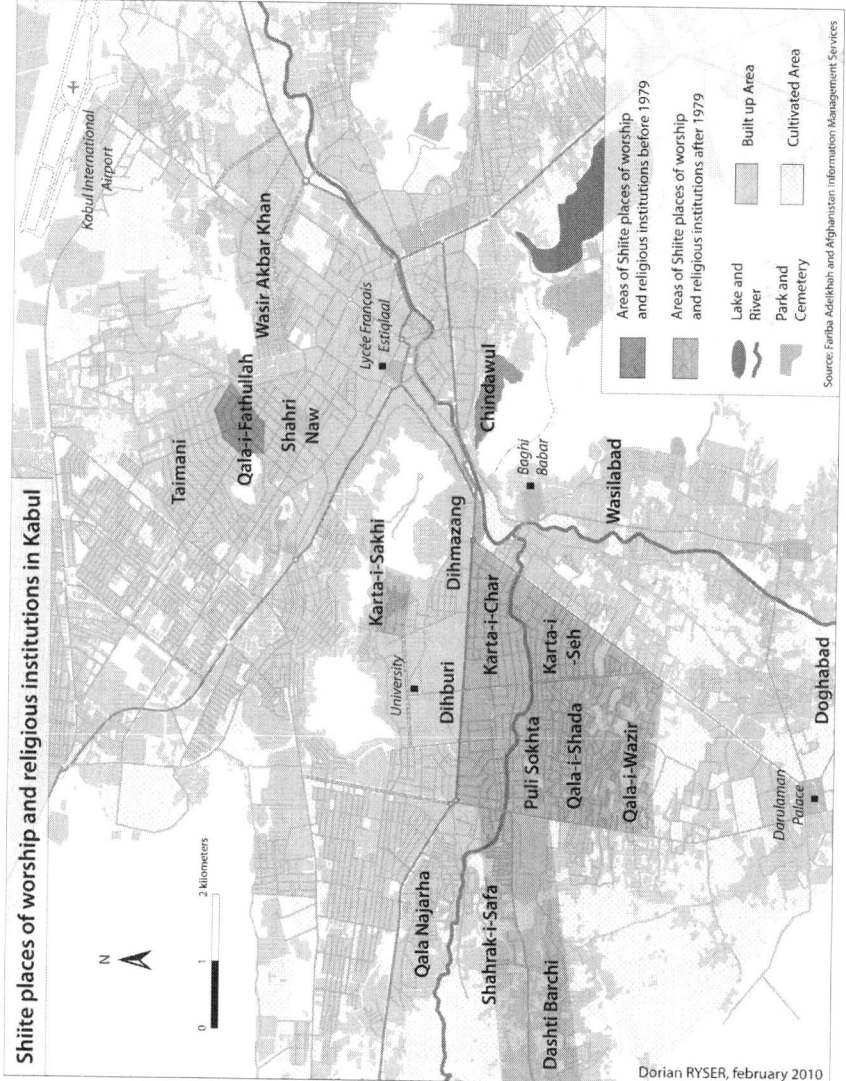

Figure 6.1 Shia places of worship and religious institutions in Kabul

Funding of Shiite religious education is provided by resources collected during the Jihad against the Soviets, money raised by émigrés and those affected by the Diaspora, the Islamic Republic of Iran, business donations, religious taxes collected by Ayatollahs Kaboli, Mohseni and Salehi, not to mention the Supreme Leader, Ayatollah Ali Khamenei, whose main Afghani interlocutor appears to be the old Ayatollah Moghaddasi, who has never set foot outside his country, and finally financial gifts from the faithful. The salient point here is the crucial importance of remittances sent by émigrés and refugees, or, more broadly, the Diaspora, in financing the madrasa. This is not exclusive to Afghanistan, but the phenomenon is possibly a lot greater there than in other countries. As it happens, virtually all the Shia schools I have seen are run by people who have lived, or are still living, abroad. It is impossible to dissociate the madrasas' political economy from import–export activities, the *hawala* system and, in all likelihood, the laundering of various revenues accumulated in the informal economy. Two questions remain on this topic. Why are the madrasa more suited to laundering than other activities, commercial or industrial for instance? And what are the social remittances that accompany financial remittances, in accordance with logics that have been described well in other migratory contexts (Levitt, 2001)? Although not able to provide a full answer to these two questions, we would like to elaborate on the moral economy of those madrasas that succeed to respond to social demands.

Madrasa, a response to social demand

Religious education comprises two degree courses: the first, generalist and preliminary, is called Darulquran (the home of the Koran). Its purpose is focused on guidance (*irshad*) or on doctrinal propaganda (*tabligh*) but, in reality, because of the dearth of public schools and access to instruction, it provides education. The second is theological (*hawza* or *madrasa*) and it addresses educated believers who are, increasingly, subjected to bureaucratic rules like the possession of a high-school diploma, passing entrance exams and/or having to sit exams regularly throughout the school year.

It is impossible to assess the exact number of students studying in Shia religious schools due to the lack of statistics. First, most schools do not keep accurate records of those registered, even in well-known schools; second, teaching methods are traditional, which means there are neither exams nor regular roll-calling in some of these schools. Finally, women are not yet included in the statistics. Nevertheless, thanks to the recent bureaucratization, and notably to the foundation of Kabul's religious school on 2002 (*Hawza-i Ilmiyya-i Kabul*), following the Iranian model (*Hawza-i Ilmiyya-i Qom*), we know that there were 978 males registered as religious students (*talabih*) in October 2007—or rather, we know that 978 male students were entitled to receive a monthly grant. They were studying mainly at Hawza-i Risalat, Madrasa-i Madinatulilm, Madrasa-i Jamiatulislam, Madrasa-i Muhammadyyih, Hoseynieh Qala Fathullah. Another 1,000 or so students are studying in similar courses in other cities like Herat, Mazar Sharif, Daikondi, Ghazni and Kandahar.[29] In contrast, the number of female students studying in religious schools but not provided with a monthly grant due to the fact that they do not pass the obligatory exams to evaluate their abilities remains unknown, although we do know that 300 of them study at the khadijatalkubra school, the female branch of Khatamulnabyyin.

Students generally come from poor areas and/or rural families; for this reason, many of them board at the school where they are studying. However, and since 2001, a few of them, notably those who used to be emigrants to Iran, come from urban backgrounds, and they belong to the merchant class. The female students are unusual, in that many of them come from emigrant backgrounds (living notably in either Iran or Pakistan) and that the great majority, due to the lack of boarding facilities, hail from urban areas—which in this case study means Kabul. The important point is that an increasing number of students now come from émigré communities. For instance, it appears that most of the students of the Khadijatalkubra School, the female branch of Khatamulnabyyin, as well as numerous boys attending various establishments, who had to leave Iran under pressure of the government, are seeking to finish their studies and to obtain a diploma that would be recognized there, allowing them to return legally as students. Migrants increasingly represent a social category in themselves, which transcends the traditional split between rural and urban categories, or between ethnic and denominational differences. The madrasa, which, as we have seen, they help finance, are an Islamic way in which to gain social advancement.

Although religious motivations are usually cited to explain a student's decision to study at a religious school, other strategies cannot be ruled out, including social or professional advancement through subsidized or free education and grants. The fact is that religious education is increasingly being used to gain qualifications and to allow access to university education.

As we will see, the links between religious instruction and lay school are clearer in Afghanistan than in Iran, where there is a large measure of differentiation between the two types of teaching, even though the Hawza has adopted a university-style organization and can demand that its diplomas be seen as the equivalent of a university degree. It is revealing that a single parliamentary commission is responsible for religious, cultural, educational and university affairs in Afghanistan, under the chairmanship of Hazara Jihad fighter Mohammad Mohaghegh.

Unfortunately, my fieldwork did not help me to discover more about the non-religious motivations of the students; it was difficult to get beyond the stereotypes and clichés of their religious ones. Nevertheless, it seems that students, both men and women, who have a mastery of the Koran are very much in demand during the religious months of the Islamic calendar, Muharram and Ramadan. They run prayer meetings and vigils, not only in their own neighborhoods, but also in other neighborhoods and even other cities. As such, and as in other Muslim countries, religious education is feeding other strategies like social ascension and fame. And in the context of the development of public schools in Afghanistan, religious schools have become one of the primary sources of teaching staff. Moreover, because of the rivalry and the on-going dialogue existent between different religious denominations in contemporary Afghanistan, the increasing prominence of women on the religion scene appears to be another tool for the Shiite community to assert its progressive outlook in regard to that of the Sunni. The presence of girls in the madrasa must be seen in the context of migration: their local implantation and the flexibility of their administration allow religious schools to facilitate the insertion of young girls who attended school abroad when they return to Afghanistan, the recognition of courses or diplomas giving them entry into public schools; in addition, the Iranian model under which girls attend school becomes an important reference for families that have spent time in the Islamic Republic and for their extended families in Afghanistan.

Two points need to be underlined. First, most of the founders of religious establishments were Jihad fighters and spent some time in Iran or in Pakistan throughout the war that started in 1979. Second, the Shia religious schooling institutions have witnessed the growing ascendancy of a new category of relatively young managers, who share the latter's background. Taking into account my fieldwork, the kin or clientelist ties between the young managers and the founders, who usually are older and have fewer bureaucratic skills, reduce the possibility of conflicts between them. Moreover, both categories are made up of people who are generally used to traveling outside the country, especially in Iran, Pakistan and Germany.

Shia religious teaching seems to meet a genuine social demand rather than satisfying a taste for theological speculation or mysticism, although a few people do require this aspect to be taught. There is more synergy between the Shia religious institutions and the public or secular schooling institutions than competition. This is especially true for the latest created institutions, the Shia religious schools provide the students with courses that deal with matters beyond religion and intend to contribute to the overall education of the society. Hawza-i Ilmyya-i Khatamulnabyyin would like to be seen as a genuine university and agreements are currently being prepared allowing the students of Maktab-i Nargues to have their degrees recognized, to apply to the Afghan Ministry of Education, and in Iran to the World Centre of Religious Sciences, which has full university status. In the same way, 500 religious students in Hawza-i Kabul obtained a school diploma by being granted an equivalent, thus to be able to pass an exam to enter the University. Therefore more than 150 students follow the two courses, one at the University and the other at Hawza since 2006–2007.

In the same way and in a context characterized by an official acknowledgement of Shiism after the American military intervention and the establishment of the Karzai administration, the Shia educational sector entertains warm relations with the current political authorities: Ayatollah Salehi, founder of the Risalat School, was appointed special presidential adviser for Islamic affairs in 2007; Ayatollah Sheikh Assef Mohseni, founder of the Khatamulnabyyin, was honored by the Academy of Sciences in 2006; Ayatollah Mohaghegh Kaboli, founder of Jamiatulislam, obtained the state's financial commitment to build a new school in 2006.

We must now turn back to the madrasas' political and moral economy as centers of social change. It may be worthwhile to compare Afghani madrasa with the interest-free loan funds (qarzul hasanih) that developed in Iran even before the 1979 Revolution and which have prospered since then. These institutions obviously had a religious and charitable dimension, but also contributed to the penetration of banking services in Iranian society, at a time when a large part of the population did not have access to the modern banking system. From this point of view, they were relatively similar to savings and loan institutions or the *monte di pietà*. Given the amounts they collected and the loans they made, they helped society become less dependent on the state and restore the exchange value of money. Similarly, the Afghani madrasa by definition dispense religious teaching and remain faithful to the Timurid tradition of charity that is attached to them according to Said Amir Arjomand (1999): under the waqf in Islamic law, they previously had various other charitable works attached to them, such as orphanages, hospitals or caravanserais; today, they continue to welcome people, lodging and supporting students from rural families, housing orphanages and carrying out the bathing and enshrouding of the dead. But the madrasa also increasingly have a money-earning dimension. While money cannot be charged for teaching the Koran,[30] this is not the case for English or computer skills, and these revenue sources are all the more appreciable that it is hard to determine the true value of this type of service. The madrasa also rent out rooms for family meetings for various important occasions (funerals, return from pilgrimage— but not yet for weddings) or for major religious festivals (Ashura, Ramadan). This was taken to its extreme by the Khatamulnabyyin in Kabul, which in 2008 opened an international conference centre with booths for interpreters, sound and projection systems that not even the government had, and which it will now be able to use. In short, the madrasa are located at the junction of the religious field, welfare and accumulation, or from another perspective the sacred, social economy (not for profit) and entrepreneurial activities. In this way, they stem, through their independence relative to the government, from civil society as well as from what goes by the term 'development,' without this prejudicing their orientation or the effectiveness of what they provide. The madrasa are today an undeniable force in favor of schooling, their constellation is one of the articulations between migrants and their homeland, and they have become a factor for urban development, in the western part of Kabul, for instance, where places like Pul-i Sokhta, Karta-i Seh and Dasht-i Barchi have benefited from investments in Shia religious schools and the capacity of the Risalat school to have the road linking two predominantly Hazara districts, namely Qala-i Shada and Qala-i Wazir, sealed.

Afghan Shiism in position of religious dependence

The Afghan current religious arena and especially its Shia component, has been reframed through three different moments: first, the jihad against the Soviet Union that provided an opportunity to get huge funding and pushed the commanders to behave as religious authorities wanted (some commanders being first religious authorities); second, the migration of five to six million Afghans, who subsequently sent home remittances and also promoted back home new social behavior and know-how (thanks to these aspects, many socio-ethnic categories—including Shia—were able to improve their daily life); third, the emergence due to the American intervention and the new political process, of new actors and new political references that have legitimized the acceptance of religious and ethnic pluralism and created new opportunities for female emancipation.

From this viewpoint, Afghan Shiism is in a very peculiar situation. As we have seen, having been marginalized and segregated since the early nineteenth century, it was unable to construct its own institutions and became dependent on Najaf and later Qom, in terms of both human resources and financing. The main sources of imitation (*marja-i taqlid*) for its believers were Hakim, Khoi and today Shirazi and Sistani. Imam Khomeini also had his supporters. From 1994 onwards, the Supreme Leader, Ali Khamenei, has offered himself as the *marja-i taqlid* for non-Iranian Shia, including those living in Afghanistan (Adelkhah, 1995). Nowadays, Ayatollah Assef Mohseni intends to make Kabul inherit the Najaf and Qom periods. However, one must acknowledge the fact that this attempt at radical reform or renewal seems to rely heavily on the Iranian model of religious teaching, which is increasingly focused on its specialized sections and increasingly bureaucratized in order to improve its efficiency and to allow it to rise to the demands of the modern world, if Islamic. Moreover, while 978 theology students are registered in Kabul, more than 8,000 Afghans follow the same syllabus in Iran, according to official figures provided by Ayatollah Kaboli's office in Qom, in 2007; yet the latter figure is very likely underestimated, and one should add the students who have no grants—in particular women—and those who have no legal clearance to stay in Iran. The only two clerics who can be considered as *marja-i taqlid*, Ayatollah Fayyaz and Mohaghegh Kaboli, prefer to stay in Najaf for the former and Qom for the latter. There, they could enjoy a larger audience than in Kabul where students have in their view not yet reached a high enough level. Incidentally, most of the Afghans responsible for Shia religious institutions stay alternatively in the two countries and have settled their family in Iran, in Qom, Shiraz, Mashhad, Karadj or Teheran, which is a way to remind us that academic nomadism is not a secular privilege (Roy, 2002: 60). They just follow the example provided by other sections of the Afghan Shia political and economic elites. In any event, most of the latter have been trained in the Iranian educational system, either public or religious. The figure of 8,000 students should be seen in this context. Iran is not only one of the main contributors to Afghan Shia education, but also provides it with most of its teaching materials; books, cassettes, CDs, syllabus, teachers and lecturers. Afghanistan's dependency on Iran still functions beyond the Afghan borders and in the Diaspora. The places of worship and religious centers visited by Afghan expatriates in Europe, in Hamburg or Frankfurt, or in the USA, in New Jersey, are led by Afghans trained in Iran. In the Iranian Republic itself, Afghan students or lecturers have not been able to organize themselves in an autonomous way, as Arabs did: there is only one Afghan religious school in Mashhad, the Ghaem School, supervised by Ayatollah Jayyed Sajedi, and another for girls, the Itrat va

Quran Centre, supervised by Hojjatoleslam Rajabzadeh, which moved to Herat in 2004 but still has a branch in Mashhad.

In this historical context, particular importance should be given to the Abbasgholi school in Mashhad and the World Centre for Islamic Sciences in Qom, whose influence extends beyond the sole sphere of religion. We have seen how the latter is a major source for the training and recruiting of founders or managers of madrasa. In addition to that, numerous members of the Afghan elite attended them: these include Justice Minister Sarvar Danesh; two of the four parliamentarians from Bamian; two of the 17 parliamentarians from Herat; one parliamentarian from Kabul, Qazni, Sar-i Pul; governors and mayors, including that of Bulkhab; and, of course, academics.

Founded at the end of the seventeenth century by Abbasgholi khan Biglarbeygi in Mashhad and located at the start of Navvab Safavi Street (formerly known as Pain khyaban) in the Tullab quarter, which is also home to the famed Afghan Bazar, the Abbasghol school has been attended, at least since the end of the nineteenth century—we do not have sources for the period before this—by Afghan Shia students, providing a launching pad towards Najaf or, especially since 1922, Qom (Pasandideh, 1385/2006). It was a vital channel in the training of the Afghan clergy as well as the intellectual elite that were behind the country's political and religious movements, as well as its literary circles. It was the alma mater of Allameh Seyed Esmail Balkhi, born in Bulkhab, in Jozjan (1295–1347/1916–1968), the founding father of the modern Islamic movement to which we owe the revitalization of the alliance between Shias and Sunnis; Allameh Modarres Afghani (1284–1365/1905–1986), born in Kharbid, in Jaghouri, a highly respected professor of Arabic literature, who taught at Najaf and Qom; Ayatollah Sheikh Mohammad Eshagh Fayyaz (1314– /1935–), born in Sobeh, in Ghazni, one of the two greatest surviving students of Ayatollah Khoi, who lives in Najaf; Ayatollah seyed Sarvar Vaez Behsoudi (1295–1358/1916–1979), born in Behsoud, the director of Kabul's oldest religious school; Mohammadiyih Abdul Ali Mazari (1326–1373/1947–1995), originally from Balkh, founder of the Nasr Organization and leader of the vahdat (unity) party, founded in 1368/1989. It was also the focus of the main Shia political organizations in the Afghani Jihad movement, including Nasr Organization, Pasdaran-i Jihad, Harakat-i Islami (of Ayatollah Assef Mohseni), the unity party, as well as other cultural or religious institutions, including the Bureau of Afghan Literature, whose members, except Kazem Kazemi, were all Talabih, or the Durr-i Dari Institute, which publishes the journal *Khatt-i Sivvum* (literally The Third Line) (Olszewska, 2007).[31]

Last of all, one must not forget the role played by the city of Qom in the formation of intellectual Afghan circles,[32] politicians,[33] or even religious reform movements,[34] without forgetting the contribution made by Afghan students to the Iranian revolution, often serving as couriers between Najaf and Qom in the 1970s, as they were not under the same amount of surveillance by SAVAK (National Intelligendce and Security Organization).

Afghanistan's Shia religious dependency on Iran seems irreversible, especially since Afghan students and lecturers settled in Iran are unlikely to go back to their homeland, as job opportunities there are too few. Inexorably, the Iranian model asserts itself in Afghanistan through the religious schooling institutions and other forms of bureaucratization of the religious arena such as associations, Islamic NGOs, publications, boards of religious institutions. However, the success of the Iranian model is encountering resistance, bypasses or reinvention by Afghan religious actors. On the one hand, the Iranian model is prompting reactions of refusal and annoyance because of nationalistic feelings. On the other, it is creating social dynamics and social movements that cannot be reduced to the Iranian influence and has allowed the inclusion of the Afghan Shias in the state, an unprecedented phenomenon.

Religious differentiation as a national frontier

Shia Afghans—as others—prefer not to use Persian expressions coming from Iran, sometimes going so far as to substitute terms taken from English: driver, engineer etc.! They criticize people who return after spending time in Iran for their Iranian accent or the way in which they dress. The simple fact of having an Iranian accent can keep people off Tamaddon, a Shia television network controlled and funded by Ayatollah Mohseni, who is keen to mark his autonomy with respect to Qom and Tehran, despite the fact that he continues to live there part of the time. And as we have seen earlier, note 28, Mohammed Hossein Jafari was not able to legally register his religious school under the name of Maktab Najris (because too close to the Iranian model) and had to modify its name in Maktab Nargues to make its activity fully legal. Shia Afghans hide their relations with Iran or the aid they receive from there. They express their rancor at having been marginalized, or even looked down upon, during their stays there. 'The Iranians do not want us as teachers, only as students. It is not the same for Arabs, who are given classes to teach', said Afghan students in Qom.[35]

But there is more to the problem than just frustration. The head of the Khadijatalkubra religious school, the female section of Khatamulnabyyin, expressed the discomfort felt by Shia Afghanis in their relations with Iranians:

> Foreign students following the teaching of the Hawza are fed up with reading about or sitting exams on questions like *The origins of the Islamic Revolution* or *The testament of Imam Khomeini*. We want to learn and gain a better understanding of Islam, but all we get in Iran is *tabligh* (propaganda). What we need most of all is our independence. The Iranians go on and on about the *hijab*, but they don't respect it. We don't want to wear the chador, and especially not the Iranian one, we prefer our *hijab*. The *maqnaih*, as a souvenir, OK, but not as national dress. Young Afghan women need to cast it off. What Afghanistan needs is unity, in two areas: between Sunnis and Shias; between universities and religious schools. We don't want to export the Iranian Islamic Revolution. Imam Khomeini was the Guide of the Iranian people, not ours. We don't want to be a mouthpiece for an authority

that is not ours, we want to remain independent. (Interview with author at Khatamulnabyyin in Kabul, 2007).

Words like this show that the Iranian situation is a problem at three levels: the fact that Shia Afghanis are in the minority, with at least 80 per cent of the population being Sunnis; the fact that they need to deal with the government which is more or less dominated by Pashtuns, who are also Sunnis; the fact that they do not share the conception of modernity that prevails in Iran, despite being big consumers—in the fields of architecture and urbanism for instance—and that they also depend on other references, including the West, beginning with England for obvious historical reasons. The theory of *vilayat-i faqih* crystallizes this distancing with respect to Iran: 'It bears in itself its own limits. While the *vilayat-i faqih* signifies the structuring of a Shia society, it is impossible to see it without defining one's interests and priorities. And the interests of Afghan society are not the same as those of Iranian society,' said the head of the Risalat school. 'This year, we followed Iran in celebrating the end of the holy month of Ramadan, but if an Ayatollah from Afghanistan had seen the moon, we certainly would not have done so, and we would have avoided the problems this raised. It is not in the interests of Shia Afghan society to be dependent on Iran.' (In 2007, the press was very critical of the Shia clergy's reliance on Iran, a charge quickly taken up by Shia intellectuals.) Similarly, pro-reform jurist Abdulghayoum Sajjadi, a member of parliament representing Ghazni, a political scientist and a former student of the World Centre of Religious Sciences in Qom said:

> We wanted to avoid adopting the Iranian system, and specifically the Guardian Council of the Constitution responsible for vetting laws to ensure they comply with Islam. In Afghanistan, there is no need for a law to comply with Islam, as long as it doesn't contradict Islamic principles. A supervisory commission elected by parliamentarians from within Parliament should deal with this, but everyone, including the President, agrees that this is a matter for the judicial power. We wanted to avoid the presence of a body that would hinder the work of Parliament.[36]

As we have seen, the singularity claimed by Afghan Shia stems mainly from their minority status. Bearing this in mind, what they seek to highlight is *ishtirakat*, characteristics they share with the Sunnis: the Koran, the Prophet and the *Kaba*, obviously, but also the fundamental principles, the Oneness of God (*tawhid*), the Prophethood (*Nubuvvat*) and Day of Judgement (*Maad*). Shia Afghans, with the experience gained in Iran (or thanks to Iran) and the fact that this allowed them to cast off their minority condition, consider themselves to be the privileged messengers of union (*vahdat*) and brotherhood (*ukhuvvat*). They gather books, hold debates and draw up institutions preparing the road to rapprochement (*taqrib*), such as the Council of Brotherhood. But the desire for unity is probably less religious than it is national, in a society that is still traumatized by denominational discrimination and civil war. From this perspective, the US intervention was a veritable blessing, on the one hand by overthrowing the Taliban, who are Sunni and suspicious of any form of social mobilization, and on the other hand promoting political correctness favorable to multi-denominationalism. Dr Mohseni, brother of Ayatollah Mohseni and the executive manager of the Khatamulnabyyin project, who lived in Iran for 30 years, for a long time working for the Reconstruction Crusade, says: 'We are not afraid of anyone and we want to discuss our convictions even with atheists.' In the face of ethnic demands and the rise of specificities, the Khatamulnabyyin school is aiming to become a tribune for competency and tolerance:

> We do not want to go to war with all and sundry. The world will never be united. We are here to tell the Sunni that the Shia are not demons. Our school does not want to be a strictly religious establishment. It is a university of theological, social and economic science. Some books published in Pakistan are badly presented and describe us as infidels to our Sunni brothers. We do not want to practice our religion in secret. Since the adoption of the Constitution, which recognizes Shiism as it is and as the foundation of our personal rights (*ahwal-i shakhsiyya*), we have sought to make a public and official call for dialogue with our Sunni brothers. We want to be a meeting place for opinions of all sorts. We want to have exchanges with the outside world and send students abroad, to France for instance. We have used the expertise of many people, Americans for the library, Iranians for building design, and we are probably going to hand catering over to the French, as we have to feed 2,000 people on a daily basis.[37] We want to know and be known. We do not want to convert people to Islam, as no one can change our religion. We just want to live together.

The national dimension of this ecumenical and inter-religious dialogue comes out clearly when Dr Mohseni acknowledges that Iranians have 'a certain intelligence when they have to define the boundaries between their own interests and national interests: ... Iranians never stop complaining, but in time of crisis they stick together and support the state.' His brother, Ayatollah Mohseni, the founder of the Khatamulnabyyin school, which he is building to plans by Iranian architects and the library of which benefited from the support of the Astan-i Quds,[38] regularly visits Islamic centers in Qom. He had no qualms about protesting to the clergy in the holy city following the publication of books that could have prompted discord with his Sunni brothers: his fear was that these works, if they came across the border, could lead to bloodshed and could ruin efforts made by the Islamic Republic of Iran to forge closer ties, and he warned against a possible crackdown in Iran itself, where the majority of Sunnis are losing patience about the discrimination they are suffering; he demanded that all copies of these books should be recalled.[39]

Getting Shia Afghans out of their minority situation will require interdenominational emulation at the same time as the breaking-down of barriers between religious instruction and university teaching. The Khatamulnabyyin requires new students to have a secondary school diploma recognized by the Education Ministry, and now has the right to award both bachelor's and master's degrees, as well as doctorates. Its staff will readily tell you that the authorities consider it as a university, and that it receives funding from American and British money received during the Jihad, as well as from *khums* and *zakat* collected from the faithful. This means it is founded on a dual paradox: the West is financing an Islamic school, and the Muslim faithful an establishment with claims to being a university. In the same vein, the grandson of Ayatollah Mohseni, Javad Mohseni, head of the Tamaddon TV network and a former student of the American University of Beirut, says that a *talabih* must demonstrate not only religious sensibility, but also the will to gain scientific knowledge. The director of the Fatimyyun school in Kandahar says, 'We want to train experts, not just clerics. We need to introduce mathematics, geography and physics to understand the divine message. We cannot limit ourselves simply to purification. There aren't that many mice falling into wells these days. In fact, there isn't much water left in the wells, as it now comes out of taps. We need to learn to speak foreign languages, starting with Pashtun, Arabic and English.'

At the same time, the Shia are proud of the religious performances of their women preachers. The head of the Risalat school, Javad Salehi, said, 'Last year, at Mawlid, we asked Halimeh Hosseini,[40] a professor in the female school of Khatamulnabyyin and a former student of Jamiat al-Zahra in Qom, to present a paper. She was the only woman in a group of men, who were largely Sunni! It was a great success and we broke a taboo.'

If we had to summarize the ambivalent relations between Shia Afghanis and their Iranian brothers, we would say that while they both view each other with suspicion, it should not be forgotten that birds of a feather flock together. Shia Afghanis readily acknowledge their debt to Iran. Mrs Shahin, who runs a family girls school in Kabul, says that 'without Iran we would not have any schoolbooks.' And the head of the Risalat school makes no bones about saying that the Iranian religious instruction model, bureaucratic and academic, is in his view unavoidable: 'If we leave students to their own devices, they do not work properly and the Muslim treasury (*bayt ol-mal*) is squandered. The Iranian system of about eleven years' study, the equivalent of a university system, featuring regular exams, is very successful, and we should apply it in Kabul.' Moreover, the Islamic Republic of Iran is seen as an advanced model, particularly among émigrés or people in contact with the Afghan Diaspora across the border, with the respect for the treatment of women and the education of girls (Hoodfar, 2004, 2007; Rostami-Povery, 2007).

At the same time, however, Shia Afghans do not think that Iranians can be taken at their word. They say that they only ever made hollow promises during the Jihad. They preferred working with the mainly Sunni Tajik and put their political interests ahead of the Shia brotherhood. The head of the Fatimyyun school, in Kandahar, provides the perfect illustration of this sentiment. Wanting to double the size of his school under a five-year plan (should this be taken as a homage to the Soviet occupation or to the Iranian experience?), he has had 'as usual, all nature of promises' from the Iranians, but their only gift to date is a water cooler, which he is still waiting to have installed. This disillusionment has obviously been exacerbated in recent years by the fight in Iran against illegal immigrants coming from Afghanistan. 'The Iranians aspire to being a nuclear power, but while they wait to achieve this goal they attack a few defenseless Afghan migrants,' said Sheikh Moussa Rezai in a public declaration in March 2008, during the commemoration of the thirteenth anniversary of the death of Shahid Mazari, leader of the Hazara Unity Party, at the Afghan Consulate in Mashhad.[41]

The Iranians do not have a better opinion of the Afghans. 'They don't like studying. That's why Afghan students in Najaf were used to getting smaller scholarships than other students. They study here in the morning, but they don't deign to change their cleric's robes for mason's clothes to do building work in the afternoon. There are more Afghans than Arabs in Qom, but unlike the Arabs do not have any religious schools there,' say people in Qom. However, Iran is in its own way dependent on its religious clientele. How brightly would the country's educational and religious star shine without the 8,000 Afghan students that no doubt make up the biggest contingent of about 15,000 foreign students attending the International Center for Islamic Studies, not only in Qom, but also in Mashhad, Shiraz and Karadj?

Conclusion: complex relations

That is why the 'dependency concept' related to Latin America school that initially was framed by historians and economists, should be understood in its whole complexity. The dependence of the Afghan religious arena does not mean its submission to a foreign power. It can also be understood as a resource that Afghan actors mobilize for their own autonomous strategies. Relations between Afghan Shiism and its older Iranian brother should allow us to refine the concept of religious dependence that could be used in other contexts either in the Christian or Islamic World in a contemporary perspective.

Afghan Shia religious dependence on the Iranian religious experience is not just a two-way relationship. They also have other relationships, with Pakistan, for instance, or Najaf. Afghan religious authorities can cross Iran to go to Najaf or take the road to Pakistan. Conversely, they can move from Najaf into Iran. What we term 'dependency' in an abstract manner is in reality a series of routes taken by numbers of real people, in very specific historical contexts. The route taken by Ayatollah Mohseni—the founder of the Khatamulnabyyin school, and the embodiment of the three faces of madrasa' legitimacy, namely the relationship to Iranian Shia theological teaching, jihad and emigration—is telling in this respect. Born in Kandahar in 1936, he started secondary school in Pakistan in 1949, where he learnt to speak Urdu. He then returned to Kandahar, but was quick to leave again, to study theology in the Hazarajat, in Jaghuri in 1952. He set off again for Najaf in 1953, where he attended classes by Ayatollahs Khoi and Hakim. In 1965, he returned home to look after the Shia minority in his hometown, founding the Fatimyyun hoseynieh. In 1978 he fled the communist police, he left to go to Mecca, then for Syria, before settling in Iran and setting up a political party, Harakat, in Qom. He again returned home after the Soviet withdrawal, but was unable to remain during the period of internal fighting among Jihad members, and returned to Pakistan. During the Taliban regime, citing 'certain considerations' (sic), he went to Iran and settled in Qom, where he taught. He then returned to Kabul, dividing his time between the two countries, and founded his large Khatamulnabyyin religious school in 2005 in order to perpetuate the traditions of Najaf and Qom.

At the same time, it will be remembered that Ayatollah Mohseni has support from religious schools in Qom and in all likelihood Astan-i Quds in Mashhad, and funds from Afghans emigrates. His sons live abroad, in Pakistan, the United States, Germany and Saudi Arabia. As for Ayatollah Sajedi, he studied in Qom, Mashhad and Najaf before founding the Ghaed school in Mashhad and the Zeynabieh in Kabul, as we saw. Under the Taliban regime, he was invited to Quetta, in Pakistan, to assist the Hazara community living in that city, and it was while living there that he was asked to move to New Jersey, where he still lives. It is these serpentine routes that inform the religious relationship between Afghan madrasa and the Iranian religious field.

The second important point that we have stressed is the close relationship between Shia religious schools in Afghanistan and migration. We do not think it is far-fetched to see religious schools as a social expression of emigration. In any event, the madrasa should not be seen solely as local institutions, isolated and focused close in on themselves. They are key factor in the country's involvement in its environment, in the same way as NGOs or companies that work there, and they have to keep up with the social changes of the day. The importance given to broadcasting media, which is shared beyond the Afghan clergy, is telling (Louër, 2008: 271–272). Afghanistan's main TV networks are controlled by former Jihad members and all have a religious bent. The Shia have not been left behind on this count: they have Ayatollah Mohseni's Tamaddon (civilization) network, and Ayatollah Moghaddasi, despite being an aging traditionalist, has launched his Kowsar (paradise) network in Spring 2009. As these networks are trying to offset the often somewhat risqué influence of Bollywood, they are inevitably buying programs not only from Arab countries, but also from Iranian TV, which is tending to cement ties with the Islamic Republic even further.

Lastly, we noted that the madrasa movement, which stemmed from the Islamic movement in the 1980s, helps provide a boundary for a religious arena that shifts from one epoch to another. In this respect, the madrasa can help define what is public and what is private, for instance by schooling young girls or people from rural areas, or by having their private school syllabus recognized by the public schools, or by having equipment provided by the public sphere; saying that the instruction of girls is a Prophetic tradition is in effect to bring girls out of the private or family sphere (or to legitimize their departure from the family) to attend a school, to move freely outside and, possibly, to obtain a public school diploma, giving them the possibility of achieving financial independence. This is how we must see the decision by the Khatamulnabyyin school to open a branch for girls, Khadijatalkubra, three years before its boys' branch, and to take in Shia as well as Sunni, going against family prejudice for each of these two denomination. What is also at stake here is the emergence of a civil society independent of the state, for which the madrasa are one of the main vectors. This brings us back to the notion of public denominational space. This notion is relevant in the context of the Islamic Republic of Iran, but it remains to be seen whether it corresponds to transformations in Afghan society.

More generally speaking, the Iranian religious instruction model, which Afghans helped greatly to emerge, has now been brought back home to Afghanistan. The question is now not so much whether it is viable as how it will change in a society in which the Shia have historically been in a position of inferiority compared with the Sunni, divided by political faction fighting, or even by war, and confronted by the problems of the creation of an independent central state. Perhaps Ayatollah Mohseni is correct when he asserts that it is Kabul's turn, after Najaf and Qom, to lead the future of Islam.

Acknowledgenents

Many thanks to Dorian Ryser for making the map on Shiite places of worship and religious institutions in Kabul.

Notes

1 The most tragic of such events is the attack on the Babri mosque in the town of Ayodhya in India, in 1992, which left thousands dead, or the attack against the sanctuary of Imam Reza in Mashhad, in 1994.
2 The two authors speak of Islam's irreconcilable differences with modernity.
3 Mehrzad Boroujerdi 1996, Negin Yavai 2003 and Yadullah Shahibzadeh 2008 describe the nature of this connexion between religious and secular intellectuals in Iran notably from 1950s till the 1979 Revolution.
4 Jamil Malik (2008: 6) points out that, 'with the introduction of new systems of education, madrasa largely lost its function as a general training institute and turned into an institution exclusively for religious education.'
5 It is difficult to estimate the size of the Shia population in Afghanistan because of lack of statistics. Estimated as 15 per cent in the early 1980s (Roy 1984: 68), it represented 20 per cent of the total population of about 22 million in 2001 (Afghanistan Statistical Yearbook 2004, Central Statistics Office). Shia are composed mainly of Hazara, which represents the vast majority, Turkmen, Qizilbash, Bayat, and Sayyid.
6 For instance, Yiki bud yiki nabud (Once upon a time), a book by Mohammad Ali Jamalzadeh, published in Berlin on 1921, criticized clerics, attacking their distance from the people because of their use of Arabic. This book sparked a huge mobilization of ulama in Tehran. The book was burned and its author was excommunicated. <http://www.alefbe.com/articleDjamalzadeh.htm> (accessed March 25, 2009); see also (Katouzian 1382/2003).
7 Ahmad Kasravi was born in a clerical family in Tabriz and was expected to take over his grandfather's mosque, but he became the most virulent critic against the clergy. He was eventually assassinated in the winter of 1946 by people close to Navvab Safavi, when he was leaving a court that had been hearing charges that he had shown 'disrespect to Islam,' before the ruling had been handed down. Roy Mottahedeh (2000: 104) wrote about him: 'Kasravi's autobiography, for all his interest in "scientific history," is in some ways sectarian history in which the role of progressive mullahs, essential to the success of the first phase of the constitutional movement, is noticeably played down.' See also (Pakdaman 1380/2001).

8 Mohagheghnasab was sentenced to two years in prison, but was freed after 86 days. Concerning Mir Hossein Mahdavi, see his leading article in Aftab (no 20, 28 Joza 1382/2003).

9 That seems to be the Iranian version of what Deobandis call 'asri 'ulum (Sikand 2005: 74–75).

10 These new schools intend to offer educational opportunities for children coming from religious families and an alternative to modern institutions such as Alborz, Hadaf, and Kharazmi high school that were founded by lay intellectuals whose goal was sending students to Europe.

11 One might also recall Mrs Seyed Nosrat Beygom Amin, the first mojtahad, or recognized as such, who in competition with modernists of her time, founded in 1965 a girl high school where all professors were women in order to convince reluctant traditional families to send their daughters to a modern school.

12 These two schools are where the first executions after the Revolution took place. <http://www.aftabnews.ir/vdcceoqp.2bqem8laa2.html> (accessed March 26, 2009).

13 Although it is not possible to quote all recent works that emphasize these connexions and diversities, we would like to illustrate this trend by a few examples of publications (Robert H. Hefner and Muhammad Qasim Zaman (eds) 2007; Cahiers de la Méditerranée 2007; Sikand and Youginder 2005; Eickelman 1992).

14 Even throughout his mandate as Prime Minister (1953–1963), Dawoud was hostile toward the Shia population but the coup against his uncle, Zaher Shah, seems to have been the turning point to Hazar departure to Iran (Roy, 1985: 70–71). For a good description of the Islamic movements and their diversity during the 1970s, see Kakar (1995: chap. 4).

15 In the same manner, the madrasas' role in politically integrating Muslim Indians throughout the British colonial period has been underlined by Barbara Daly Metcalf (1982).

16 Concerning the Islamic Shi'a movements in the Gulf, Laurence Louër goes as far as underlining an 'Unavoidable attraction of the political movement and activists towards the domestic space' (2008: 259).

17 This kind of discussion and disagreement extends to other Islamic scholars and quite often readers send comments that underline a clear opposition to the fact that sunni ulamas are hijacked by shia ones. See Muasisih amuzishi-i imam khomeini (1980/2001: 63–66).

18 Founded by Ayatollah Mohseni in 1382/2003 with Ustad Burhaneddin Rabbani's (the former President of Afghanistan) support, the Council publishes a quarterly review Payam-i ukhuvvat (The fraternity's message).

19 According to Gilles Dorronsoro, because of the usual confusion between Shia and Hazara, and with the stigma resulting from the Sunni people, the non-Shia Hazaras generally tend to reject their ethnic belonging and declare themselves to be Tajik (2000: 56).

20 The value placed on the Pashtuns' identity and culture by the monarchy was concurrent with the exaltation of the aryanity of the Persians and the Turks against the backdrop of nationalist movements in the late nineteenth and early twentieth centuries, in Iran and Turkey. It is a modern phenomenon of inventing a tradition linked to the emergence of a nation-state.

21 Islam also penetrated Afghanistan through Zaranj, later, in the third century of the rule of Hijra under the Saffarid dynasty. It appears that the entire country was converted to Islam at that time, with the exception of Nuristan Province, which remained Buddhist until the nineteenth century.

22 According to Monsutti Hazara, conversion to Shia could be a way to distance themselves from the surrounding populations (2004: 45).

23 Born in Kabul, he followed the standard route for Afghani students of religion. He emigrated at the age of 11 to Mashhad in the early twentieth century, studying at the

Abdal Khan school. He left Mashhad, apparently to attend classes held by Abdolkarim Haeri, the founder of the religious school in Qom. Then he left for Najaf to complete his studies, returning home in around 1930 after having become an Ayatollah <www.hojjat.net/zendeginamah> (accessed January 24, 2009).

24 It is interesting to note that Ayatollah Assef Mohseni also recently announced that the Shia call to prayer on TV dates from 2007, which corresponds to the inauguration of his own TV network, Tamaddon. (Interview with Payam-i Aftab, 1386.09.14/ Dec. 2007) <http://afterwar.blogfa.com/post-17.aspx> (accessed March 5, 2010).

25 Interview, a member of the Sadat family.

26 According to Sarvar Danish, Minister of Justice, the difference between Shias and Sunnis is not related to their fiqh which are very similar but it concerns precisely a very limited section of it, personal law, which covers notably prayers, marriage, divorce, inheritance, guardianship. <http://www.moj.gov.af/?lang=da&p=events&nid=221> (accessed March 25, 2010).

27 Afshar and Hoseynieh in Qala-i Fathullah (1341/1962), both founded by Ayatollah Mohammad Amin Afshar (1288–1357/1909–1979); Muhammadiye in Karta-i Sakhi (1347/1968), founded by Ayatollah Seyed Mohammad SarvarVaez Behsoudi (1295–1358/1916–1979); Madinatulilm, Pul-i Sokhta (1344/1965), founded by Ayatollah Taghaddosi. The school remained open during the Soviet occupation, the civil war and the Taliban regime; Jamiatulislam, Pul-i Sokhta (1351/1972), founded by Ayatollah Ghorbanali Mohaghegh Kaboli; Risalat, Qala-i Shada (1373/1994), founded by Ayatollah Salehi Modarres; Baghirululuum, founded by Senator and Ayatollah Erfani (1318–/1939–); Khatamulnabyyin, in Karta-i She (1383/2004), founded by Ayatollah Mohseni (1314– /1935–). Various schools such as Maktab-i Nargis in Karta-i Sakhi, founded by hojjatoleslam Ali Jafari, Ayatollah Sajedi's Zeynabieh School in Kartai-i Char, and Ayatollah Hojjat's Hoseynieh in Chindawul must also be added to this list.

28 The school should have been recorded under the name of Maktab Narjis, following the Iranian model, which is analysed by Keiko Sakurai in this volume, but under pressure and in order to emphasize his autonomy toward Iran, hojatoleslam Jafari had to give it up and he modified the name to Maktab Nargues. It is worth mentioning that the manager of the school, Mrs Fouzieh Nemati, is a former student of Maktab Narjis in Mashad during the Taliban.

29 Source: interview with Javad Salehi, head of the Risalat school (Kabul, October 2007). In September 2010 the student number reached 1127.

30 Actually, Iranians seem to have recently broken this taboo when they published the tariffs of what is called 'Quranic activities.' Lecturers are divided in three categories; furthermore, oral and written teachings are not paid for in the same way. National and international exams do not cost the same. <http://www.farsnews.net/newstext.php> (accessed September 15, 2009).

31 In fact, the journal, Durr-i dari, was published by the Cultural Centre for Afghan Writers, which, for financial reasons, was unable to publish beyond issue number 13. But the chief editor, Seyed Aboutaleb Mozaffari, and his editorial staff decided to extend the experience by founding the Dorr-i Dari Cultural Institute, which gave birth to the journal Khatt-i sivvum in autumn 1381/2002.

32 These include the Valiasr Cultural and Scientific Circle, the Yassin Cultural Association, the Institute for Fundamental Research, the Bisharat Cultural Institutes and the Cultural Foundation of Afghanistan, which respectively publish the following quarterlies: Ummat, Payam-i Yasin (the Yasin message), Andishih-i Farda (tomorrow's thought), Bisharat (the happy promise) and the bimonthly Parwaz (flight).

33 We could cite some of the former students of the World Centre for Islamic Education: apart from Gholam Sarvar Danish, the Justice Minister and Abdolghayoum Sajjadi, the parliamentary member for Ghazni and editor of the only—and very good—quarterly political journal, Discourse, Karim Khalili, the advisor of Afghan President Hamed Karzai and Ghorbanali Erfani, member of meshranu jerga, the Senate.

34 This is the case of Ayatollah Ali Mohagheghnasab, who, it will be remembered, was arrested in Kabul, in October 2005, following complaints made against him by Shia as well as Sunni clerics, as well as by President Karzai's religious affairs advisor, Muhyiddin Balouch. Chief Editor of the journal Huquq-i zanan (women's rights), Mohagheghnasab was accused of having defended declarations deemed disrespectful to sacrosanct Islamic principles in his writings.

35 For a total number of 115,000 foreigners who are living in Qom, the population is made up of 59,000 Afghans, 8,000 Arabs. Cf. <http://ghom.ir/old-sit> (accessed November 12, 2008).

36 This is a very clear allusion to the situation prevailing in Iran, where there is recurrent conflict between the Majlis and the Guardian Council of the Constitution, necessitating constant intervention by the Expediency Discernment Council, even though the parliamentarian for Ghazni that we cite readily acknowledged having to 'fight against the vacuum of bad interpretation' created by superposing the parliamentary commission and the judicial power with respect to constitutionality. (interview with the author at the Journal Quarterly discourses HQ in Kabul, 2007)

37 Dr Mohseni was obviously aware of the fact that I come from France.

38 <http://Shianews.org> (accessed February 7, 2007).

39 <http://Baztab.com> (accessed on May 15, 2006).

40 She is, with Tahereh Rohani, one of the authors of Azadi wa iradih-i insan dar kalam-i islami (Freedom and will in the Islamic words) (1381/2002).

41 <http://katebhazara.blogfa.com/post-433.aspx> (accessed March 25, 2010).

7   Epilogue

Madrasas – vitality and diversity

Dale F. Eickelman

The Moral Economy of the Madrasa takes a fresh approach to the *madrasa* tradition by focusing principally on its contemporary social and political roles. All the chapters in this book are based on recent field research—often in places where North American and European social scientists are reluctant to tread. The book focuses on the contemporary role of madrasas in Afghanistan, Iran, Pakistan, Bangladesh, and China. Adelkhah and Sakurai's introductory chapter places the contributions in an appropriate historical and social context equally relevant to the general reader and to the specialist familiar with the Muslim world. Even for such specialists, however, *Moral Economy* stands apart because of its comparative approach in highly diverse contexts and the editors' ability to indicate how the study of contemporary madrasas informs studies in history, politics, and social thought.

For example, Adelkhah and Sakurai's focus on 'moral economy' is distinctly modern, although the term invokes its antecedents in the heyday of the Scottish Enlightenment in the late eighteenth century. E.P. Thompson (1971) projected the term into common usage in the 1960s and 1970s, and it has since become a point of departure for scholars in contexts as diverse as Indochina in the 1930s (Scott 1976) and Iran in the 1940s (McFarland 1985). Thompson's use of the term was avowedly Marxist, but the concept as now used, including in this book, reaffirms the religious practices, habits of thought, and the deep and popular roots of madrasas. Even as some Muslims and others claim that madrasas are rooted in a nearly timeless past, others see them as short-term opportunistic fronts that disseminate militant radicalism. In the aftermath of September 11, 2001, George Bush, Dick Cheney, and Donald Rumsfeld all claimed at one time or another that 'madrasas' were a threat, and the conservative *Insight Magazine* at one point in 2007 claimed that Barack Obama had actually attended a 'radical' *madrasa* as a child (http://www.cnn.com/2007/POLITICS/01/22/obama.madrassa/). At least Fox News, which gave a wider audience to *Insight*'s reporting, distinguished between radical and non-radical madrasas.

Yet in both the Sunni and Shi'a religious traditions, madrasas have a strong resilience. Najaf, long the major center for Shi'a religious learning, survived the first decades of Ba'th rule in Iraq, but after the collapse of the American-encouraged uprising against the Saddam Hussein regime in 1991, its leadership and institutions suffered savage reprisals. After 2003, however, the *hawza* (as the major centers of learning are called in the aggregate), began quickly to rebuild both as centers of religious pilgrimage and of learning, attracting students at all levels from Iraq, Iran, South Asia, and elsewhere, as well as donations from the faithful (author's interviews with *hawza* leadership, Najaf, November 20–21, 2009). As madrasas in Iran come under increasing government state restrictions, Najaf is bound to regain its prior role as the major center of Shi'a religious learning, complete with multilingual websites and ready Internet access to the outside world to counter the continued difficulties of physical access.

In social anthropology, formal education has long been stepchild until recently to studies of childhood and child socialization, and the study of madrasas, mosque-universities, and the habits of thought inculcated in them have been no exception. Most studies have focused on madrasas in the Arab world and their Indonesian equivalent, the *pesantaran* (Eickelman 1985; Hefner and Zaman 2007; this volume, Chapter 1).

Rather than seeing madrasas in South and Southeast Asia as a pale reflection of a historically known or imagined past, these studies begin with the present or the near-present. As the editors of *The Moral Economy of the Madrasa* remind us, the term *madrasa* taken at its most basic, means (in Arabic) a place of learning, and this learning is not now and never has been exclusively Islamic. Since the nineteenth century, madrasas have existed alongside secular and state institutions. Throughout the Muslim world, from the late Ottoman Empire, British India, Egypt, to Morocco, *madrasa* leadership has sought since the nineteenth century to innovate and adapt—and such adaptation is integral to *madrasa* structure, not solely a reaction to Western encroachment. *Not exclusive, but acknowledged*

In some contexts, as in Bangladesh (this volume, Chapter 5), governments have in recent years sometimes seen madrasas as a low-cost way of extending mass education, especially in remote regions, a notion to which UNESCO contributed in the 1980s (Eickelman 1987). *Madrasa* education, like state-supplied mass education, has become 'objectified' at all levels—a commodity that, as the editors indicate (Chapter 1), is as subject to 'management science' and 'human resource management' as any other institution or organization. Yet like the *hawwala* system for the transfer of money and messages over great distances and into remote areas which is more adaptive, trustworthy, and flexible than the modern banking system (see Monsutti 2005), so madrasas are often more adaptive and flexible in the educational sphere than are modern state schools or many of their secular private counterparts.

So Yamane's chapter on Pakistan's Federally Administered Tribal Area (FATA) gets immediately to the heart of the political role of madrasas in contemporary Pakistan. In the time of the Soviet occupation of Afghanistan, Pashtun refugees from Pakistan were in refugee camps in Pakistan, and with American, Saudi, and Pakistani support they were encouraged to join the anti-Soviet Taliban. In 1996, Arabs, together with young Pashtun supporters fighting the Soviets in Afghanistan, entered a village and tried to kill the traditional tribal leadership. This leadership resisted and successfully drove the invaders away. In Spring 2008, 'those who opposed the traditional tribal system' were 'said' to have caused bombs to fall on a tribal *jirga*, or gathering of its senior leadership. Yamane is circumspect on who could cause bombs to fall, but forcefully presents this leadership as related to 'newly established' madrasas. In these schools, the students are not necessarily Pashtun or respectful of *Pashtunwali*, the tribal code of honor, nor do they accept the coexistence of their politicized version of Islam with the tribal code.

As in many other parts of the Muslim world, the idea of Islamic law, the *shari'a*, encompasses those aspects of local custom (Ar., *'adat*) that are compatible with formal Islamic law. In social practice, the Pashtun of Afghanistan's south share much in common with their kin in Pakistan's FATA, although by the 1970s the Pashtun of Afghanistan had more access to education than their Pakistani counterparts.

Pre-1980s madrasas in the FATA remained largely under local control, although they were strongly influenced by wider intellectual and political currents, notably the Deobandi movement. In the newly established madrasas of the 1980s, just as with the Deobandi-inspired predecessors of the 1920s, doctrines of *jihad* were emphasized. With massive foreign and state support, including from Pakistan's Inter-Services Intelligence (ISI), the new madrasas thrived, and Pakistan, according to Yamane, became a 'hotbed' of religious extremism. Some madrasas are under state supervision, while others remain independent, and they vary in their acceptance of external support. Traditional notables were not neglected in the distribution of state and private largesse during the Soviet occupation of Afghanistan. After the Soviet withdrawal, however, this funding suddenly ceased, the region was abandoned, and the youth attracted to the *jihad* movement were left to fend for themselves.

The growth of madrasas in Pakistan since 1947 is stunning. From 245 registered in West Pakistan at the time of independence, Yamane reports that their number reached 2,056 by the 1980s, with many of those in the FATA located along the Pakistan–Afghanistan border. Unlike their older counterparts, the newer madrasas of the 1980s tended to be built away from the residences of local tribal leaders, and the influx of refugees also made these new schools, including their teachers and their leadership, independent from local authorities. Antagonism between the traditional leadership and the mullahs of the new madrasas grew. As the mullahs, including Taliban militants, were also heavily armed, they could paralyze the more moderate leadership of the traditional tribal elders and ignore the decision making of the *jirgas*. Ironically, the traditional leadership was more open to the introduction of modern education and the education of girls, but was also powerless to act effectively.

Southern Afghanistan lapsed into lawlessness following the Soviet withdrawal. By 1994 the Taliban ('students'), many of whom were trained in madrasas in Quetta and Kandahar, were initially welcomed. The 'pure-hearted,' as they were called at the time, reduced banditry in the region and merchants supported them. By 1997, the Taliban controlled 90 per cent of Afghanistan. Following the September 11, 2001 attacks on the United States, the Americans ousted the Taliban government. Nonetheless, as Yamane points out, the Pakistani government declared that the students in the newly established madrasas in Pakistan were 'local' Taliban and therefore not subject to attack. Private support for these madrasas and for the Taliban continued to pour in.

Yamane's argument highlights the underlying conflict between the existing religious hierarchy and tribal leadership in the FATA region and southern Afghanistan and the increasingly powerful Taliban movement. Implicit in his argument is the powerful challenge that the Taliban posed to the legitimacy of the existing political and religious order, both in Pakistan and Afghanistan. It is convenient to claim that the Taliban became ascendant through fear and external support alone, but as Yamane argues, some villagers and external supporters welcomed them in the early 1990s as a stabilizing force based on the *shari'a* as villagers and tribesmen understood it. In this respect, the Taliban are distinctly modern and may prove more resilient than outsiders and state authorities care to admit.

Sakurai's discussion of women's seminaries in Iran and Pakistan gets to the heart of popular legitimacy. Most contemporary conservative Muslims in these countries acknowledge that women's opportunities for education have until recently lagged behind those of men, although modern state schooling, at least in Iran, has been more open to them. In both Iran and Pakistan, the religious seminaries were marginalized in favor of state schooling, with its opportunities for employment and state advancement. In 1968, I had an opportunity to visit several male madrasas in various parts of Iran. The most striking thing about them was the significant number of students who had failed the highly competitive entrance examinations for *lycée* education or the subsequent examinations for entrance to Reza Shah Pahlevi University. The graduation rate for *lycée*s hovered around 10 per cent, and many failed students then shifted to religious education. The consequence, however, was that many *madrasa* students were thoroughly familiar with secular subjects. In this way, the Iranian state indirectly contributed to the health of the women's seminaries. In Pakistan, in contrast, at least for the Shi'a population (15 per cent of Pakistan's population), the seminary system there is more dependent at the advanced level on studies in Iran and Iraq.

In 1984, Ayatollah Khomeini established Iran's first full-scale women's seminary, and the idea spread throughout Iran and into Pakistan. Unlike the male madrasas, largely independent of the Iranian state, female seminaries were creations of the state. Their curriculum, an academic credit system, and formal ways to accept non-Iranian students made the seminaries increasingly attractive because such manifestations of bureaucracy and management enhanced the 'modernity' of the institutions.

Women seminary graduates formally participate in education and propagation (*tabligh*) implicitly to alter the balance between male and female authority in domestic settings. Sakurai reports that the seminaries have become so popular that they can accept only 10 per cent of their applicants. As in Indonesia and elsewhere, seminary education is equivalent to secular higher education, and also attractive to students who prefer a gender-segregated environment.

The administrative and curricular details that Sakurai provides indicate how women's seminaries are fully the equivalent of secular institutions in organization and administration. Her example of how graduates of these institutions work in Pakistan also indicates the pervasiveness of both male and female religious networks. The father of one student from Skardu in Pakistan, for example, studied in Najaf for 14 years, represents Ayatollahs Sistani and Khamenei, and has founded seminaries in Skardu, where his daughter, having studied in Iran, is accorded prestige in her own educational and *tabligh* activities.

An important byproduct of the women's seminary movement has been to encourage the explicit discussion of women's rights in the Islamic context. Although not an explicit threat to the male hierarchy, there is now a critical mass of women with advanced scholarly credentials, although they still are not regarded as capable of issuing legal opinions on their own. Mir-Hosseini (1999) argued nearly two decades ago that educated women often assumed male names to enter into debates in religious magazines. This practice now seems to yield to direct participation. In Pakistan, where there are fewer educational opportunities for women and men, as in Iran, women are concerned with implementing all Islamic ideals and practices, not just those that apply to gender issues.

Adelkhah has had a long-standing interest in religious space as part of social space, and draws attention to the growing proliferation of religious spaces. Yamane's chapter documents the different forms that madrasas can take, and Adelkhah focuses on how madrasas encapsulate and sometimes advocate religious and social change, redefining the role of religion in society. In post-2001 Afghanistan, madrasas have become a key provider of education. To adapt a phrase from the Russian literary critic Mikhail Bakhtin (1990), madrasas provide a space for an 'excess of seeing.' Foreigners and locals mingle in them, outsiders see or misperceive their activities, and they provide networks for wide-ranging intellectual contacts and networks if trust.

Shi'a madrasas are places where highly diverse groups can interact, debate, and respond to innovation—and adjust their actions both to what works and how others see them. The Shi'a madrasas are also cosmopolitan, both in Iran and in Afghanistan, where they have strong ties with their Iranian counterparts. What is new since the 1990s is the accelerated pace at which accommodation to changed circumstances occurs and the wider range of audiences that must be taken into account. Adelkhah also underscores the 'hybrid' nature of religious and state education, where the more successful Islamic intellectuals effectively connect many audiences.

Since 2001, she argues that the same holds for Afghanistan, and that the Shi'a madrasas there provide a model for 'cultural, social, and economic modernization.' The model includes English language acquisition, the use of computers, and as in the past, participation with the Sunni majority in discussions of national and ethnic identities—most Afghan Shi'a are Hazara while most Pashtun are Sunni.

Both Sunni and Shi'a participated in resistance to Soviet rule after 1979, and by the 1980s the category 'Jihad fighter' emerged, in which ethnic and sectarian identities became less important. Emigration to Iran for religious learning was earlier for Shi'a seminarians. Afghan seminaries have benefited intermittently from Iranian government and private funding. The channeling of such funds is made easier by the networks of personal ties that leading scholars have built up from the time of their own studies outside of Afghanistan. *Madrasa* students often come from poor backgrounds, but religious studies often are a form of upward social mobility facilitated by the regular stipends and lodging for which *madrasa* students are eligible. Many, as former anti-Soviet jihadis, have added leadership credentials, and some have traveled to Iran, Pakistan, and Europe. The Iranian model of bureaucratized Islamic associations and schooling predominates, but in terms of language, dress, and the use of media, Afghan Shi'a seek to distance themselves from their Iranian counterparts in order to attenuate accusations of antagonism to the Pashtun and Sunni majorities.

As Adelkhah concludes, dependence on Iran does not mean submission to a foreign power. The Afghan Shi'a minority also has ties with Najaf in Iraq and with its counterparts in Pakistan. Migration, both for the purpose of knowledge and for commerce—the two often are intertwined—plays an important role in defining the complex roles that madrasas and religious education play. As with minorities elsewhere, transnational educational networking, migration, and increasingly the new communications technology contribute to allowing Afghanistan's Shi'a minority more complex forms of empowerment and participation in religious and social fields.

Madrasas in Bangladesh also play pivotal roles in defining and contesting what it means to be Muslim. As with the other chapters in this volume, Bangladeshi madrasas vary from state-subsidized to independent and in terms of sectarian, or *maslaki*, orientation. Aliya madrasas are regulated and often funded by the Bangladesh Madrasa Education Board, part of the Ministry of Education. Quomi (Arabic *qawmi*) madrasas are privately funded, perhaps in emulation of the Aliya madrasas, those have also sought to organize since 1978. In the Brahmanbaria municipality, the subject of Kabir's study, the Aliya schools are grade-based, as are most secular schools; Qoumi schools are subject-based, although the subjects are also partly organized in a grade-based way. Thus Quranic memorization and recitation constitutes the first stage of learning, followed by more advanced subjects.

Since the 1980s, schools for girls have also been formed. These Quomi schools are fee-based and provide religious scholars with a livelihood. The number of students enrolled in Quomi schools is uncertain, but Aliya madrasas nationwide constitute around 27 per cent of national enrolment, with secular schools constituting the rest. As with other parts of the Muslim world, the introduction of state-sponsored Western-style schooling has not eclipsed *madrasa* education.

Madrasas, and the religious scholars associated with them, continue to play vital public roles. The state does not fully recognize degrees earned at Aliya madrasas, but this is better than the Quomi degrees, which receive no state recognition. Nonetheless, Quomi students can achieve community recognition and network in their own community and beyond to maintain a livelihood.

This notion of networking is salient in the context of Bangladesh and beyond. As Stefan Reichmuth (2000) has shown for other contexts, tracing the regional and transregional networks now and in the past sheds significant light on the spread of ideas, practices, and identities. Understanding these networks, as Kabir reminds us, sheds light on how the 'ulama create social and religious space. Sponsoring madrasas can also influence social advancement. Among 'ulama, debate over doctrinal points also serves to delineate market spheres and solidify one's primary base. Quomi 'ulama can argue that the modern disciplinary subjects of the Aliya schools detract students from a 'proper' Islamic education. Aliya teachers in turn can argue that the Quomi rigidity is preserving tradition that detracts students from proper critical thinking. These debates remind us of British philosopher Walter Gallie's notion of 'essentially contested concepts,' notions that are so value-laden that agreement on alternate interpretations is impossible. Yet such debates, when carried out in public space, have the potential to transform that space.

The Shimbo and Matsumoto chapter on Hui women's Islamic education in China traces the rise and fall of its subject. Estimated at 9.8 million in China's 2000 census the Hui are perhaps half of the Chinese Islamic community and 0.75 per cent of China's total population. The Hui are marginalized by reason of language, religion, and economic disadvantage. In addition, Hui Muslims were reluctant to educate their girls alongside boys or to have them mix in public places. Nonetheless, in the Republican era (1912–1949) some male religious and other community leaders noted the importance of female education and established several female madrasas (*nüxue*). After 1949, the Communist government enhanced public education to promote national gender integration, although both religious and secular schooling ground to a halt during the 1966–1976 Cultural Revolution.

At the end of this period, Hui leaders worked with the government to make secular and religious education coexist and to integrate women into it. Even UNESCO provided funding, indicating how Hui leaders could use international concerns about gender equality to leverage international private contributions. The result was a shift away from *nüxue* to state schooling. Although *nüxue* were built by the private sector to promote women's education 'without sacrificing religious identity,' the government paid overheads and teachers' salaries and demanded a shift away from Islamic subjects and toward 'national integration and secularization' and a demanding curriculum geared to national school entrance examinations.

The reluctance to allow women to be educated early in the twentieth century has now been replaced by agreement on the economic advantages of secular schooling, with secular schools as the first choice and the possibility of teaching as a career. Although *nüxue* have been marginalized, they remain privately supported. Their focus has shifted to the study of Arabic and to eliminating illiteracy among older women. Many pursue religion-related careers, and some older women study in preparation for the pilgrimage to Mecca. The study of Arabic offers others the possibility of serving as interpreters in the business world and at the same time cementing their credentials as 'Muslim feminists,' playing greater roles in society while adhering to Islamic values.

Several underlying themes emerge from these chapters. The first is that *madrasa* education everywhere remains important and is strongly shaped by national policy or, as in the case of Pakistan, the lack of a clear national policy or interest in educational reform (Witte 2010). Second is the growing globalization of *madrasa* education. This does not lead to a greater homogenization, but to the ability to learn from successful *madrasa* models elsewhere and to seek to emulate the most successful innovations of state-sponsored education. At the same time, *madrasa* students and their teachers are increasingly aware of alternative ideas of education and their 'market value' both in terms of social status and of locally and regionally shared Islamic values. Third is the extent to which *madrasa* education shapes pervasive notions of what is right and just in both Muslim and non-Muslim societies. These notions are contested and have been subject to strongly competing claims.

The role that madrasas play in society remains highly varied and is sensitive to the societies in which they are embedded. Madrasas everywhere continue to shape religious, social, and political beliefs and practice.

In the epilogue, D.F.E. notes the shortcomings Pak govt pol & int in edu as the exception to 'transregional networks' of madrasas continuing to "share rel, soc, & pol bel & prac.

It is evident that obst to edu for women & girls persists where the counter intelligence of female role models are not present to influence "cultural, social, and eco modernization." (134)

Glossary

adab   manner or proper rules of conduct

ahung, akhund   Islamic religious leaders or experts

ahwal-i shakhsiyya   personal law

akhirat   life after death, hereafter

akhlaq   good qualities, virtue

akhund   see *ahung*

alim, pl. ulama   religious scholar

Alim   degree obtained after completion of grade 12 at Aliya madrasa

aqida   faith, creed

aseke rasul   devotee of the Prophet

ashura   day of mourning for the martyr Imam Hossein on tenth of Muharram

awqaf   plural of waqf, religous endowment

ayatollah   lit. sigh of God. Modern honoric title in the Shia clerical institutions

Bahai   followers of the reformer movement in the mid-19th century related to the religious dissidents Mirza Husain Ali Nuri, known as Bahaullah (1817–1892), and his son (1844–1921)

bayt ul-mal   historically, it was a financial institution responsible for the administration of the treasury (taxes or spoils of war) belonging to muslims in Islamic states, particularly in the early Islamic Caliphate; public or national treasury

bidaat   reprehensible innovation often considered as heretical and sinful

Brahman   Hindu priests

Dakhil   degree obtained after completion grade 10 at Aliya madrasa

dar al-harb   land of the war

dar al-Islam   land of Islam

dars-i nizami   syllabus of Islamic education devised by Mullah Nizamuddin (d. 1748) which continues to influence religious education in South Asia

Daura-i Hadith   the degree for obtaining expertise on the Prophetic tradition

din   religion; often refers to Islam

dua   supplication and invocation to Allah for seeking favor from Him

eid-e miladunnabi   celebration of the birth of the Prophet

fatwa   religious expertise or verdict based on Islamic legal schools

Fazil   degree obtained after completion of grade 14 at Aliya madrasa

fiqh   Islamic jurisprudence

fitna   secession, disorder and chaos; also refers to disagreement and division in Islam

furfura pir   a clan of Sufi master originated from the village of Furfura in Hooghly district in West Bengal, India

hadia   gift often given to a Sufi master in exchange of healing

hadith   tradition of the words and deeds attributed to the Prophet

Hanafiate   school of Islamic law ascribed to Abu Hanifa (699–767)

hawala   lit. transfer of funds; informal network of payment system

hawza, hawza-i ilmiyya   Shia religious school

Hazara kushi   to bring down the Hazara

Hazara sitizi   to make war with the Hazara

hazir u nazir, hadir wa nazir   theological precepts that allow the barrier of time–space, able to be present at one time in different places

hijab   veil; set of moral or Islamic rule to dress or to behave

hoseynieh   place dedicated to Imam Hossein for the use of religious meetings

Hossein, Husayn   third Shia imam, grandson of the Prophet Muhammad (d. 680)

Hui   Muslim people in China

ijaza   lit. authorization; a certificate enabling a clergy to exercise ijtihad

ijtihad   independent reasoning in the interpretation of Islamic law; effort to interpret the Islamic laws

ilm   knowledge; also it refers to religious knowledge

ilm-i ghayb   the knowledge of the unseen

iman   faith

irshad   put on track; give the correct orientation

ishtirakat   lit. common ground; principle based on making common ground between Shia and Sunni to prevent tension

itrat   Prophet's lineage

jamia   center of higher education

jihad   lit. exertion; holy war

Kamil   degree obtained after completing 16 grade, similar to Masters degree, at Aliya madrasa

khanqah   sufi meetinghouse

khatib   the prayer leader of a mosque who provides khutbah, congregational religious sermon; also refers to religious leader

khums   religious tax

kitabkhana   the division of text, usually begins at post-primary level at Quomi madrasas

kuttab   religious school

lailat-ul barat   night of forgiveness, the night preceding the 15th day of Shaban month in Arabic calendar

lailat-ul miraj   the night of ascent of the Prophet to Allah, the 27th day of Rajab month in Arabic calendar

lungis   lifetime tribal chiefs

maad   resurrection

madaris   plural of madrasa

maduli   amulet containing sacred text or incantation for healing illness or evil spirits

mahfil   public gathering, especially where religious sermons and opinions are delivered

majar   Sufi shrine or spiritual preceptor's grave

majhab, mazhab   the four schools of law considered as legitimate in Sunni Islam; often also refers to religion in South Asia

maktab   religious school

maliks   hereditary tribal chiefs who receive allowances from the government

marja-i taqlid   the highest authority in Islamic law among the Shia clergy

markaz   center

mashayekh   pl. of sheikh, a religious scholar or Sufi master

masla   rules of guidance

maslaki   particular interpretative aspects of Islamic doctrine

maulana   scholar of religious learning

maulvi, maulavi   scholar of religious learning

mawajib   regular allowances paid to maliks and lungis

mawlid   prophet's birthday

Menhuan   sufi orders in China

mian   descended from holy men

mufti   jurist qualified to issue fatwas

muhaddith   scholar of prophetic tradition

muhtamim   manager or director; often refers to the head of a madrasa

mujtahid   high-ranking cleric who has the authority to interpret religious laws according to his judgment

murshid   leader or teacher in a sufi order; They are often called laorenjia, which is the translation of Pir

naeb-e mufti   deputy Islamic jurist-consultant

nowruz   new year

nüahong   female teachers in women's madrasa; some of them conduct religious rituals for women

nubuvvat, nubuwwat   prophecy

nur   light, illumination

nüxue   lit. women's school; in the context of Islam in China, women's madrasa

pani-pora   form of Islamic healing where Islamic preceptor utters some sacred passages onto water, as remedy for curing illness or evil spirits

parda   lit. separation; it is related to gender segregation

Pashtunwali   the Pashtun's basic concepts of social life

pir   spiritual preceptor, a Sufi master

qarzul hasana   lit. loan made with no interest; Islamic banking

qazi   judge applying Sharia

qingzhen   lit. 'pure and true'; it evokes Islam in China

Quran   Koran, the Islamic sacred book

riwaj a loosely collected set of old customs

sadaka voluntary religious donation

sadat plural from Sayid; family descends from Prophet Mohammed

saiyid, sayyid, sayda, sayid descended from the Prophet

sanad royal ordinance

sharif noble, descended from the Prophet

shirk polytheism

suba-i ifta department of practical lessons for issuing religious verdicts

sunna/sunnat the normative practices of Prophet's deeds and actions or traditions

tabiz amulet containing sacred text or incantation for healing illness or evil spirits

tabligh propagation of the faith

talib, talabih, pl. taliban madrasa student

taqiya lit. to conceal, to hide; principle based on denial of one's religious views when it is necessary to protect oneself

taqrib lit. rapprochement; principle to bring together the Islamic denominations, notably Shias and Sunnis

tawhid unicity; the first principle of the five pillars of Islam

ukhuvvat, ukhuwwat brotherhood

ulum-i ruz modern sciences

umma Muslim community

ushr religious tax

vahdat, wahdat unity

vilayat-i faqih the government of jurist consult

wali holy men

waqf, pl.awqaf religious endowment

zakat obligatory almsgiving/religious tax; one of the five pillars of Islam

zakat al-fitr religious tax to discharge at the end of Ramadan

zakira the female religious authority in charge of reciting the story of the martyrdom of Husayn at Karbala

Zeynabieh place dedicated to hazrat-i Zeynab for the use of religious meetings

References

Books and journals

Aaftaab, Naheed Gina (2005) '(Re)Defining public spaces through developmental education for Afghan women', in Falah Ghazi-Walid and Caroline Nagel (eds) *Geographies of Muslim Women: Gender, Religion, and Space,* New York: Guilford Press.

Abou Zahab, Mariam (2008) 'Between Pakistan and Qom: shi'i women's madrasas and new transnational networks', in Farish A. Noor, Yoginder Sikand and Martin van Bruinessen (eds) *The Madrasa in Asia: Political Activism and Transnational Linkages,* Amsterdam: Amsterdam University Press.

Adelkhah, Fariba (1991) *La Révolution sous le voile: femme islamique d'Iran,* Paris: Karthala.

—— (1995) 'L'ayatollah Khamenei, source d'imitation?', *Esprit,* mai: 165–9.

—— (1999a) *Being Modern in Iran,* London: Hurst & Company.

—— (1999b) 'Un évergétisme islamique: les réseaux bancaires et financiers en Iran', *Revue des mondes musalmans et de la méditerranée,* 85/86: 63–79.

Adelkhah, Fariba and Olszweska, Zuzanna (2007), 'The Iranian Afghans', *Iranian Studies,* 40(2): 137–65.

Ahmad, Hafiz Nadhar (1987) 'Pakistan men dini madaris : mukhtasar jaiza', in Institute of Policy Studies (ed.) *Dini Madaris ka Nizam-e Talim,* Islamabad: Institute of Policy Studies.

Ahmad, Irfan (2005) 'Between moderation and radicalization: transnational interaction of Jamaat-e-Islami of India', *Global Networks,* 5(3): 279–99.

—— (2008) 'Power, purity and the vanguard: educational ideology of the Jama'at-i-Islami of India', in Jamal Malik (ed.) *Madrasas in South Asia: Teaching Terror?,* London: Routledge.

Ahmadi, Fereshteh (2006) 'Islamic feminism in Iran: feminism in a new Islamic context', *Journal of Feminist Studies in Religion,* 22(2): 33–53.

Ahmed, Akbar S. (1986) *Pakistan Society: Islam, Ethnicity and Leadership in South Asia,* Karachi: OUP.

Ahmed, Leila (1992) *Women and Gender in Islam,* New Haven, CT: Yale University Press.

Ahmed, Rafiuddin (1988) 'Conflict and contradictions in Bengali Islam: problems of change and adjustment', in Katherin P. Ewing (ed.) *Shari'at and Ambiguity in South Asian Islam,* Berkeley, CA: University of California Press.

——(1996) *The Bengal Muslims 1871–1906: A Quest for Identity,* Delhi: Oxford University Press.

Ahmed, Sufia (1996) *Muslim Community in Bengal 1884–1912,* Dhaka: University Press.

Alam, Arshad (2008a) 'The enemy within: madrasa and Muslim identity in North India', *Modern Asian Studies*, 42 (2–3): 605–27.

——(2008b) 'Making Muslims: identity and difference in Indian madrasas', in Jamal Malik (ed.) *Madrasas in South Asia: Teaching Terror?*, London and New York: Routledge.

Alatiqi, Imad (2009) 'Male–female encounters in early Islamic society—examples and case study', paper presented at the American University of Kuwait, the International Conference March 10–12, 2009, titled 'University Development and Critical Thinking: Education in the Arabian Peninsula for a Global Future'.

Ali, A.K.M. Ayyub (1983) *History of Traditional Islamic Education in Bangladesh (Down to A.D. 1980)*, Dhaka: Islamic Foundation.

Ali, Mansur (1987) 'Mubahith: ijlas cahlm', in Institute of Policy Studies (ed.) *Dini Madaris ka Nizam-e Talim*, Islamabad: Institute of Policy Studies.

al-Alwani, Taha Jabir (1935) *Adab al-Ikhtilaf fi al-Islam*, trans. Abdul Wahid Hamid (2007) *The Ethics of Disagreement in Islam*, Herndon, VA: International Institute of Islamic Thought.

Arjomand, Said Amir (1999) 'The law, agency, and policy in medieval Islamic society: development of the institutions of learning from tenth to the fifteenth century', *Comparative Studies in Society and History*, 41(2): 263–93.

Asad, Talal (1986) *The Idea of an Anthropology of Islam*, Washington DC: Center for Contemporary Arab Studies, Georgetown University.

——(1993) *Genealogy of Religion*, Baltimore, MD: Johns Hopkins University Press.

Badie, Bertrand (1987), *Les Deux Etats: pouvoir et société en occident et en terre d'islam*, Paris: Fayard.

Bakhtin, M. M. (1990), 'Author and hero in aesthetic activity', in *Art and Answerability: Early Philosophical Essays* eds. Michael Holquist and Vadim Liapunov, and trans. Vadim Liapunov, pp. 4–256. Austin, TX: University of Texas Press.

Balandier, Georges. (1974) *Anthropo-logiques*, Paris: Presses Universitaire de France.

Bangash, Mumtaz A. (2005) 'FATA: towards a new beginning', in Cheema, Pervaiz Iqbal and Nuri, Maqsudul Hasan (eds) *Tribal Areas of Pakistan: Challenges and Responses*, Islambad: Islamabad Policy Research Institute.

Bangladesh Bureau of Educational Statistics (BANBEIS) (2006) *National Education Survey (Post-Primary)-2005 Final Report*, Dhaka: Ministry of Education.

Banglapedia National Encyclopedia of Bangladesh (2003) Dhaka: Asiatic Society of Bangladesh.

Banki, Purfard, and Amir, Husayn (eds.) (2002) *Ayine-i Zan*, Qom: Daftar-i Mutaliat wa Tahqiqat-i Zanan, Markaz-i Mudiriyat-i Hawzaha-i Ilmiyya-i Khaharan.

Bano, Masooda (2007) 'Beyond politics: the reality of a Deobandi madrasa in Pakistan', *Journal of Islamic Studies*, 18 (1): 43–68.

Barelvi, Saiyid Mustafa Ali (1980) *Musalmanan-e Suba-e Sarhad ki Talim*, Karachi: All Pakistan Educational Conference.

Basic Education and Policy Support (BEPS) Activity (2004) *Bangladesh Educational Assessment: Pre-primary and Primary Madrasah Education in Bangladesh*, United States Agency for International Development: Creative Associates International in collaboration with CARE, George Washington University and Ground Work.

Bayart, Jean-François (2007) *Global Subjects: A Political Critique of Globalisation*, Cambridge: Polity Press.

Berkey, Jonathan P. (1992a) *The Transmission of Knowledge in Medieval Cairo: A Social History of Islamic Education*, Princeton, NJ: Princeton University Press.

——(1992b) 'Women and Education in the Mamluk Period', in *Women in Middle Eastern History: Shifting Boundaries in Sex and Gender*, ed. Nikki Keddie and Beth Baron, New Haven, CT: Yale University Press, 1992: 143–57.

——(2003) *The Formation of Islam: Religion and Society in the Near East, 600–1800*, New York: Cambridge University Press.

——(2007) 'Madrasa, medieval and modern: politics, education, and the problem of Muslim identity', in Hefner W. Robert and Muhammad Qasim Zaman (eds) *Schooling Islam: The Culture and Politics of Modern Muslim Education*, Princeton, NJ: Princeton University Press.

Bilgrami, Akeel (1992) 'What is a Muslim? Fundamental commitment and cultural identity', *Critical Inquiry*, 18 (2): 821–42.

Boroujerdi, Mehrzad (1996), *Iranian Intellectuals and the West: The Tormented Triumph of Nativism*, Syracuse, NY: Syracuse University Press.

Bowen, John R. (1993) *Muslims through Discourses*, Princeton, NJ: Princeton University Press.

——(2003) *Islam, Law and Equality in Indonesia: An Anthropology of Public Reasoning*, Cambridge: Cambridge University Press.

Boyle, Helen N. (2004) 'Modernization of education and Kura'nic adaptation in Morocco', in Holger Daun and Geoffrey Walford (eds) *Educational Strategies among Muslims in the Context of Globalization*, Leiden: Brill.

——(2006) 'Memorization and learning in Islamic schools', *Comparative Education Review*, 50 (3): 478–95.

Bruinessen, Martin van (2008) 'Traditionalist and Islamist Pesantrens in contemporary Indonesia' in Farish A. Noor, Yoginder Sikand and Martin van Bruinessen (eds) (2008). *The Madrasa in Asia: Political Activism and Transnational Linkages*, Amsterdam: Amsterdam University Press.

Cheema, Pervaiz Iqbal and Nuri, Maqsudul Hasan (eds) (2005) *Tribal Areas of Pakistan: Challenges and Responses*, Islamabad: Islamabad Policy Research Institute.

Cooke, Miriam and Lawrence, Bruce B. (2005) *Muslim Networks from Hajj to Hip Hop*, Chapel Hill, NC and London: University of North Carolina Press.

Cornell, Vincent J. (1998) *Realm of the Saint: Power and Authority in Moroccan Sufism*, Austin, TX: University of Texas.

Cui Xiangsu and Lao Kaisheng 崔相肃, 劳凯声 (1995) *Jiaoyufa Shimu Quanshu* 『教育法事务全书』 (Book on Educational Law), Beijing: Yuhan Chubanshe 宇航出版社.

Daftar-i Mutaliat wa Tahqiqat-i Zanan (n.d.) *Rayhana*, Qom: Daftar-i Mutaliat wa Tahqiqat-i Zanan.

——(2006) *Haura : mahnama-i ilmi: farhangi wa ijtimai-i zanan*, Qom: Daftar-i Mutariat wa Ijtimai-i Zanan, 21: 10–11.

Datta, Pradip Kumar (1999) *Carving Blocs: Communal Ideology in Early Twentieth Century Bengal*, New Delhi: Oxford University Press.

Deoband, Darul-Uloom (2007) 'The track (Maslak) of Darul Uloom', available online at: <http://darululoom-deoband.com/english/index.htm> (accessed 25 January 2007).

Ding Guoyong 丁国勇 (1992) 'Huizu nüzi jiaoyu de xingban yu fazhan' 「回族女子教育的兴办与发展」 (Initiation and development of Hui girls' education), in Guojia bawu zhexue shehui kexue zhongdian keti<Nongcun nütong jiaoyu xianzhuang wenti ji duice yanjiu>ketizu 国家八五哲学社会科学重点课题＜农村女童教育现状问题及对策研究＞课题组 (The 8th national five-year plan key theme team about philosophy and social science) <Research of problem and counter measure of girl education in rural area>)

(ed.) *Nüzi Jiaoyu Yanjiu Wenxian Ciliaoji*, 『女子教育研究文献资料集』(Collection of Documents on Women's Education) Internal document.

—— 丁国勇 (ed.) (1993) *Ningxia Huizu* 『宁夏回族』(Hui People in Ningxia), Yinchuan: Ningxia Renmin Chubanshe 宁夏人民出版社

Dorronsoro, Gilles (2005) *Revolution Unending: Afghanistan, 1979 to the present*, trans. J. King, London and New York: Hurst and Columbia University Press.

Durrrani, Abd al-Wajed (ed.) (2002) *Madaris Dinya Dairiktari*, Lahore: Wafaq al-Madaris al-Shia.

Eaton, Richard M. (1994) *The Rise of Islam and the Bengal Frontier, 1204–1760*. Delhi: Oxford University Press.

Eickelman, Dale F. (1978), 'The art of memory: Islamic education and its social reproduction', *Comparative Studies in Society and History*, 20(4): 485–516.

——(1979) 'The political economy of the meaning', *American Ethnologist* 6 (2): 386–93.

——(1982) 'The study of Islam in local contexts', *Contributions to Asian Studies*, 17: 1–16.

——(1985) *Knowledge and Power in Morocco: The Education of a Twentieth Century Notable*. Princeton, NJ: Princeton University Press.

——(1987) 'Rapport de séminaire de l'IIPE, Paris, 10–12 decembre 1984', in *Les formes traditionnelles d'education et la diversification du champ éducatif: le cas des écoles coraniques*, pp. 81–112. Paris: Institut International de Planification de l'Education.

——(1992) 'Mass higher education and the religious imagination in contemporary Arab societies', *American Ethnologist*, 19 (4): 643–55.

——(2007) 'Madrasas in Morocco: their vanishing public role', in Hefner W. Robert and Muhammad Qasim Zaman (eds) *Schooling Islam: The Culture and Politics of Modern Muslim Education*, Princeton, NJ: Princeton University Press.

——(2008) 'Gender and religion in the public and private spheres', Kazuo Ohtsuka and Dale F. Eickelman (eds) *Crossing Boundaries: Gender, the Public, and the Private in Contemporary Muslim Societies*, Tokyo: Research Institute for Languages and Cultures of Asia and Africa.

——(2009) 'Afterword: re-reading Bourdieu on Kabylia in the twenty-first century', in Jane E. Goodman and Paul A. Silverstein (eds) *Bourdieu in Algéria: Colonial Politics, Ethnographic Practices, Theoretical Developments*, Lincoln, NB: University of Nebraska Press.

Eickelman, Dale F. and Anderson, Jon W. (eds) (2003) *New Media in the Muslim World*, Bloomington, IN: Indiana University Press.

Eickelman, Dale F. and Piscatori, James (eds) (1990) *Muslim Travellers: Pilgrimage, Migration, and the Religious Imagination*, Berkeley, CA: University of California Press.

——(1996) *Muslim Politics*, Princeton, CA: Princeton University Press.

Eickelman, Dale F. and Salvatore, Armando (2004) 'Muslim publics', in Armando Salvatore and Dale F. Eickelman (eds) *Public Islam and the Common Good*, Leiden: Brill.

El-Guindi, Fadwa (1999) *Veil: Modesty, Privacy and Resistance*, New York: Berg.

Elias, Norbert. (1978) *What is Sociology*, New York: Columbia University Press.

Fair, C. Christine (2008) *The Madrassah Challenge: Militancy and Religious Education in Pakistan*, Lahore: Vanguard Books.

Faruqi, Ziyaul Hasan (1963) *The Deoband School and the Demand for Pakistan*. N e w Delhi: Asia Publishing House.

Fischer, Michael M.J. (1980) *Iran: From Religious Dispute to Revolution*, Cambridge, MA: Harvard University Press.

Friedmann, Yohanan(2003/1989) (1989) *Prophecy Continuous: Aspects of Ahmadi Religious Thought and its Mediaeval Background*, Berkeley, CA: University of California Press.

Gaudiosi, Monica M. (1988) 'The influence of the Islamic law of waqf on the development of the trust in England: the case of Merton College', *Law Review*, 136: 1231–61.

Geaves, Ron (2005) 'Tradition, innovation, and authentication: replicating the "Ahl as Sunna wa Jamaat" in Britain', *Comparative Islamic Studies*, 1(1): 1–20.

Geertz, Cliford (1960) 'The Javanese Kijaji: the changing role of cultural broker', *Comparative Studies in Society and History*, 2(2): 228–49.

Gellens, Sam I. (1990) 'The search for knowledge in medieval Muslim societies: A comparative approach', in Dale F. Eickelman and James Piscatori (eds) *Muslim Travellers: Pilgrimage, Migration, and the Religious Imagination*, Berkeley, CA: University of California Press.

Ghiyasi, Ghulam Riza (1383/2004–5) *Talim wa Tarbiyat dar Islam wa Hawza-i Ilmiyya*, Iran: Intisharat-i Bayan al-Haqq.

Goodman, Jane E. and Silverstein, Paul A. (eds) (2009) *Bourdieu in Algéria: Colonial Politics, Ethnographic Practices, Theoretical Developments*, Lincoln, NB: University of Nebraska Press.

Graham, William A. (1993) 'Traditionalism in Islam: an essay in interpretation', *Journal of Interdisciplinary History*, 13 (3): 495–522.

Gul, Imtiaz (2008). 'Afghanistan Imbroglio: implication for Pakistan's tribal areas', *Policy Perspectives*, 5(2): 67–86.

Hairu Nüzi Zhongxue (1996) *Hairu Nüzi Zhongxue Xiaoyoulu*『海如女子中学校友录』(Roster of graduates of Hairu Girls' Junior High School), Tongxin: Hairu Nüzi Zhongxue.

Haroon, Sana (2008) 'The rise of Deobandi Islam in the north-west frontier province and its implications in colonial India and Pakistan 1914–1996', *Journal of Royal Asiatic Society*, Series 3, 19: 47–70.

Harris, Winifred (1947) 'Moslem womanhood', typed manuscript April 30 (SOAS, CIM PP2, Botham Papers 1939–52).

Hartung, Jan-Peter (2006) 'The Nadwat al-'ulama': chief patron of *Madrasa* education in India and a turntable to the Arab world', in Jan-Peter Hartung and Helmut Reifeld (eds) *Islamic Education, Diversity and National Identity*, New Delhi: Sage.

Hartung, Jan-Peter and Reifeld, Helmut (2006) *Islamic Education, Diversity and National Identity*, New Delhi: Sage.

Hashmi, Saiyid Matin (1987) 'Dars Nizami men Tabdili ka Masala' in Institute of Policy Studies (ed.) *Dini Madaris ka Nizam-e Talim*, Islamabad: Institute of Policy Studies.

Hefner, Robert W. (2007) 'Introduction: the culture, politics and future of Muslim education', in Robert W. Hefner and Muhammad Qasim Zaman (eds) *Schooling Islam: the Culture and Politics of Modern Muslim Education*, Princeton, NJ and Oxford: Princeton University Press.

Hefner, Robert W. and Zaman, Muhammad Qasim (eds) (2007) *Schooling Islam: The Culture and Politics of Modern Muslim Education*, Princeton, NJ: Princeton University Press.

Herrera, Linda (2006) 'Islamization and education: between politics, profit, and pluralism' in Linda Herrera and Carlos Alberto Torres (eds) *Cultures of Arab Schooling: Critical Ethnographies from Egypt*, Albany, NY: State University of New York Press.

Herrera, Linda and Torres, Carlos Alberto (eds) (2006) *Cultures of Arab Schooling: Critical Ethnographies from Egypt*, Albany, NY: State University of New York Press.

Hodgson, Marshall G.S. (1974) *The Venture of Islam: Conscience and History in a World Civilization*, vol.1, Chicago, IL: University of Chicago Press.

Holland, Dorothy, Lachicotte Jr., W., Skinner, D. and Cain, C. (1998) *Identity and Agency in Cultural Worlds*, Cambridge, MA: Harvard University Press.

Hoodfar, Homa (2004) 'Families on the move: the changing role of Afghan refugee women in Iran', *Hawwa*, 2(2): 141–71.

——(2007) 'Women, religion and the Afghan education movement in Iran', *Journal of Development Studies*, 43(2): 265–93.

Hoodfar, Homa and Sadr, Shadi (2009) 'Can women act as agents of a democratization of theocracy in Iran?', Final Research Report prepared for the project Religion, Politics and Gender Equality, United Nations Research Institute for Social Development (UNRISD) and Heinrich-Böll-Stiftung. 1–37.

Huq, Maimuna (2008) 'Reading the Quran in Bangladesh: the politics of "Belief" among Islamist women', *Modern Asian Studies*, 42 (2–3): 457–88.

Hussain, Syed Iftikhar (2005) 'Inaugural address', in Cheema, Pervaiz Iqbal and Nuri, Maqsudul Hasan (eds), *Tribal Areas of Pakistan: Challenges and Responses*, Islamabad: Islamabad Policy Research Institute.

Hussain, Syed Talat (2001) 'Breeding ground of extremisms', in *Dawn* (Karachi), 3 December.

Institute of Policy Studies (2002) *Pakistan: Religious Education Institutions—An Overview*, Islamabad: Institute of Policy Studies.

International Crisis Group (2002) *Pakistan: Madrasas Extremism and the Military*, ICG Asia Report No.36, July.

Jalal, Ayesha (2008) *Partisans of Allah: Jihad in South Asia*, Lahore: Sang-e Meel Publications.

Jamiat al-Zahra (2006–7) *Prospectus for Full and Part-time Entry for Overseas Students 2006–2007*, Qom: Deputy of International Affairs, Jamiat al-Zahra.

Jaschok, Maria and Shui, Jingjun (2000) *The History of Women's Mosques in Chinese Islam*, London: Curzon Press.

Kakakhel, S. Siyah al-Din (1987) 'Dars Nizami: nisab men tabdili?', in *Dini Madaris ka Nizam-e Talim*, Islamabad: Institute of Policy Studies.

Kakar, Hasan K. (1979) *Government and Society in Afghanistan: The Reign of Amir 'Abd al-Rahman Khan*. Austin, TX: University of Texas Press (Modern Middle East Series 5).

Kakar, M. Hassan (1995) *Afghanistan: The Soviet Invasion and the Afghan Response, 1979–1982*, Berkeley, CA: University of California Press.

Kamalkhani, Zahra (1998) *Women's Islam: Religious Practice Among Women in Today's Iran*, London: Kegan Paul International.

Kasemi, Maulana Muhammad Ali Akbar (2005), *Buda'atider Kotipoi Prosner Jabab* (Responses to some Questions of Bidaatis), Nabinagar, Brahmanbaria: collected from YM office.

Katouzian, Muhammad Ali Homayoun (1382/2003) *Darbara-i Jamalzada wa Jamalzada-shinasi* (Jamalzadeh and Jamalzadehlogy), Tehran: Nashr-i Shahab.

Kazmi, Sayyid Muhammad Saqalain (ed.) (2004) *Imamiyah Dini Madaris Pakistan*, Lahore: Wafaq al-Madaris al-Shia, Pakistan.

Keddie, Nikki R. (ed.) (1978) *Scholars, Saints, and Sufis: Muslim Religious Institutions*, Berkeley, CA: University of California Press.

Kepel, Gilles and Richard, Yann (eds) (1990) *Intellectuels et militants de l'Islam contemporain*, Paris: Seuil.

Keddie N.and Baron B. (ed.)(1992) *Women in Middle Eastern History: Shifting Boundaries in Sex and Gender*, New Haven, CT: Yale University Press.

Khadija 罕戈 (1994) 'Nüxing de shiming' 「女性的使命」 (Missions of women), *Peilei* 『蓓蕾』 1: 2.

Khalid, Salim Mansur (2002) *Dini Madaris men Talim*, Islamabad: Institute of Policy Studies.

Khan, Azmat Hayat (2005) 'FATA (Federally Administrated Tribal / Areas of Pakistan)', in Pervaiz Iqbal Cheema and Maqsudul Hasan Nuri (eds) *Tribal Areas of Pakistan: Challenges and Responses*, Islamabad: Islamabad Policy Research Institute.

Khan, Rashid Ahmad (2005) 'Political developments in FATA: a critical perspective', in Pervaiz Iqbal Cheema and Maqsudul Hasan Nuri (eds) *Tribal Areas of Pakistan: Challenges and Responses*, Islamabad: Islamabad Policy Research Institute.

—— (2008) 'FATA after Independence: 1947–2001' in *Federally Administrated Tribal Areas of Pakistan*, Islamabad: Islamabad Policy Research Institute.

Kramer, Martin (ed.) *Shi'ism, Resistance, and Revolution*, Boulder, CO: Westview Press.

Lagrée, Michel (1992) *Religion et cultures en Bretagne 1850–1950*, Paris: Fayard.

Laycock. (n.d.) 'Little Chinese girls learning Arabic in a Lanchow mosque' (CIM photograph File 286) London: SOAS.

Levitt, Peggy (2001) *The Transnational Villagers*, Berkeley, CA: University of California Press.

Lewis, Bernard (1988) *The Political Language of Islam*, Chicago, IL: University of Chicago Press.

Li Xiaojiang李小江 (2005) 'Zhongguo nüxing xue de guoji ziyuan yu benduhua wenti yanjiu' 「中国女性学的国际资源与本土化问题研究」 *Yunnan Minzu Daxuebao* 『云南民族大学报』 22 (1): 31–7.

Li Xinghua 李兴华 (2008) 'Weizhou Yisilanjiao Yanjiu' 「韦州伊斯兰教研究」 (Research of Islam in Weizhou), *Huizu Yanjiu* 『回族研究』, 2: 73–88.

Li Xinghua, Chen Huibin, Feng Jinyuan and Sha Qiuzhen (李兴华、秦惠彬、冯近源、沙秋真) (eds) (1998) *Zhongguo Yisilanjiao Shi* 『中国伊斯兰教史』 (The History of Islam in China), Beijing: Zhongguo Shehui Kexue Chubanshe.

Li Zongdao 李宗道, Wang Kelin 王克林 (2000) 'Tongxin xian de Huizu jiaoyu' 「同心县的回族教育」 (Hui education in Tongxin prefecture), *Huizu Yanjiu* 『回族研究』, 3: 62–4.

Louër, Laurence (2008) *Transnational Shia Politics: Religious and Political Networks in the Gulf*, New York: Columbia University Press.

Majidi, Musa (1986) 'Tarikhcha-i mukhtasar-i kitabha-i darsi wa sayr-i tahawwul-i an dar Iran', *Faslnama-i Taalim wa Tarbiyat*, 1 (4): 65–95.

Makdisi, George (1981) *The Rise of Colleges: Institutions of Learning in Islam and the West*, Edinburgh: Edinburgh University Press.

Madrase-i Ali-i Shahid Bint al-Huda (2006–7, 2007–8) *Huda: faslnama-i farhangi wa ijtimai*, Qom: Madrase-i Ali-i Shahid Bint al-Huda.

Ma Lan 马兰 (2001) *Xibu Zhonghun* 『西部忠魂』 (The spirit of the Northwest) Hongkong: Yinhe Chubenshe 银河出版社.

Malik, Jamal (1998) *Colonialization of Islam: Dissolution of Traditional Institutions in Pakistan*, New Delhi: Monohar.

——(1999) *Colonialization of Islam: Dissolution of Traditional Institutions in Pakistan*, Dhaka: The University Press Limited.

Malik, Jamal (ed.) (2008) *Madrasas in South Asia: Teaching Terror?*, New York: Routledge.

Mallat, Chibli (1993) *The Renewal of Islamic Law: Muhmmad Baqer as-sadr, Najaf and the Shi'i international*, Cambridge: Cambridge University Press.

Ma Qiang 马强 (2003) 'Funü jiaoyu yu wenhua zijue—Linxia Zhong-A nüxiao ge-an diaoyan' 妇女教育与文化自觉—临夏中阿女校个案调研 (Female education and women's cultural awareness—a study on Linxia women's Islamic school), *Zhongguo Musilin* 『中国穆斯林』 (China Muslims), No. 1, <http://islambook.net/xueshu/list.asp?id-1951> (accessed 10 November 2006).

Markaz-i Jahani-i Ulum-i Islami (2007) *Shinasan*, Qom: Markaz-i Jahani-i Ulum-i Islami.

Markaz-i Mudiriyat-i Hawzaha-i Ilmiyya-i Khaharan (1383–4/2004–5) *Rahnama-i Pazirish-i Nizam-i Amuzashi Tamam Vaqt: madaris-i ilmiyya-i khahran*, Qom: Markaz-i Mudiriyat-i Hawzaha-i Ilmiyya-i Khaharan.

Ma Shinian 马士年 (1988) 'Shitan Tang-Song shiqu Yisilanjiao zai woguo dongnan diqu de chuanbo', 「试谈唐宋时期伊斯兰教在我国东南地区的传播」 (A Study on the spread of Islam in southeast China during the Tang and Song period), in Zhongguo Yisilanjiao Yanjiu Wenji (ed.) *Zhongguo Yislanjiao Yanji Wenji*, 『中国伊斯兰教研究文集』 (Studies on Islam in China), Yinchuan: Ningxia Renmin Chubanshe 宁夏人民出版社

Matsumoto, Masumi (1999) *Chuugoku Minzoku Seisaku no Kenkyuu* (A Study on China's Policy toward Ethnic Minorities) Tokyo: Taga Shuppan.

——(2001) 'Chuugoku seihoku ni okeru Islam fukkou to joshi kyouiku: Rinka chuu-a jogaku to Ishuu chuu-a jogaku wo reitoshite' (Islamic revival and women's education in the Northwest China) *Keiwa Gakuen Daigaku Kenkyuu Kiyou* (*Bulletin of Keiwa College*), 10: 145–70.

Mawdudi, Abul Ala (1988/1977) *Towards Understanding Islam*, trans. and ed. Khurshid Ahmad, Lahore: Idara Tarjuman-ul-Quran.

Ma Xinlan 马新兰 (1995) 'Wo yu Huizu nütong jiaoyu', in Yang Liwen (ed.) *Chuangzao Pingdeng* 『创造平等』 (Create equality), Beijing: Minzu Chubanshe 民族出版社 (Nationality Press).

McFarland, Stephen L. (1985) 'Anatomy of an Iranian Political Crowd: The Tehran Bread Riot of December 1942,' *International Journal of Middle East Studies* 17 (no. 1, February): 51–65.

Meijie 梅洁 (1999) *Chuang Shiji Qingsu: Laizi Zhongguo Xibu Nütong Jiaoyu de Baogao* 『创世纪情愫－来自中国西部女童教育的报告』 (*Creating True Feeling－Report of Girls' Education in Western District of China*), Shijiazhuang: Hebei Jiaoyu Chubanshe 河北教育出版社.

Menashri, David (1992) *Education and the Making of Modern Iran*, Ithaca, NY: Cornell University Press.

Merry, Michael S. (2007) *Culture, Identity and Islamic Schooling: A Philosophical Approach*, New York: Palgrave Macmillan.

Messick, Brinkley (1988) 'Kissing hands and knees: hegemony and hierarchy in Shari'a discourse', *Law & Society Review*, 22 (4): 637–59.

Messick, Brinkley (2005) 'Madhabs and modernities', in Peri Bearman, Rudolph Peters and Frank Vogel (eds) *The Islamic School of Law: Evolution, Devolution, and Progress*, Cambridge, CA: Harvard University Press.

Metcalf, Barbara Daly (1982) *Islamic Revival in British India: Deoband 1860–1900*, Princeton, NJ: Princeton University Press.

——(2007) 'Madrasas and minorities in secular India', in Robert W. Hefner and Muhammad Qasim Zaman (eds) *Schooling Islam: The Culture and Politics of Modern Muslim Education*, Princeton, NJ: Princeton University Press.

Mir-Hosseini, Ziba (1999) *Islam and Gender: The Religious Debate in Contemporary Iran*, Princeton, NJ: Princeton University Press.

——(2002) 'Religious modernists and the "woman question": challenges and complicities', in Eric Hooglund (ed.) *Twenty Years of Islamic Revolution: Political and Social Transition in Iran since 1979*, New York: Syracuse University Press.

Momen, Moojan (1985) *An Introduction to Shi'i Islam: The History and Doctrines of Twelver Shi'ism*, New Haven, CT: Yale University Press.

Monsutti, Alessandro (2005) *War and Migration: Social Networks and Economic Strategies of the Hazaras of Afghanistan*. London: Routledge.

——(2004) *Guerres et migrations: réseaux sociaux et stratégies économiques des Hazaras d'Afghanistan*, Neuchâtel and Paris: Institut d'ethnologie et Maison des sciences de l'homme.

Mottahedeh, Roy P. (1985) *The Mantle of the Prophet: Religion and Politics in Iran*, New York: Simon and Schuster.

——(1998) 'Traditional shi'ite education in Qom', in Amelie Oksenberg Rorty (ed.) *Philosophers on Education: New Historical Perspectives*, London: Routledge.

Mousavi, Sayed Askar (1985) *The Hazaras of Afghanistan: An Historical, Cultural, Economic and Political Study*, Richmond: Curzon.

Muassisa-i Amuzishi-i Imam Khumayni (1980/2001) *Mashahir-i tashayyu dar Afghanistan* (Shia celebrities in Afghanistan), Jild-i duwwum, Qom: Muassiasa-i amuzishi-i Imam Khumayni.

Muhammad Qutb 穆罕默德 · 古图布 (n.d.) *Ershi shiji mengmei zhuyi* 『二十世紀蒙昧主義』 (Jahiliya of the twentieth century) Internal document.

——穆罕默德 · 古图布 (1995) 'Yisilan he funü ' (Islam and women) trans. Anonymous, in *Musilin Funü* 『穆斯林妇女』 No. 6, July 24.

Munir, Ahmed D. (1987) 'The Shi'is of Pakistan', in Martin Kramer (ed.) *Shi'ism, Resistance, and Revolution*, Boulder, CO: Westview Press.

Mutahheri, Allamah Murtaza (1992) *Women and Her Rights*, trans. M.A. Ansari, Accra: Islamic Seminary Publications.

Nakash, Yitzhak (1994) *The Shi'is of Iraq*, Princeton, NJ: Princeton University Press.

Nasr, Seyyad Hossein (1987) *Traditional Islam in the Modern World*, London: KPI.

Nasr, S.V.R. (1994) *The Vanguard of the Islamic Revolution: the Jama'at-i Islami of Pakistan*, Berkeley, CA: University of California Press.

——(2000a) 'International politics, domestic imperatives, and identity mobilization, sectarianism in Pakistan, 1979–1998', *Comparative Politics*, 32 (2):171–90.

——(2000b) 'The rise of Sunni militancy in Pakistan: the changing role of Islamism and the ulama in society and politics', *Modern Asian Studies*, 34(1): 139–80.

Ningxia Huizu Zizhiqu Tongjiju, Guojia Tongjiju Ningxia Diaochadui 宁夏回族自治区统计局，国家统计局宁夏调查 (2008) *Ningxia Tongji Nianjian 2008* 『宁夏统计年鉴』 (Statistics of Ningxia 2008), Beijing: Zhongguo Tongji Chubanshe.

Ningxia jiaokesuo guojia nütong jiaoyu yanjiu ketizu 宁夏教科所国家女童教育研究课题组(National project team of research on girl's education, Research Institute of Educational Science in Ningxia) (ed.) (1992) *Ayu Liangbaiju (Shiyong-ben)* 『阿语二百句(试用本)』 (Arabic 200 Sentences <Trial edition>), Yinchuan: Ningxia Jiaokesuo 宁夏教科所.

Ningxia Jiaoyu Kexue Yanjiusuo 宁夏教育科学研究所 (Ningxia Institute for Education and Science). (ed.) (2001) *Ningxia Nütong Jiaoyu Zhiliang yu Xiaoyi Yanjiu* 1997–2000 『宁夏女童教育质量与效益研究 (1997–2000)』 (Research of quality and effect about girl education in Ningxia), Yinchuan: Ningxia Jiaoyu Kexue Yanjiusuo. 宁夏教育科学研究所.

Ningxia nütong jiaoyu yanjiu ketizu宁夏女童教育研究课题组 (Research team of girls' education in Ningxia) (1995) 'Ningxia pinkun diqu Huizu nütong jiaoyu de yanjiu baogao' 「宁夏贫困地区回族女童教育的研究报告」 (Report on education of Hui girl on poor area in Ningxia), *Zhongguo Xibu Nütong Xingdong Yanjiu* 『中国西部女 童教育行动研究』 (Action research on girl education in western China), Yinchuan: Ningxia Renmin Chubanshe 宁夏人民出版社.

Noor, Farish A., Sikand, Yoginder and Bruinessen, Martin van. (eds) (2008) *The Madrasa in Asia: Political Activism and Transnational Linkages*, Amsterdam: Amsterdam University Press.

Olesen, Asta (1995) *Islam and Politics in Afghanistan*, Richmond: Curzon Press.

Olszewska, Zuzanna (2007) 'A desolate voice: poetry and identity among young Afghan refugees in Iran', *Iranian Studies*, 40(2): 203–24.

Pakdaman, Nasser (1380/2001) *Qatl-i Kasrawi* (Kasravi's Murder), Germany: Intisharat-i Furugh.

Pasandideh, Mohammad (1385/2006), *Hawza-i Ilmiyya-i Khurasan. jild-i awwal:, madaris-i ilmiyya-i Mashhad* (Religious school in Khorasan. vol. 1, Madrasa in Mashhad), Mashhad: Bunyad-i Pazhuhishha-i Islami.

Paygah-i Ittilarasani-i Hawza-i Ilmiyya-i Qum (1380/2001), *Bashir 80: Rahnama-i Jama-i Muassasat-i Farhangi-i Islami-i Ustan-i Qum*, Qom: Intisharat-i Markaz-i Mudiriyat-i Hawza-i Ilmiyya-i Qum.

Pickens Collection (1934–5) 'Muslim girls and boys with hornbooks' (photograph), Archive of Harvard Yenching Library. <http://via.lib.harvard.edu/via/deliver/chunkDisplay?_collection=via&inoID=219500&recordNumber=41&chunkNumber=1&method=view&image=full&startChunkNum=1&endChunkNum=1&totalChunkCount=1&offset=0> (accessed 12 August 2008).

Prothom Alo, (2006) April 3, Dhaka

Qiu Shusen 邱树森 (1996) *Zhongguo Huizu Shi* 『中国回族史』 (History of the Hui in China), Yinchuan: Ningxia Renmin Chubanshe. 宁夏人民出版社

Qureshi, Rashida and Rarieya, F.A. Jane (eds) (2007) *Gender and Education in Pakistan*, Oxford: Oxford University Press.

Rabita al-Madaris al-Islamiya Pakistan (n.d.) *Dastur aur Nisab-e Ta'lim*, Lahore: (n.p.).

Rahman, Khalid and Bukhari, S. Rashad (2005) 'Religious education institutions (REIs): present situation and the future strategy', *Policy Perspectives*, 2(1): 55–82.

Rahman, Tariq (2004) *Denizens of Alien Worlds: A Study of Education, Inequality and Polarization in Pakistan*, Karachi: Oxford University Press.

——(2008) 'Madrasas: the potential for violence in Pakistan?', in Jamal Malik (ed.) *Madrasas in South Asia: Teaching Terror?*, Londond: Routledge.

Rais, Rasul Bakhsh (1994) *War without Winners*, Karachi: OUP.

Raju, Zakir Hossain (2008) 'Madrasa and Muslim identity on screen: nation, Islam and Bangladeshi art cinema on the global stage', in Jamal Malik (ed.) *Madrasas in South Asia: Teaching Terror?*, London: Routledge.

Reichmuth, Stefan (2000) '"Netzwerk" und "Weltsystem": Konzepte zur neuzeitlichen "Islamichen Welt" und ihrer Transformation,' *Saeculum* 51(2): 267–93.

Riaz, Ali (2005) *Global Jihad, Sectarianism and the Madrassahs in Pakistan*, Singapore: Institute of Defence and Strategic Studies.

——(2008) *Faithful Education: Madrassahs in South Asia*, New Brunswick, NJ: Rutgers University Press.

Robinson, Francis (1993) 'Technology and religious change: Islam and the impact of print', *Modern Asian Studies*, 27(1): 229-251.

——(2000) *Islam and Muslim History in South Asia*, New Delhi: Oxford University Press.

——(2001) *The 'Ulama of Farangi Mahall and Islamic Culture in South Asia*, London: Hurst & Company.

Rohani, Taherhe and Hoseyni, Halima (1381/2002) *Azadi wa Irada-I Iinsan dar Kalam-i Islami* (Freedom and Will in the Islamic Words), Qom: Markaz-i Jahani-i Ulum-i Islami (World Centre for Islamic Sciences).

Rostamy-Povery, Elaheh (2007) 'Gender, agency and identity, the case of Afghan women in Afghanistan, Pakistan and Iran', *Journal of Development Studies*, 43(2): 294–311.

Roy, Asim (1983) *The Islamic Syncretistic Tradition in Bengal*, Dhaka: Academic Publishers.

——(1995) *Généalogie de l'islamisme*, Paris: Hachette

——(2002) *L'Islam mondialisé,* Paris: Le Seuil.

——(2005) *La laïcité face à l'islam*, Paris: Stock.

Roy, Olivier (1985) *L'Afghanistan: Islam et modernité politique*, Paris: Seuil.

Rubin, Barnett R. (1995) *The Search for Peace in Afghanistan—From Buffer State to Failed State*, New Haven, CT: Yale University Press.

Sabrina, Mervin (2007), *Les mondes chiites et l'Iran,* Paris: Karthala.

Safdari, Mehrab Ali (1384/2006) '*Ruhaniyyat wa hukumat dar Afghanistan: Zaminiha, mavani wa rahkarha* (The Clergy and the Political System in Afghanistan)', unpublished masters thesis, Qom: Markaz-i Jahani-i Ulum-i Islami (World Centre for Islamic Sciences).

Sakurai, Keiko (2004) 'University entrance examination and the making of an Islamic society in Iran: a study of the post-revolutionary Iranian approach to konkur', *Iranian Studies*, 37(3): 385–406.

Saleem, H. Ali (2008) 'Pakistani madrasas and rural underdevelopment: an empirical study of Ahmedpur east', in Malik, Jamal (ed.) *Madrasas in South Asia: Teaching Terror?*, London: Routledge.

——(2009) *Islam and Education: Conflict and Conformity in Pakistan's Madrassahs*, Oxford: Oxford University Press.

Salvatore, Armando and Eickelman, Dale F. (eds) (2004) *Public Islam and the Common Good*, Leiden: Brill.

Sanyal, Usha (1996) *Devotional Islam and Politics in British India: Ahmad Riza Khan Barelwi and his Movement*, New Delhi: Oxford University Press.

Sanyal, Usha (1998) 'Generational changes in the leadership of the Ahl-e Sunnat movement of North India in the twentieth century', *Modern Asian Studies*, 32 (3): 635–56.

——(2008) 'Ahl-i Sunnat madrasas: the madrasas Manzar-i Islam, Bareilly and Jamia Ashrafiyya, Mubarakpur', in Jamal Malik (ed.) *Madrasas in South Asia: Teaching Terror?* London: Routledge.

Schimmel, Annemarie (2003) *Islam in the Indian Subcontinent*, Lahore: Sang-e-Meel Publications.

Shahibzadeh, Yadullah (2008), *From Totalism to Perspectivisme, An Intellectual History of Iranian Islamisme From Shariati to the Advent of Kahtami*, Oslo: Faculty of Humanities (University of Oslo).

Scott, James C. (1976) *The Moral Economy of the Peasant*. New Haven, CT: Yale University Press.

Shimbo, Atsuko (1995) 'Chuugoku ni okeru joji mishuugaku mondai: Neika kaizoku jichiku wo megutte' (Problems of Girls' School Enrolment in China: Focusing on Ningxia). *Gakujutsu Kenkyu* 43: 1–13.

——(2007) 'Globalization no moto deno Chuugoku Musim josei shidousha: koukyouiku to shuukyo kyoiku no hikaku kentou' (An examination about female education leaders of Muslim women in China under globalization: Comparison and discussion between public education and religious education), *Gakujutu Kenkyu*, 55: 1–10.

Shinwari, Naveed Ahmad (2008) *Understanding FATA: Attitudes Towards Governance, Religion and Society in Pakistan's Federally Administrated Tribal Areas*, Islamabad: CAMP.

Shirkhani, Ali and Zari Abbas (1384–6) *Tahawwulut-i Hawza-i Ilmiyya-i Qum*, Tehran: Markaz-i Asnad-i Inqilab-i Islami.

Shoushtari, Mir Abd ol-Latif Khan. (1363/1984) *Tuhfat al-Alam*, Tehran: Tahuri.

Sikand, Yoginder (2005) *Bastions of the Believers: Madrasas and Islamic Education in India*, New Delhi: Penguin Books.

Statistical Centre of Iran (2004–5) *Iran Statistical Year Book 1383*, Iran: Statistical Centre of Iran.

Taleghany , M.A.R. (trans.) (1995) *The Civil Code of Iran*, Littleton, CO: Fred B. Rothman & Company.

Taylor, Charles (1989) *Sources of the Self: The Making of the Modern Identity*, Cambridge, MA: Harvard University Press.

Teepu Mahabat Khan (2008) *The Tribal Areas of Pakistan: A Contemporary Profile*, Lahore: Sang-e Meel Publications.

Thompson, Edward P. (1963) *The Making of the English Working Class*, London: Victor Gollancz.

——(1971) 'The moral economy of the English crowd in the eighteenth century,' *Past and Present* 50: 76–136.

——(1993) *Customs in Common*, New York: The New Press.

Tijani Tunisi, Muhammad (1383/2004) *Ahl-i Sunnat-i Waqii* (True Sunni), Qom: Bunyad-i Maarif-i Islami.

Tongxinxian jiaoyuzhi bianzuan xiaozu/Tongxinxian jiaoyuju 同心县教育志 · 同心县教育局 (Editorial team of educational history of Tongxin prefecture and department of education in Tongxin government) (ed.) (1991) *Tongxin Xian Jiaoyuzhi* 『同心县教育志1880–1990』 (History of Education in Tongxin Prefecture from 1880–1990), Tongxin: Tongxinxian Jiaoyuju. 同心县教育局

Torab, Azam (2002) 'The politicization of women's religious circles in post-revolutionary Iran', in Sarah Ansari and Vanessa Martin (eds) *Women, Religion and Culture in Iran*, Richmond: Curzon.

Troeltsch, Ernst (1912) *Protestantism and Progress: The Significance of Protestantism for the Rise of the Modern World*, London and New York: Williams and Norgate, J.P. Puttnam's Sons.

Tsukamoto, K. (2006) 'Rapid increase of Muslim merchants—Yiwu, China', *Asahi Shinbun*, 24 May.

Uddin, Sufia M. (2006) *Constructing Bangladesh: Religion, Ethnicity, and Language in an Islamic Nation*, Chapel Hill, NC: University of North Carolina Press.

Veyne, Paul (2007) *Quand notre monde est devenu chrétien* (312-394), Paris: Editions Albin Michel.

Wadud, Amina (2006) *Inside the Gender Jihad: Women's Reform in Islam*, Oxford: Oneworld.

Walbridge, John (2001) 'Muhammad-Baqir al-Sadr: The Search for New Foundations', in Linda S. Walbridge (ed.) *The Most Learned of the Shi'a*, Oxford: Oxford University Press.

Wang Jianxin王建新 (2001) 'Seihoku chihou no Kaizoku—keizai hatten wo meguru minzoku to shuukyou no yukue' (Muslims in the Northwest—ethnicity and religion in the economic development), in Sasaki Nobuaki (ed.), *Gendai Chugoku no minzoku to keizai* (Ethnicities and Economics in Contemporary China) Tokyo: Shakai Shisousha.

Wang Zhengming王正明 and Tao Hong陶红 (2003) *Houtu—Xihaigu de Huihui men* 『厚土：西海固的回回们』 (Piled Land—Hui in Xiji, Haiyuan, Guyuan of Ningxia), Yinchuan: Ningxia Renmin Chubanshe.

Wickham, C. Rosefsky (2002) *Mobilizing Islam: Religion, Activism and Political Change in Egypt*, New York: Columbia University Press.

Wiktorowicz, Quintan (2004) *Islamic Activism: A Social Movement Theory Approach*, Bloomington, IN: Indiana University Press.

Witte, Griff (2010) 'Poor schooling slows anti-terrorism effort in Pakistan,' *Washington Post*, January 17, p. A10.

Xibu sishengqu nütong jiaoyu yanjiu zonghe ketizu 西部四省区女童教育研究综课题组 (Research team of girls' education in four provinces of west China) (1999) *Nütong Jiaoyu Yanjiu zai Zhongguo* 『女童教育研究在中国』 (Study of girls' education in China), Yinchuan: Internal document.

Yao Jide *et al.* (eds) 姚继德他編 (2005) *Yunnan Yisilanjiao Shi* 『云南伊斯兰教史』 (History of Islam in Yunnan), Kunming: Yunnan University Press 云南大学出版社.

Yavari, Negin (2003) *Intellectuals and the State in Iran: Politics, Discourse, and the Dilemma of Authenticity*, Gainesville, FL: University Press of Florida.

Zaman, Haider (2005) 'Problems of education, health and infrastructure in FATA', in Cheema, Pervaiz Iqbal and Nuri, Maqsudul Hasan (eds) *Tribal Areas of Pakistan: Challenges and Responses*, Islamabad Policy Research Institute.

Zaman, Muhammad Qasim (1998) 'Sectarianism in Pakistan: the radicalization of Shi'i and Sunni identities', *Modern Asian Studies*, 32 (3): 689–716.

——(2002) *The Ulama in Contemporary Islam: Custodians of Change*, Princeton, NJ: Princeton University Press.

——(2005) 'Pluralism, democracy and the 'ulama', in Robert W. Hefner (ed.) *Remaking Muslim Politics: Pluralism, Contestation, Democratization*, Princeton, NJ: Princeton University Press.

——(2007) 'Epilogue: competing conceptions of religious education', in Hefner W. Robert and Muhammad Qasim Zaman (eds) *Schooling Islam: The Culture and Politics of Modern Muslim Education*, Princeton, NJ: Princeton University Press.

Zaman, Muhammad Qasim (2008) 'Reformisme, islamismes et libéralismes religieux', *Revue des mondes musalmans et de la Méditerranée*, 123: 17–35.

Zastoupil, Lynn and Moir, Martin (1999) *The Great Indian Education Debate: documents Relating to the Orientalist–Anglicist Controversy, 1781–1843*, London: Curzon.

Zeghal, Malika (1996) *Gardiens de l'Islam: les oulémas d'al-Azhar dans l'Egypte contemporaine*, Paris: Presses de Sciences-Po.

——(2007) 'The 'recentering' of religious knowledge and discourse: the case of al-Azhar in twentieth-century Egypt', in Hefner W. Robert and Muhammad Qasim Zaman (eds) *Schooling Islam: The Culture and Politics of Modern Muslim Education*, Princeton, NJ: Princeton University Press.

——(ed.)(2008) 'Réformismes, Islamismes et libéralismes religieux', *Revue des mondes musulmans et de la méditerranée*, 123, juillet.

Zhongguo Renmin Gongheguo Guojia Tongjiju 中国人民共和国国家统计局 (ed.) (2008) *Zhongguo Tongji Nianjian* 『中国统计年鉴』 (China's Annual Statistics), Beijing: Zhongguo Tonji Chubanshe.

Zhouwei 周卫 (1997) *Pinkun zhong de Qipan* 『贫困中的期盼』 (Hope in poverty), Nanning: Guangxi Jiaoyu Chubanshe 广西教育出版社.

Online journals and newspapers

Alef, http://www.alefbe.com

Ayandi-i Rushan, http://www.bfnews.ir

Gulbarg, http://www.hawzah.net/Hawzah/Magazines/MagArt.aspx?id=14959

Iran Daily, http://www.iran-daily.com

Nama-i Jamia, http://jz.ac.ir

Payam-i Hawza, http://www.hawzah.net/Per/Magazine/PH/Index.htm

Rasa news agency, http://www.rasanews.com

Index